CLEVELAND BROWNS A–Z

ROGER GORDON

FOREWORD BY MIKE PRUITT

SPORTS
PUBLISHING

Sports Publishing books may be purchased in bulk at special discounts for sales promotion, corporate gifts, fund-raising, or educational purposes. Special editions can also be created to specifications. For details, contact the Special Sales Department, Sports Publishing, 307 West 36th Street, 11th Floor, New York, NY 10018 or sportspubbooks@skyhorsepublishing.com.

Sports Publishing® is a registered trademark of Skyhorse Publishing, Inc.®, a Delaware corporation.

Visit our website at www.sportspubbooks.com.

10 9 8 7 6 5 4 3 2 1

Library of Congress Cataloging-in-Publication Data is available on file.

Cover design by K. Jeffrey Higgerson
Cover photo credit: AP Photo/Mark Duncan

ISBN: 978-1-61321-810-5
Ebook ISBN: 978-1-61321-858-7

Printed in the United States of America

TABLE OF CONTENTS

IV Cleveland Browns A–Z

FOREWORD

The first time I ran onto the Cleveland Municipal Stadium field for a regular season game, I was in awe. We were playing the New York Jets. Joe Namath was on that team! I was thinking, "I can't believe I'm actually here, competing with guys who I've watched for years!" And the Cleveland fans were remarkable. I'd never seen anything like it. Never had I seen a city so covet a team like Cleveland does the Browns.

I went on to enjoy a successful nine-year career as a running back with Cleveland, something I never dreamed would happen—and definitely not with the Browns. Not only was I taken aback when they selected me in the 1976 NFL Draft, I was in utter shock WHERE they picked me—No. 7 overall! I expected to be drafted, yes, but in the second or third round. Upon returning to earth, I realized I was headed to a team that, although having gone through recent tough times, had loads of tradition. Guys like Jim Brown, Leroy Kelly, and Marion Motley played for this team!

The Kardiac Kids days were the most thrilling times, moments like the Monday night shocker over the Cowboys in a rocking Cleveland Stadium in 1979, the upset of the Oilers in the Astrodome the next year, and the division-clincher three weeks later in Cincinnati.

There were also moments I'd like to file away forever. The 1982 players' strike. The excruciating loss to the Vikings two years before that nearly cost us a playoff berth. The worst one, though, should come as no surprise to Browns fans—Red Right 88.

The moment I recall most though, was a good one. It occurred in 1978 in a home game against Buffalo. I scored on a 71-yard run, one of two touchdowns I had that day, that helped us to a 41-20 victory. Benchwarming had been my calling for the most part during my two-plus seasons with the Browns. I was beginning to doubt my abilities. That long run against the Bills gave me the confidence boost I desperately needed. For the first time, I truly believed I belonged in the NFL.

Whether pleasant memories or not, I'll always cherish my days with the Cleveland Browns.

Cleveland Browns A–Z offers fans the chance to relive the rich history of the Browns franchise, from the glory days of yesteryear to the present that will hopefully bring the same kind of success in the not too distant future.

—Mike Pruitt
*Running Back, Cleveland Browns, 1976-84

PREFACE

I look at the alphabet in a whole new way now.

That's what happens after countless hours of research and writing in compiling a book called *Cleveland Browns A–Z.*

Now, when I think of the letter "A," instead of a one-word article coming to mind I think of the All-America Football Conference. When I think of the letter "D," rather than my college report cards coming to mind I think of The Dawg Pound. And when I think of the letter "M," instead of May 3, 1980, the day of my Bar Mitzvah, coming to mind I think of Alex Mack.

When Sports Publishing approached me in the spring of 1999 to write *Cleveland Browns A–Z,* it was a no-brainer. Authoring an alphabetic history of the Browns was a project I could not resist. I have been a Browns fan for years—from the early '80s days of Brian Sipe, Mike Pruitt, and Dave Logan; to the Dawg Days of Bernie Kosar, Webster Slaughter, and Earnest Byner; to mainstays from both eras like Ozzie Newsome, Clay Matthews, and Hanford Dixon; to the new era that featured Tim Couch, Kevin Johnson, and Jamir Miller and now features a pair of Joes—Thomas and Haden.

In addition, I have always been an ardent researcher, fascinated by the history of the Browns all the way back to their pre-National Football League days when they were members of the All-America Football Conference.

Cleveland Browns A Z was at times a challenging work, but well worth it. I hope you enjoy the final result.

ACKNOWLEDGMENTS

I would like to thank Mike Pearson of Sports Publishing first and foremost for giving me the opportunity to write this book. Without him, it never would have happened. Also from Sports Publishing, I would like to thank Jennifer Polson for the time and energy she put into the book, and Joe Bannon, Jr. Thanks, too, goes out to Niels Aaboe of Skyhorse Publishing for allowing me to update the book.

I also appreciate the assistance I received from the staff of the Pro Football Hall of Fame archives library, specifically Chad Reese for his diligent effort in furnishing me with much of the research material I needed.

Gratitude is also owed to the staff of the Cleveland State University Cleveland Press Collection department for furnishing me with photos.

Special thanks goes to Mike Pruitt for writing the foreword.

ABBREVIATIONS KEY

AAFC: All-America Football Conference
ABC: American Broadcasting Company
AFC: American Football Conference
AP: Associated Press
CBS: Columbia Broadcasting Company
CFL: Canadian Football League
C&O: Coaches & Officials
ESPN: Entertainment and Sports Programming Network
FD: *Football Digest*
FWA: Pro Football Writers Association
INS: International News Service
MAC: Mid-American Conference
MAX: Maxwell Club
NBC: National Broadcasting Company
NCAA: National Collegiate Athletic Association
NEA: Newspaper Enterprise Association
NFC: National Football Conference
NFL: National Football League
NYN: *New York Daily News*
OFF: official teams
PFI: *Pro Football Illustrated*
PFW: *Pro Football Weekly*
SI: *Sports Illustrated*
SN: *The Sporting News*
SP: Sportswriters Inc.
UP: United Press
UPI: United Press International
USFL: United States Football League
WFL: World Football League

CHARACTERS KEY

The following notations denote their meanings:

#: Does not include Browns games against the Buffalo Bills on December 4, 1949, and Los Angeles Rams on December 24, 1950, for Otto Graham and Marion Motley and the Browns game against the New York Giants on December 17, 1950, for Motley

##: Does not include Browns games against the New York Giants on December 17, 1950, and Los Angeles Rams on December 24, 1950, and a portion of the Browns game against the Buffalo Bills on December 4, 1949

###: Does not include the Browns game against the New York Giants on December 17, 1950, and a portion of Browns games against the Buffalo Bills on December 4, 1949, and Los Angeles Rams on December 24, 1950

####: Does not include a portion of Browns games against the Buffalo Bills on December 4, 1949, and Los Angeles Rams on December 24, 1950

#####: Does not include the Browns game against the Los Angeles Rams on December 24, 1950, and a portion of the Browns game against the Buffalo Bills on December 4, 1949

######: Does not include fumble return yardage for part of Browns history

#######: Does not include Browns games against the Brooklyn Dodgers on December 8, 1946, and Baltimore Colts on December 7, 1947

Notes

1. Overtime in the regular season began in 1974.

2. Players' career statistics are comprised of regular-season play only unless indicated otherwise.

3. Preseason games are not included unless indicated otherwise.

4. Sacks have been an official NFL statistic since 1982.

5. The statistic "combined net yards" (also called all-purpose yards) comprises the following yardage totals: rushing, receiving, punt return, kickoff return, interception return, and fumble return.

6. The statistic "total net yards" comprises rushing yards and net passing yards.

7. When an individual is described as having led the league/conference in an "average yards per" category, it is assumed that individuals with higher averages, but a minute amount of attempts, are not included.

8. When a player is described as being drafted, it is the AAFC or NFL drafts only unless indicated otherwise.

9. When a team and/or league record being set is described, it is assumed that the record still stands unless indicated otherwise.

10. When there were two teams playing in the same city in lists that are rankings of particular games, the city's abbreviation is followed by the nickname.

11. When a touchdown is described, and the resulting game score results in seven points, the point after touchdown (PAT) is assumed successful unless indicated otherwise.

DECADE-BY-DECADE TIMELINE

1940s

The 1940s began with the Browns' domination of the AAFC in their—and the conference's—first year of existence in 1946 under head coach Paul Brown, whom the team was named after. The Browns' dominance continued through 1949, when the AAFC folded. Cleveland won three Western Division Championships from 1946-48 and all four conference titles (in 1949, the two-division format was scratched). The Browns rolled through the 1946 season, finishing 12-2 and defeating the New York Yankees 14-9 in Cleveland in the title game. The Browns were 12-1-1 in 1947 and beat New York again 14-3. This time, Cleveland took the conference crown in Yankee stadium.

In 1948, the Browns put together a perfect 14-0 record and routed Buffalo 49-7 in the AAFC title game at home. The Browns wound up 9-1-2 in 1949 and knocked off Buffalo at home 31-21 in an opening-round playoff before dismantling the 49ers in the AAFC's final title contest 21-7 in Cleveland.

The Browns' record in the 1940s was 47-4-3, 24-2-1 at home and 23-2-2 on the road. Their postseason record in the 1940s was 5-0, 4-0 at home and 1-0 on the road.

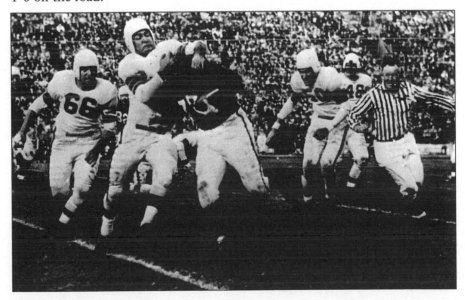

Browns in action, 1946. Photo courtesy of the Cleveland Press Collection.

The Browns against the Rams, 1951. Photo courtesy of the Cleveland Press Collection.

Conference again in 1954 and '55 and claimed the NFL crown both years, beating the Lions in 1954 and Rams in 1955.

After a down year in 1956 in which they finished 5-7 due in large part to several retirements, rookie running back Jim Brown led the Browns back to the NFL Championship Game in 1957, but Cleveland was routed by the Lions 59-14. The Browns had a chance to repeat as conference champion in 1958 but lost a heartbreaker to the Giants on the

Action from 1954. Photo courtesy of the Cleveland Press Collection.

1950s

The Browns began the 1950s by continuing their stellar play upon joining the NFL. Under head coach Paul Brown they finished 10-2, tying the Giants for first place in the American Conference in 1950. They beat the New Yorkers 8-3 in a playoff to claim the conference title. They beat the Los Angeles Rams 30-28 for the NFL title on Lou Groza's 16-yard field goal with 28 seconds left.

Cleveland won the American Conference title in 1951 and '52 with 11-1 and 8-4 records, respectively, but was upended in the league title game each time—by the Rams in 1951 and Lions in 1952. The Browns won the renamed Eastern Conference in 1953, but lost to the Lions again in the league championship game. They won the Eastern

final Sunday 13-10 in New York that forged a tie with the Giants at 9-3. New York won a playoff 10-0 the next week in Yankee Stadium.

The Browns finished 7-5 in 1959. Cleveland's record in the 1950s was 88-30-2, 45-15 at home and 43-15-2 on the road. Its postseason record in the 1950s was 4-5, 3-1 at home and 1-4 on the road.

1960s

The Browns began the 1960s as a team treading in mediocrity – at least for a franchise with the championship tradition that the Browns had built. They were 8-3-1 in 1960, 8-5-1 in 1961 and 7-6-1 in 1962, finishing second, third, and third, respectively, in the Eastern Conference. Majority owner Art Modell, deciding a change was needed, fired the only head coach the franchise ever had, Paul Brown, on January 9, 1963. Modell replaced Brown with offensive backfield coach Blanton Collier.

Collier implemented a more wide-open offensive attack, and led by quarterback Frank Ryan and running back Jim Brown, Cleveland improved to 10-4 in 1963. However, the Browns still finished one game behind the Eastern

Frank Ryan is taken down as Jim Brown (32) looks on in the background in 1962. Photo courtesy of the Cleveland Press Collection.

Jim Brown finds a hole against the Steelers on November 25, 1962. Photo courtesy of the Cleveland Press Collection.

Conference Champion Giants. In 1964, the Browns finished in first place at 10-3-1 and upset heavily-favored Baltimore 27-0 in the NFL Championship Game in Cleveland. The Browns returned to the title game the following year but fell to the Packers 23-12 in the snow and mud of Green Bay. Cleveland finished 9-5 in 1966 but missed the postseason.

In 1967 the Eastern Conference split into two divisions—the Capitol and Century. The Browns won the Century, repeating their 9-5 mark from the year before, but were creamed by the Cowboys in the Cotton Bowl 52-14 in the conference championship game. Bill Nelsen replaced Ryan as the starting quarterback early in the 1968 season and directed the Browns on an offensive binge that Browns fans had never seen before—the team scored at least 30 points in seven straight games, winning them all. Cleveland wound up 10-4 and Century Division titlists once again. They upset the Cowboys in the Eastern Conference Championship Game in Cleveland but were buried by Baltimore 34-0 at home for the NFL Championship.

The Browns won their third straight Century Division title in 1969, finishing 10-3-1. They beat Dallas with ease in the conference championship game in the Cotton Bowl, then fell to the Vikings 27-7 in the NFL Championship Game on January 4, 1970, in frigid Minnesota.

The Browns' record in the 1960s was 92-41-5, 48-18-3 at home and 44-23-2 on the road. Their postseason record in the 1960s was 3-4, 2-1 at home and 1-3 on the road.

1970s

The 1970s began with one of the biggest trades in Browns history. The team traded exceptional wide receiver Paul Warfield to the Miami Dolphins for the third pick in the next day's draft in order to select sensational Purdue University quarterback Mike Phipps. Veteran Bill Nelsen, however, was the starter when the 1970 season began. That season got off to a rousing start as the Browns helped inaugurate the ABC *Monday Night Football* series by hosting its very first game, a 31-21 Browns victory over the Joe Namath-led New York Jets on September 21, 1970, in front of 85,703 fans, the largest home crowd in team history. The Browns, though, were a model of inconsistency all season and finished 7-7, a game behind the Cincinnati Bengals in the first year of the AFC Central Division.

Don Cockroft's punt is blocked by the Cowboys' Richmond Flowers in the Browns' 6-2 loss at home on December 12, 1970. Photo courtesy of the Cleveland Press Collection.

Under new head coach Nick Skorich, the Browns easily won the weak Central in 1971 with a 9-5 record but lost to Baltimore in an AFC Divisional Playoff at home. In 1972, Phipps took over as the starter early in the season and directed Cleveland to a 10-4 finish and the AFC Wild Card spot. The Browns took the undefeated Dolphins down to the wire before falling 20-14 in a divisional playoff in the Orange Bowl, a game in which Phipps was intercepted five times. The Browns seemed headed for the playoffs once again in 1973 but collapsed late in the season and finished in third place in the Central at 7-5-2.

The Browns won just seven games during the next two seasons, the second of which was under new head coach Forrest Gregg. They finished in last place both years. In 1976, the Browns rebounded by finishing 9-5 and were in playoff contention through the final weekend. Cleveland began 1977 with high hopes and came through in the first half of the season—they were 5-2 and in first place. Then the bottom fell out, and the team won just one of its last seven games, winding up 6-8 and in last place. Gregg was fired with one game left in the season (defensive coordinator Dick Modzelewski coached the season finale in Seattle).

Longtime NFL assistant coach Sam Rutigliano came aboard in 1978 and instilled a more wide-open offensive philosophy. That, combined with the maturing of quarterback Brian Sipe, who had replaced the traded Phipps as

Cold Browns on the sidelines, 1974. Photo courtesy of the Cleveland Press Collection.

the starter, resulted in an 8-8 record '78 and a 9-7 mark in 1979. The '79 team earned the nickname of "Kardiac Kids," due to several close finishes. The team barely missed the playoffs that year.

The Browns' record in the 1970s was 72-70-2, 41-30-1 at home and 31-40-1 on the road. Their postseason record in the 1970s was 0-2, 0-1 at home and 0-1 on the road.

1980s

The 1980s began with a bang when the Browns—rather, the Kardiac Kids—won the AFC Central Division title in 1980 in thrilling fashion, dethroning 1970s kingpin Pittsburgh in the process. Twelve games that year were decided by seven points or less en route to an 11-5 record. The Browns tied Houston for the best record in the division, but the Browns were awarded the title on the basis of a better record within the AFC than the Oilers (8-4 to 7-5). Sipe, a multi-award winner that year, passed for a team-record 4,132 yards. Cleveland's Super Bowl dreams came to a crashing halt against Oakland in the AFC Divisional Playoffs when Mike Davis intercepted a Sipe floater in the end zone with less than a minute to play, clinching the Raiders' 14-12 victory in arctic-like temperatures.

The Browns fell on hard times during the next four seasons (5-11 in 1981, 4-5 in '82, 9-7 in '83, and 5-11 in '84). The 1982 club actually qualified for the strike-induced expanded playoff tournament despite its losing record, but lost in Los Angeles to the Raiders 27-10 in the first round. Paul McDonald replaced Sipe as the starting quarterback after six games that year. The 1983 squad, with Sipe back as the starter for most of the season, just missed qualifying for the playoffs on a tiebreaker, the only one of five 9-7 teams in the league that year that missed the postseason. The '83 team posted consecutive shutouts when it blanked Tampa Bay and New England in November, becoming the second Browns team ever—and first since 1951—to do so.

Defensive coordinator Marty Schottenheimer replaced the fired Rutigliano midway through the disastrous 1984 campaign that culminated in a 5-11 record. With rookie Bernie Kosar as the starting quarterback for part of the season and a pair of 1,000-yard running backs in Kevin Mack and Earnest Byner, the Browns won the Central Division title in 1985 despite an 8-8 record. They nearly upset heavily-favored Miami in the divisional playoffs, blowing a 21-3 third-quarter lead. The 1986 and '87 Browns not only won the Central Division but advanced to the AFC Championship game, the first due to a remarkable comeback victory over the Jets in the divisional playoffs. The

Browns lost in heartbreaking fashion to the John Elway-led Denver Broncos in both conference title tilts. *(Please see Drive, The and Fumble, The).*

Cleveland persevered through countless injuries that resulted in four starting quarterbacks in 1988 but lost to Houston in the AFC Wild Card Game. Under new head coach Bud Carson (Schottenheimer had resigned soon after the 1988 season), the Browns recaptured the division title in 1989 but lost to the Broncos again in the conference title game.

The Browns' record in the 1980s was 83-68-1, 46-28-1 at home and 37-40 on the road. Their postseason record in the 1980s was 3-7, 3-3 at home and 0-4 on the road.

1990s

The 1990s began in horrific fashion as the Browns finished just 3-13 in 1990—the worst season in team history to that point—after five straight playoff appearances. Carson was replaced by assistant coach Jim Shofner nine games into the season, the day after a 42-0 home loss to Buffalo, the worst shutout loss and worst home defeat for the Browns up to that point. With Bill Belichick as head coach, the Browns improved to 6-10 in 1991 and 7-9 in both 1992 and '93.

The Browns, who had released Kosar midway through the 1993 season, finally came through in 1994 with quarterback Vinny Testaverde, an ex-teammate of Kosar's at the University of Miami, finishing 11-5, mostly due to the fact that they yielded just 204 points, the fewest in the league. A wild card win over New England was all but forgotten when the Browns were obliterated 29-9 by Pittsburgh the next week in an AFC Divisional Playoff, Cleveland's third loss to the Steelers that season.

As bad as the decade had begun for the Browns with their miserable 1990 season, what happened in 1995 made that seem like nothing. Rumors circulated for the first two months of the season that Modell was planning on relocating the franchise to Baltimore after the season, but the Browns still won three of their first four games. They hit a cold spell but recovered as rookie quarterback Eric Zeier replaced the benched Testaverde (who was actually leading the AFC in passing at the time) and led the team to a thrilling overtime victory, and a 4-4 record, against the Bengals in Cincinnati on October 29. The next week, on November 5 in a home game against Houston the uninspired Browns, aware that Modell's official announcement of the relocation was coming the next day, were crushed 37-10. Modell made his team's impending move to Maryland official to the public the following day in Baltimore.

The rest of the season was basically a moot point, as the Browns won just one more game—a 26-10 victory over the Bengals on December 17 in what many thought to be the final home game in the history of the franchise. The team finished 5-11 and in third place, ahead of only the expansion Jacksonville Jaguars. The Browns did leave, and move to Baltimore, where they were renamed the Ravens. Thus, football-crazed Cleveland was without a pro football team for three seasons from 1996-98.

On June 12, 1996, the city of Cleveland, and the NFL, announced terms of a historic public-private partnership that would continue the Browns franchise and guarantee a new state-of-the-art stadium in Cleveland in 1999. On March 23, 1998, at a league meeting in Orlando, NFL owners agreed that the Cleveland Browns would be an expansion team in 1999. On September 8, 1998, the NFL awarded majority ownership of the franchise to Al Lerner. The Browns didn't have much time, but they spent months putting together a team through free agency, the expansion draft and the regular draft, in which University of Kentucky standout quarterback Tim Couch was their top pick and the first overall selection.

Under head coach Chris Palmer, the "reborn" Browns took the field for the first time on September 12, 1999, against the Pittsburgh Steelers in brand new Cleveland Browns Stadium for a nationally-televised game broadcast on ESPN. The Browns not only lost 43-0 but were only able to muster 40 total yards! The Browns, as expected, had a rough season in 1999, but at times showed flashes of a bright future. They finished 2-14 and in last place in the AFC Central.

Cleveland's record in the 1990s was 41-71, 22-34 at home and 19-37 on the road. Its postseason record in the 1990s was 1-1, 1-0 at home and 0-1 on the road.

2000s

The 2000s began roughly for the Browns as they finished just 3-13 in 2000 after a 2-1 start. Number-one overall draft pick Tim Couch broke his right thumb in a practice session on October 19, sidelining him for the year. With castoff Doug Pederson and 2000 Browns sixth-round draft choice Spergon Wynn calling the signals the rest of the way, Cleveland lost eight of nine games.

With new head coach Butch Davis now running the show, the Browns got off to a surprisingly fine start in 2001 behind a strong defensive effort, winning four of their first six games. They had a golden opportunity to go 5-2, but a shocking overtime defeat to the Bears in Chicago—they blew a 14-point lead with just 28 seconds left—and another heartbreaker in Pittsburgh left them at 4-4. Playoff hopes were renewed with wins over the Ravens and Bengals, but the Browns dropped five of their last six games—including the infamous "Bottlegate" defeat to Jacksonville—to wind up 7-9.

The 2002 season, in one respect, might have been the most exciting in Browns history. Thirteen games were decided by nine points or less. Some were actually decided with 0:00 on the clock, with literally no time left. There was Dwayne Rudd's gaffe in the season opener agasnt Kansas City. There was Couch looking like John Unitas in thrilling comeback road wins over the Titans, Jets and Ravens. There was Quincy Morgan hauling in a Hail Mary from Couch in Jacksonville to keep the playoffs from becoming a pipe dream. There was the heartbreaking home loss to the Colts. There was Kelly Holcomb directing two wins, including the finale against the Falcons in which Cleveland Browns Stadium had the sound and feel of . . . Cleveland Stadium. There was the waiting and wondering regarding the Dolphins-Patriots and Jets-Packers games. And, of course, there was the trifecta of three-point defeats to the hated Steelers, the last of which came in the playoffs.

Things seemed to be continuing in the right direction for Cleveland as the 2003 season approached. But, due to a salary-cap quandary, the Browns' hierarchy gutted the team of several veteran defensive players who contributed mightily to the team's success the year before. Amid a quarterback carousel with Couch and Holcomb, the Browns lost eight of nine after a 3-3 start and finished 5-11 and in the AFC North cellar. The next season Couch was gone, Jeff Garcia was in and Holcomb was the backup. After a season-opening squashing of the Ravens had a number of delusional fans thinking Super Bowl, reality quickly set in. Kellen Winslow, Jr. got hurt. In a repeat of the previous season, a 3-3 start disintegrated into a nightmare. Davis quit Thanksgiving weekend. Assistant Terry Robiskie finished out the 4-12 season.

Despite a new regime—including head coach Romeo Crennel—running the show, it was much the same story for the 2005 Browns. Another retread quarterback in Trent Dilfer. More dropped passes by receivers who complained they didn't get the ball enough. Tight defeats to bad teams. A 6-10 record, tied for last place. But on the bright side, there did seem to be a glimmer of hope for the future. A young, homegrown quarterback who finally got his shot and showed some promise in Charlie Frye. A 1,000-yard rusher who battled for every inch in Reuben Droughns. A number-one draft pick who showed flashes of brilliance in Braylon Edwards. A defense that played over its head but notched a year under its belt. And, finally, a league in which jumping from last place to first in one season is not so far-fetched.

When it comes to the Browns, though, jumping from last to first in one season *is* far-fetched. As the 2006 season approached, Dilfer was gone, and Frye, a third-round draft pick the year before, was now the main man at quarterback. The Browns hoped the 6-4, 225-pound University of Akron alum would buck the odds and become their quarterback of the future. Frye was not awful, completing nearly 65 percent of his passes. Neither was he exactly a Pro Bowler, as he tossed 17 interceptions to just 10 touchdown passes. The team got off to a poor start, dropping five of its first six games on its way to a 4-12 last-place finish.

It did not look like the same old Browns as the 2007 season got underway—it looked worse. Frye, who had somehow won the starting quarterback job again in training camp over Derek Anderson, was so bad in the season opener at home against Pittsburgh—he was 4-of-10 with an interception and five sacks before getting yanked late in the first half—that he was traded to Seattle two days later, causing many to observe that they couldn't remember an opening-day NFL starting quarterback being traded after just one game.

Enter backup Derek Anderson as the starter—or was it a clone of Dan Fouts?—and all of a sudden, out of nowhere, the Browns, with Edwards and Winslow on their way to career years, looked like Air Coryell in a 51-45 win at home against the Bengals. During a span of 12 games, the Browns scored fewer than 21 points just once (and that was against the soon-to-be 16-0 Patriots), and tallied 33 or more four times! In the end, Pro Bowler Anderson's dreadful performance in a loss at Cincinnati in Game 15 wound up costing Cleveland, which finished 10-6 and in second place, a playoff berth.

The 2008 Browns very simply could not put points on the board. Two primetime wins—over the Giants and Bills—were pretty much the only bright spots as the team scored just 31 points in its last six games in finishing 4-12 and in last place. With new head coach Eric Mangini running the show in 2009 and minus the traded Winslow, Brady Quinn and Anderson played musical quarterbacks. The Browns lost 11 of their first 12 games, attaining the franchise's worst record ever after a dozen games. The offense was so anemic that the team tallied seven or fewer points seven times in their first 11 games! Four victories to close the season—including its first win over Pittsburgh in six years—left Cleveland with a 5-11 record and yet another last-place finish.

Cleveland's record in the 2000s was 57-103, 31-49 at home and 26-54 on the road. Its postseason record in the 2000s was 0-1 (road game).

2010s

Other than the fact that they didn't lose 11 of their first 12 games, with the trio of Jake Delhomme, rookie Colt McCoy and Seneca Wallace at quarterback and one-year wonder Peyton Hillis at running back, the Browns' 2010 season wasn't much different than their 2009 campaign. They did manage to lose five of their first six games, however. Upsets of the Saints and Patriots gave fans a ray of hope. But a second straight 5-11 record was the end result. With Pat Shurmur now strolling the sidelines and Colt McCoy the main man at quarterback, the Browns won two of their first three games in 2011. They lost two straight but then won a 6-3 snooze-fest over Seattle to improve to 3-3. Nine losses in their last 10 games, however, left them with a 4-12 record and last-place finish. The Brandon Weeden era got off to an inauspicious start in 2012, as the Browns' soon-to-be twenty-nine-year-old rookie was 12-of-35 with four interceptions and a 5.1 QB rating in a season-opening 17-16 loss to the Eagles. Weeden's stats improved—how couldn't they have?—but the team kept losing, dropping to 0-5 en route to a 5-11 record and another last-place finish.

Under yet another new head coach, Rob Chudzinski, Weeden's second season opener in 2013 was better than his atrocious performance in the loss to the Eagles in the 2012 opener, but that's not saying much. In a 23-10 home loss to the Dolphins, the former Oklahoma State gunslinger went 26-of-53 for 289 yards with a touchdown pass, three picks and a QB rating of 48.4. Just like the year before, his stats improved but not enough. Third-string quarterback Brian Hoyer, a Cleveland native, inexplicably got the nod over second-stringer Jason Campbell in Week 3 at Minnesota. He led the Browns to a comeback win over the Vikings and then a solid win over the Bengals, but the next week he got hurt early, ending his season, during a primetime victory over Buffalo that upped the Browns' record to 3-2. Weeden and Campbell split the QB duties the rest of the way. Josh Gordon's record-setting season mattered little. The team lost 10 of its last 11 games in finishing 4-12 and, yes, in last place again.

New season. New head coach *again*. With Mike Pettine now the man and Hoyer the starter in 2014, the Browns shocked the world by winning seven of their first 11 games that put them right smack in the middle of the playoff race. Included was a record-setting comeback win at Tennessee and a 31-10 bashing of the Steelers. The apex of the Browns' run, though, was a 24-3 primetime spanking of the Bengals in Cincinnati that landed them in . . . first place? Yes, first place! The bottom fell out, however, as they quickly faded from playoff contention—including a forgetful sampling of Johnny Manziel—by dropping their last five games.

Cleveland's record in the 2010s is 25-55, 17-23 at home and 8-32 on the road.

A

ABC TELEVISION NETWORK

The ABC television network broadcast the NFL's first *Monday Night Football* game on September 21, 1970. The Browns won 31-21 over the New York Jets in front of 85,703 fans in Cleveland Municipal Stadium. ABC aired several other Browns prime time games since, including other Monday games and special edition Thursday and Sunday games.

ABRAHAM, ABE

Abe Abraham was the man in the brown suit who used to catch field goals and extra points at Browns home games. Born in Lebanon, he came to the United States at age three. He was working at the pass gate in week four of the 1946 season and went on the field to watch the action. He was hit by the ball and knocked down on a field goal by Lou Groza. From that point until he passed away in 1982, Abraham caught all field goals and extra points at the closed end of Cleveland Municipal Stadium.

ACCORSI, ERNIE

Ernie Accorsi was executive vice president of football operations for the Browns from 1985-91 after spending 1984 as the assistant to the president. He was instrumental in the Browns obtaining quarterback Bernie Kosar in the 1985 supplemental draft.

ADAMLE, TONY

Tony Adamle was a Browns linebacker from 1947-51 and in 1954. A product of Ohio State University, he was acquired by the Browns as a free agent. He had four interceptions for 42 return yards in 1949 and intercepted seven passes for 96 return yards in his Browns career. He was voted to All-NFL defensive teams in 1951 by NYN and UP and was selected to play in the Pro Bowl in 1950 and 1951.

ADAMS, MIKE

Mike Adams was a Browns defensive back from 2007-11. He is a product of the University of Delaware. He was the team leader in 2011 with three interceptions.

ALL - AAFC

Various news organizations voted on players for the All-AAFC, a "team" comprised of outstanding players from across the All-America Football Conference. The organizations that voted are denoted after the players' names. *Please see the abbreviations key.*

1946   Otto Graham (OFF, UP), Dante Lavelli (AP, OFF), Marion Motley (AP, NYN, OFF, UP), Lou Rymkus (SP), Mike Scarry (NYN), Mac Speedie (NYN, UP), Bill Willis (OFF, SP)

1947   Otto Graham (AP, C&O, NYN, OFF, SP), Dante Lavelli (OFF), Marion Motley (AP, C&O, NYN, OFF), Lou Rymkus (C&O, NYN, OFF, SP), Mike Scarry (C&O), Mac Speedie (AP, C&O, NYN, OFF, SP), Bill Willis (OFF)

1948   Otto Graham (AP, OFF, UP), Marion Motley (AP, NYN, OFF, SN), Lou Rymkus (AP, OFF, UP), Lou Saban (NYN, UP), Mac Speedie (AP, NYN, OFF, SN, UP), Bill Willis (AP, NYN, OFF, UP)

1949   Otto Graham (AP, NYN, OFF, UP), Marion Motley (NYN), Lou Rymkus (UP), Lou Saban (AP, NYN, OFF, UP), Mac Speedie (AP, NYN, OFF, UP); Offense: Otto Graham (INS), Lou Rymkus (INS), Mac Speedie (INS); Defense: Lou Saban (INS)

ALL - AMERICA FOOTBALL CONFERENCE

The All-America Football Conference was home to the Browns from 1946-49. It also originally consisted of the Chicago Rockets, Los Angeles Dons, and San Francisco 49ers in the Western Division, and the Brooklyn Dodgers, Buffalo Bisons, Miami Seahawks, and New York Yankees in the Eastern Division. The conference had shrunk to seven teams in a one-division format by 1949. The championship was won all four years by the Browns, who compiled an overall record of 47-4-3 and 5-0 mark in the postseason.

AAFC WESTERN DIVISION

The AAFC Western Division was home to the Browns from 1946-48. It dissolved in 1949 along with the Eastern Division, as the All-America Football Conference would have no divisions in its final season of 1949. The Browns won the division all three years, finishing 12-2 in 1946, 12-1-1 in '47, and a perfect 14-0 in '48.

ALL-AFC

Various news organizations voted on players for the All-AFC, a "team" comprised of outstanding players from across the American Football Conference. The organizations that voted are denoted after the players' names. *Please see the abbreviations key.*

1970   Offense: Gene Hickerson (FWA, UPI)

1971   Offense: Leroy Kelly (NEA), Milt Morin (AP, UPI)

1972   Defense: Don Cockroft (NEA)

1973   Defense: Clarence Scott (UPI)

1975   Defense: Jerry Sherk (SN)

1976   Defense: Jerry Sherk (AP, NEA, PFW, FWA, SN, UPI)

1978   Offense: Keith Wright (PFW); Defense: Thorn Darden (NEA, PFW, FWA, SN, UPI)

1979   Offense: Ozzie Newsome (FWA, SN, UPI), Mike Pruitt (PFW, SN, UPI); Defense: Lyle Alzado (PFW, Thorn Darden (PFW)

1980   Offense: Joe DeLamielleure (PFW, FWA, SN, UPI), Brian Sipe (AP, NEA, PFW, FWA, SN, UPI); Defense: Lyle Alzado (AP, UPI)

1983   Offense: Cody Risien (UPI); Defense: Chip Banks (AP, PFW, FWA, UPI), Tom Cousineau (UPI)

1984   Offense: Ozzie Newsome (AP, NEA, PFW, FWA, SN, UPI); Defense: Tom Cousineau (UPI), Clay Matthews (NEA, PFW, SN)

1985   Defense: Chip Banks (UPI), Bob Golic (SN)

1986   Offense: Cody Risien (PFW); Defense: Chip Banks (PFW, UPI), Hanford Dixon (AP, NEA, PFW, FWA, SN, UPI)

1987   Defense: Hanford Dixon (AP, NEA, PFW, FWA, SN, UPI), Frank Minnifield (PFW, FWA, SN, UPI)

1988   Defense: Frank Minnifield (AP, NEA, PFW, FWA, SN, UPI)

1989   Offense: Webster Slaughter (UPI); Defense: Mike Johnson (PFW, UPI), Frank Minnifield (UPI), Michael Dean Perry (AP, PFW, FWA, SN, UPI)

1990   Defense: Michael Dean Perry (AP, NEA, PFW, FWA, SN, UPI)
1991   Defense: Michael Dean Perry (PFW, SN)
1992   Defense: Michael Dean Perry (SN)
1993   Offense: Eric Metcalf (AP, PFW, SN, UPI); Defense: Michael Dean Perry (SN)
1994   Offense: Tony Jones (PFW), Eric Metcalf (SN); Defense: Michael Dean Perry (UPI), Eric Turner (AP, PFW, UPI)
2001   Defense: Jamir Miller (PFW)

ALL-NFL

Various news organizations voted on players for the All-NFL, a "team" comprised of outstanding players from across the National Football League. The organizations that voted are denoted after the players' names. *Please see the abbreviations key.*

1950   Offense: Marion Motley (AP, NYN, UP), Mac Speedie (NYN, UP), Bill Willis (UP); Defense: Bill Willis (NYN)
1951   Offense: Frank Gatski (NYN, UP), Otto Graham (AP, NYN, UP), Lou Groza (NYN, UP), Dub Jones (AP, NYN, UP), Dante Lavelli (NYN, UP); Defense: Tony Adamle (NYN, UP), Len Ford (AP, NYN, UP), Warren Lahr (NYN, UP), Bill Willis (AP, NYN, UP)
1952   Offense: Frank Gatski (AP, NYN), Otto Graham (NYN, UP), Lou Groza (AP, NYN, UP), Mac Speedie (UP); Defense: Len Ford (AP, NYN, UP), Bill Willis (AP, NYN)
1953   Offense: Frank Gatski (AP, NYN, UP), Abe Gibron (NYN), Otto Graham (AP, NYN, UP), Lou Groza (AP, NYN, UP), Dante Lavelli (NYN, UP); Defense: Len Ford (AP, NYN, UP), Ken Gorgal (NYN, UP), Tommy Thompson (AP, UP), Bill Willis (AP)
1954   Offense: Otto Graham (AP, NYN, SN, UP), Lou Groza (AP, NYN, SN, UP); Defense: Len Ford (AP, NYN, UP)
1955   Offense: Frank Gatski (AP, NYN, NEA, UP), Abe Gibron (NYN, NEA, UP), Otto Graham (AP, NYN, UP), Lou Groza (AP, NYN, NEA, UP), Mike McCormack (NYN); Defense: Don Colo (NEA, UP), Len Ford (NYN, NEA, UP), Don Paul (UP)
1957   Offense: Jim Brown (AP, NYN, NEA, UP), Lou Groza (NYN, UP), Mike McCormack (NEA); Defense: Don Colo (NYN, NEA)
1958   Offense: Jim Brown (AP, NYN, NEA, UPI); Defense: Bob Gain (NEA)

1959   Offense: Jim Brown (AP, NYN, NEA, UPI), Jim Ray Smith (AP, NYN, NEA, UPI); Defense: Walt Michaels (NYN)

1960   Offense: Jim Brown (AP, NYN, NEA, UPI), Jim Ray Smith (AP, NYN, NEA, UPI)

1961   Offense: Jim Brown (AP, NYN, NEA, UPI), Jim Ray Smith (AP, NYN, NEA, PFI, UPI)

1962   Offense: Jim Ray Smith (NEA)

1963   Offense: Jim Brown (AP, NYN, NEA, UPI), Dick Schafrath (AP)

1964   Offense: Jim Brown (AP, NYN, NEA, UPI), Dick Schafrath (AP, NYN, UPI), Paul Warfield (NEA); Defense: Jim Houston (NEA)

1965   Offense: Jim Brown (AP, NYN, NEA, UPI), Gary Collins (NYN, UPI), Dick Schafrath (AP, NYN, UPI); Defense: Jim Houston (UPI)

1966   Offense: Gene Hickerson (NEA), Leroy Kelly (AP, NYN, NEA, UPI), John Wooten (NYN)

1967   Offense: Gene Hickerson (AP, NYN, NEA, UPI), Leroy Kelly (AP, NYN, NEA, UPI)

1968   Offense: Gene Hickerson (AP, NYN, NEA, PFW, FWA, UPI), Leroy Kelly (AP, NYN, NEA, PFW, FWA, UPI), Paul Warfield (NEA, PFW, UPI)

1969   Offense: Gary Collins (AP, UPI), Gene Hickerson (AP, NYN, OFF, PFW, FWA, SI, UPI), Leroy Kelly (NEA), Paul Warfield (NEA, OFF PFW, SI)

2001   Defense: Jamir Miller (AP, FD, PFW, SI)

2007   Offense: Braylon Edwards (SN); Special Teams: Josh Cribbs (SN)

2009   Offense: Joe Thomas (AP, FWA); Special Teams: Josh Cribbs (AP, FWA)

2010   Offense: Joe Thomas (AP, FWA, SN)

2011   Offense: Joe Thomas (AP, FWA)

2012   Offense: Joe Thomas (SN); Special Teams: Phil Dawson (SN)

2013   Offense: Josh Gordon (AP, FWA, SN), Alex Mack (SN), Joe Thomas (AP, FWA, SN); Defense: Joe Haden (SN)

2014   Offense: Joe Thomas (AP, FWA)

ALZADO, LYLE

Lyle Alzado was a Browns defensive end from 1979-81. He was a Yankton product acquired by Cleveland on August 12, 1979, in a trade with the Denver Broncos for second and fifth-round draft picks in 1980. He was voted to All-AFC defensive teams in 1979 by PFW and in '80 by AP and UPI.

Dick Ambrose breaks up a pass headed for Pittsburgh's John Stallworth in the Browns' 15-9 overtime loss in Three Rivers Stadium on September 24, 1978. Photo courtesy of the Cleveland Press Collection.

AMBROSE, DICK

Dick Ambrose was a Browns linebacker from 1975-83. He was Cleveland's 12th-round draft choice in 1975 out of the University of Virginia.

AMERICAN CONFERENCE

The American Conference was the Browns' home from 1950-52. It changed names in 1953 when it became known as the Eastern Conference. It also consisted of the Chicago Cardinals, New York Giants, Philadelphia Eagles, Pittsburgh Steelers, and Washington Redskins. It was won all three years by the Browns, who finished 10-2 in 1950. The Browns tied with the Giants but won a playoff 8-3 on December 17 in Cleveland. The Browns finished 11-1 in 1951, one-and-a-half games ahead of second-place New York, and 8-4 in 1952, one game ahead of the Giants and Eagles, both of whom wound up 7-5.

AMERICAN FOOTBALL CONFERENCE

The American Football Conference was the Browns' home from 1970-95, and has been since 1999. It was formed in 1970 when the NFL and AFL merged to become the 26-team National Football League, evening the NFL's two conferences—the American Football Conference and the National Football Conference—at 13 teams apiece (in 1969 there had been 16 teams in the NFL and 10 in the AFL). There are now 16 teams each in the AFC and the

NFC. The Browns have never won the championship. They have come close three times by advancing to the title game in 1986, 1987, and 1989. Each time, though, they lost to the Broncos—23-20 in overtime in 1986, 38-33 in 1987, and 37-21 in 1989.

ANDERSON, DEREK

Derek Anderson was a Browns quarterback from 2005-09. A product of Oregon State University, he was claimed off waivers by the Browns on September 21, 2005.

Anderson came out of nowhere in Week 2 of 2007 after opening-day starter Charlie Frye was traded to complete 20 of 33 passes for 328 yards, five touchdowns, and an interception in leading the Browns to a 51-45 triumph over the visiting Cincinnati Bengals. He went on to enjoy a Pro Bowl year, completing 298 (sixth in team history) passes in 527 attempts for 3,787 yards (fifth in team history), 29 TDs, and 19 interceptions. Unfortunately, four of those 19 picks came in a 19-14 loss to the Bengals in Cincinnati on December 23 that wound up costing the Browns, who finished 10-6, a playoff berth.

Anderson was unable to continue the success in 2008 that he had enjoyed the year before as the Browns plummeted to a 4-12, last-place finish. He wound up splitting the quarterback duties in 2009 with Brady Quinn. He ranks 10th in Browns history with 7,083 passing yards and ninth with 578 completions.

ANDREWS, BILLY

Billy Andrews was a Cleveland linebacker from 1967-74. He was a 13th-round draft choice by the Browns in 1967 out of Southeastern Louisiana University. The highlight of his career was when he made a diving interception of a Joe Namath pass, got up and returned the ball 25 yards for a touchdown with 35 seconds left in the first-ever ABC *Monday Night Football* game on September 21, 1970, in Cleveland Municipal Stadium. Andrews's touchdown was the clincher in a 31-21 triumph.

ANDRUZZI, JOE

Joe Andruzzi was a Browns guard from 2005-06. A product of Southern Connecticut State University, Andruzzi was signed by Cleveland as a free agent in 2005.

ARIZONA CARDINALS

The Arizona Cardinals were opponents of the Browns in the NFL from 1950-95 and have been since 1999. The franchise was based in Chicago through 1959 and in St. Louis from 1960-87. One of the more memorable games against the Browns was on September 20, 1964, in Cleveland Municipal Stadium when the game ended in a 33-33 tie. The Cardinals' all-time record against the Browns is 13-33-3, 7-18-1 at home and 6-15-2 on the road.

ASSISTANT COACHES

John Brickels, Blanton Collier, William (Red) Conkright, Fritz Heisler, and Bob Voigts were the first assistant coaches for the Browns. *Please see Coaches and Assistant Coaches on page 213 for a full list of assistant coaches.*

ATLANTA FALCONS

The Atlanta Falcons were Browns opponents in the NFL from 1966-95 and have been since 1999. One of the more memorable games against the Browns came on November 23, 2014, in the Georgia Dome when Brian Hoyer led the Browns on a late drive that culminated in a 37-yard field goal by Billy Cundiff as time expired in a 26-24 Browns win. Atlanta's all-time record against Cleveland is 3-11, 1-6 at home and 2-5 on the road.

ATTENDANCE

The highest home attendance figure recorded was on September 21, 1970, when the Browns beat the Jets 31-21 in front of a crowd of 85,703. The lowest home attendance figure recorded was the 16,506 fans who watched the Browns beat Chicago 35-2 on November 6, 1949. *For more attendance statistics (both regular season and postseason), please see Attendance Statistics on page 217.*

AUGUST
-30, 1946

The Browns beat the Brooklyn Dodgers 35-20 in the Rubber Bowl in Akron, Ohio, in their first-ever exhibition game. *Please see Rubber Bowl.*

-9, 1999

The Browns defeated the Dallas Cowboys 20-17 in overtime in Canton, Ohio, in the "new era" team's first preseason game.

AUSTIN, MILES

Miles Austin was a Browns wide receiver in 2014. A Monmouth College product, he was signed by Cleveland as a free agent on May 15, 2014. He had 47 receptions for 568 yards and two touchdowns in '14. His receptions total ranked second on the team and his TD receptions total was tied for second.

AWARDS

Various news organizations voted on individual player awards. The organizations that voted are denoted after the players' names. *Please see the abbreviations key.*

1947	Otto Graham (AAFC Most Valuable Player by OFF)
	Paul Brown (AAFC Coach of the Year by PFI)
1948	Otto Graham (AAFC Most Valuable Player by UP; AAFC co-Most Valuable Player with San Francisco quarterback Frankie Albert by OFF)
	Paul Brown (AAFC Coach of the Year by NYN)
1949	Otto Graham (AAFC Most Valuable Player by OFF)
	Paul Brown (AAFC Coach of the Year by NYN, SN)
1951	Paul Brown (NFL Coach of the Year by NYN)
1953	Otto Graham (NFL Most Valuable Player by UP)
	Paul Brown (NFL Coach of the Year by NYN)
1954	Lou Groza (NFL Most Valuable Player by SN)
	Paul Brown (NFL Coach of the Year by UP)
1955	Otto Graham (NFL Most Valuable Player by SN, UP)
1957	Jim Brown (NFL Player of the Year by AP; NFL Rookie of the Year by AP, UP) Paul Brown (NFL Coach of the Year by NYN, UP)
1958	Jim Brown (NFL Most Valuable Player by NEA, UPI)
1963	Jim Brown (NFL Most Valuable Player by MAX, UPI; co-Most Valuable Player with New York quarterback YA. Tittle by NEA)
1965	Jim Brown (NFL Player of the Year by AP; NFL Most Valuable Player by NEA, SN, UPI)
1968	Leroy Kelly (NFL Most Valuable Player by MAX)
1976	Jerry Sherk (NFL Defensive Player of the Year by NEA) Forrest Gregg (AFC Coach of the Year by AP)
1979	Sam Rutigliano (AFC Coach of the Year by UPI)
1980	Brian Sipe (NFL Most Valuable Player by FWA, SN; NFL Player of the Year by AP; NFL Offensive Player of the Year by PFW; AFC

Most Valuable Player by UPI) Sam Rutigliano (AFC Coach of the Year by UPI)

1982   Chip Banks (NFL Defensive Rookie of the Year by AP, PFW)
1985   Kevin Mack (AFC Rookie of the Year by UPI)
1986   Marty Schottenheimer (AFC Coach of the Year by FWA, UPI)
1989   Michael Dean Perry (AFC Defensive Most Valuable Player by UPI)

B

BAAB, MIKE

Mike Baab was a center for the Browns from 1982-87 and in 1990 and
'91. He was a fifth-round draft choice of Cleveland's in 1982 out of the
University of Texas. He was traded to New England on August 29, 1988, and
then re-acquired as a free agent on March 6, 1990.

BABICH, BOB

Bob Babich was a linebacker for the Browns from 1973-78. He was a
Miami University product. He was acquired by the Browns on September 6,
1973, in a trade with the San Diego Chargers for a first-round draft choice in
1974 and a second-round pick in 1975.

BAHR, MATT

Matt Bahr was a Browns kicker from 1981-89. He was a Penn State
University product obtained by Cleveland on October 6, 1981, in a trade
with San Francisco for a 1983 draft choice. Bahr replaced Dave Jacobs, who
had supplanted long-time kicker Don Cockroft. Jacobs was released after a
terrible start. Bahr connected on 87.5 percent of his field goal attempts in
1983 (21-of-24 attempts). He scored 101 points that year. He tallied 104
points in 1988.

Bahr ranks fifth all-time for the Browns with 677 points and second
all-time in team history with 46 postseason points. He kicked a pair of 52-yard
field goals—one in the regular season and one in the postseason. The regular-
season field goal came on October 26, 1986, in a win against Minnesota, and
the postseason one occurred on January 8, 1983, in an AFC First-Round
Playoff loss to the Raiders in Los Angeles.

Bahr was as tough as kickers come, as evidenced by his courage on
November 23, 1986, at home against Pittsburgh. He tore ligaments in his right

Billy Andrews greets Bob Babich as the defense comes off the field in 1973. Photo courtesy of the Cleveland Press Collection.

knee while making a game-saving tackle off a return of his own kickoff with the Browns leading 31-28. The Browns eventually won in overtime 37-31.

BAKER, AL

Al Baker was a Browns defensive end in 1987 and from '89-90. He was a Colorado State University product obtained by Cleveland on September 3, 1987, in a trade with the St. Louis Cardinals for a fifth-round 1988 draft pick.

The Browns waived him on August 29, 1988, before he returned as a free agent on March 31, 1989. Baker totaled 14.5 sacks for the Browns.

BALDWIN, RANDY

Randy Baldwin was a Browns running back from 1991-94. He was a University of Mississippi product. He was picked up by Cleveland as a free agent on November 13, 1991. He was best known for his kickoff return duties, leading the Browns in kickoff returns and kickoff return yardage every season from 1992-94. Baldwin had an 85-yard kickoff return for a touchdown in a 28-20 opening-day victory over the Bengals in Cincinnati on September 4, 1994. That year, he totaled 753 return yards. His 1,872 kickoff return yards rank fifth in team history.

BALTIMORE COLTS (ORIGINAL)

The original Baltimore Colts were Browns opponents in the AAFC from 1947-49 and in the NFL in 1950. They were the forerunners of the Colts franchise that became quite successful in later years. Their all-time record against the Browns was 0-7, 0-4 at home and 0-3 on the road.

BALTIMORE RAVENS

The Baltimore Ravens have been Browns opponents in the NFL since 1999. They were members of the AFC Central Division through 2001. The Ravens were the original Browns franchise before their relocation in 1996. The Ravens easily defeated the Browns in the four games in 1999 and 2000 before the Browns gained many measures of revenge with two upsets of the Ravens in 2001. Another memorable Browns win over the Ravens came on December 22, 2002, in Baltimore when Tim directed a masterful 92-yard drive late in the game that resulted in a touchdown and a 14-13 Browns win that kept alive their playoff hopes. On November 18, 2007, the Browns beat the Ravens in the incredible "Ricochet" game 33-30 in overtime at Baltimore. *Please see Ricochet, The.* Baltimore's all-time record against Cleveland is 24-8, 13-3 at home and 11-5 on the road.

BANKS, CHIP

Chip Banks was a Cleveland linebacker from 1982-86. He was a Browns first-round draft choice in 1982 from the University of Southern California.

He was second on the team with three interceptions in 1983, including a 65-yard return for a touchdown in a 30-0 victory on November 20 at New England in a crucial matchup of AFC wild-card contenders. Banks led the Browns with 11 sacks in 1985, tying for fifth all-time for the Browns. His 27.5 sacks all-time rank seventh in team history. AP and PFW named him NFL Defensive Rookie of the Year in 1982. He was voted to All-AFC defensive teams in 1983 by AP, PFW, FWA and UPI, in 1985 by UPI; and in 1986 by PFW and UPI. He was voted to the Pro Bowl in 1982, 1983, 1985, and 1986.

BARNES, ERICH

Erich Barnes was a Browns defensive back from 1965-71. He was a product of Purdue University acquired by Cleveland on August 30, 1965, in a trade with the New York Giants. The deal also included a trade to the Detroit Lions for Mike Lucci and a draft choice. On October 1, 1967, against New Orleans Barnes intercepted a pass and threw a lateral pass to Ross Fichtner, who raced 88 yards deep into Saints territory en route to a 42-7 rout for the Browns' first win of the year after two defeats. Barnes was the team leader with five interceptions in 1970, including a 38-yard return for a touchdown that sealed Cleveland's 15-7 victory over Pittsburgh on October 3 in Cleveland Municipal Stadium. He had 18 career interceptions with the Browns and was a Pro Bowl pick in 1968.

BARTON, ERIC

Eric Barton was a Browns linebacker from 2009-10. A product of the University of Maryland, he signed with Cleveland as an unrestricted free agent on March 13, 2009.

BELICHICK, BILL

Bill Belichick was the Browns' head coach from 1991-95. He took over a 3-13 team from 1990. He was previously the New York Giants' defensive coordinator the year before when the Giants won Super Bowl XXV. He led the Browns to a 6-10 finish in 1991 and two 7-9 finishes in 1992 and '93 before directing the team to a playoff berth in 1994 and a wild-card win over New England. He was fired following a 5-11 finish in 1995 when the franchise announced it would be relocating to Baltimore. Belichick's all-time record as Browns head coach was 36-44, 20-20 at home and 16-24 on the road. His all-time postseason mark as Browns head coach with the team was 1-1, 1-0 at home and 0-1 on the road.

BENARD, MARCUS

Marcus Benard was a Browns linebacker from 2009-11. A product of Jackson State University, he signed with the Browns as an undrafted free agent in 2009. His 7.5 sacks in 2010 was tops on the team. Benard totaled 11.5 career sacks with the Browns.

BENJAMIN, TRAVIS

Travis Benjamin has been a Cleveland wide receiver and kickoff and punt returner since 2012. He was a fourth-round draft pick of the Browns in 2012 out of the University of Miami. The small but lightning quick Benjamin's best year receiving was in 2014 when he had 18 receptions for 304 yards and a team-leading three touchdowns. He has returned two punts for touchdowns, both in home wins—a 93-yarder against the Chiefs on December 9, 2012 and a 79-yarder against the Bills on October 3, 2013.

BENTLEY, KEVIN

Kevin Bentley was a Browns linebacker from 2002-04. He was a fourth-round draft pick by Cleveland in 2002 out of Northwestern University.

BEREA

Berea is a small Ohio town near Cleveland that was the home of the Browns' training and administrative complex from 1992-95 and has been since 1999.

BERNIE, BERNIE

"Bernie, Bernie" is a song named after quarterback and hometown hero Bernie Kosar. It was popular during the Browns' playoff run in 1986.

BERNIE'S INSIDERS

Bernie's Insiders was a publication from 2001-06 that offered news, views, features, and many other things regarding the Browns.

BIG DAWG

Big Dawg is Browns fan John Thompson who attires himself in canine paraphernalia. This behavior stems from the enormous popularity of The Dawg Pound at old Cleveland Stadium. Thompson became known nationwide. *Please see Dawg Pound, The.*

BITONIO, JOEL

Joel Bitonio has been a Browns guard since 2014. He was a second-round draft pick of Cleveland's in 2014 out of the University of Nevada.

BLOOM, TOM

Tom Bloom was a sixth-round draft choice of the Browns in 1963 out of Purdue University. He was the Boilermakers' Most Valuable Player as a running back in 1962. He was killed in an automobile accident soon after draft day while driving the car he had purchased with the bonus money he received for signing with the Browns. He had hoped to win a spot in the defensive backfield.

BODDEN, LEIGH

Leigh Bodden was a Browns cornerback from 2003-07. The Browns signed him in 2003 as an undrafted free agent. He tied for the team lead with three interceptions in 2005 and was the team leader in 2007 with six picks.

BOLDEN, LEROY

Leroy Bolden was a Browns running back from 1958-59. He was a sixth-round draft selection for the Browns in 1955 out of Michigan State University. He spent 1956 and '57 in the military. In addition to playing running back he also returned kickoffs, including a 102-yarder for a touchdown on October 26, 1958, in a 38-24 victory over the Chicago Cardinals.

BOLDEN, RICKEY

Rickey Bolden was a Cleveland offensive tackle from 1984-89. He was a fourth-round draft choice by the Browns in 1984 out of Southern Methodist University.

Leroy Bolden fumbles in preseason action in Detroit against the Lions on August 22, 1958. Photo courtesy of the Cleveland Press Collection.

BOLTON, RON

Ron Bolton was a Browns defensive back from 1976-82 and a Norfolk State University product. Cleveland acquired him on April 8, 1976, in a trade with the Patriots for Bob McKay. Bolton intercepted 17 passes in his career. One of his most memorable occurred in an AFC Divisional Playoff on January 4, 1981, when he returned a Jim Plunkett pass 42 yards for a touchdown. This gave the Browns a 6-0 second-quarter lead on the frozen field of Cleveland Stadium, but the Browns eventually lost 14-12.

BOTTLEGATE

"Bottlegate" was a bizarre incident that occurred on December 16, 2001, toward the end of the Browns' 15-10 loss to Jacksonville in Cleveland Browns Stadium. Angry fans threw thousands of plastic bottles from the stands, littering large parts of both end zones in response to the following scenario: with the Browns, trailing by five and still in playoff contention, deep in Jaguars territory late in the game, quarterback Tim Couch passed to Quincy Morgan.

The rookie wide receiver was hit by safety James Boyd and struggled to hold onto the ball. After making an apparent catch, Morgan lost the ball temporarily when he hit the ground but recovered his own fumble, which would have made it a catch and given the Browns a first down. That would have given them time for four attempts to get into the end zone. Couch quickly spiked the ball to stop the clock, which by rule ends the option for an instant replay challenge. Referee Terry McAulay, though, ruled the replay buzzer on his belt went off prior to the snap.

Jacksonville's request for a review was honored, and the ruling of a completion was overturned, causing the bottle-throwing escapade. Due to the danger of this, McAulay ruled the game over and ordered both teams to their respective locker rooms with 48 seconds still left on the clock. Nearly thirty minutes later, however, both sides returned to the field for one more snap to officially complete the game, via orders from NFL commissioner Paul Tagliabue.

BOUSMA, BOB

Bob Bousma was a Browns radio broadcaster from 1952-53.

BOWENS, DAVID

David Bowens was a Browns linebacker from 2009-10. A product of Western Illinois University, he signed with Cleveland on March 10, 2009. He had 5.5 sacks in 2009 that ranked second on the Browns. Bowens had quite a day on October 24, 2010, against the Saints in New Orleans. That day, he returned two interceptions off of Drew Brees for touchdowns—a 30-yarder in the second quarter and a 64-yarder in the fourth quarter that put the nail in the coffin as the Browns shocked the defending Super Bowl Champs 30-17.

BOWLING GREEN STATE UNIVERSITY

Bowling Green State University acted as the Browns' training-camp site from 1946-51. The Browns have drafted nine players from the university.

BOYER, BRANT

Brant Boyer was a Browns linebacker from 2001-03. He attended the University of Arizona.

BRADLEY, HENRY

Henry Bradley was a Browns defensive tackle from 1979-82. He was an Alcorn State University product acquired by Cleveland as a free agent in July 1979. He was released on August 27, 1979, and re-signed in November of that year when Jerry Sherk went down with a staph infection.

BRANDON, DAVID

David Brandon was a Browns linebacker from 1991-93. A Memphis State University product, he was acquired in 1991 by Cleveland as a free agent. He was second on the Browns in interceptions in 1991 and '92. Two were returned for touchdowns—a 30-yarder in overtime that gave the Browns a 30-24 win in San Diego on October 20, 1991, and a 92-yarder on the Bears' opening drive that fueled the Browns' 27-14 home victory on November 29, 1992.

BRENNAN, BRIAN

Brian Brennan was a Browns wide receiver from 1984-91. He was a fourth-round draft selection of Cleveland's in 1984 out of Boston College. His most productive season was 1986 when he led the team with 55 receptions and 838 receiving yards and had six touchdown catches. He had 315 receptions (tied for sixth in team history) for 4,148 yards and 19 touchdowns in his Browns career. Quite possibly, Brennan's most memorable moment came against Denver in the AFC Championship Game on January 11, 1987, when he was on the receiving end of a 48-yard touchdown pass from Bernie Kosar that gave the Browns a 20-13 lead with 5:43 left in the game. The Browns eventually lost 23-20 in overtime. He caught two touchdown passes from Bernie Kosar in the Browns' 37-21 AFC title game loss in Denver on January 14, 1990, including a spectacular, diving 10-yard catch. He also returned punts and scored on a 37-yard return against the New York Jets on December 22, 1985.

BREWER, JOHNNY

Johnny Brewer was a tight end/linebacker for the Browns from 1961-67. He was a fourth-round draft choice of Cleveland's in 1960 out of the University of Mississippi with one year of college eligibility remaining. He returned an interception 70 yards for a touchdown in a 42-37 home win over the Washington Redskins on November 26, 1967. He was selected to play in the Pro Bowl in 1966.

BREWSTER, DARREL

Darrel Brewster was a Browns wide receiver from 1952-58. He was a Purdue University product acquired by the team on July 12, 1952, in a trade with the Chicago Cardinals for Burl Toler. Brewster was the team leader in receptions and receiving yards every season from 1955-57. He was second on the team in touchdown receptions in 1954 and '55. His 182 yards receiving on December 6, 1953, against the New York Giants rank ninth in team history. He was a Pro Bowl pick in 1955 and '56.

BROADCASTS, RADIO

The following are the Browns' radio broadcasters and the flagship stations Browns games have been broadcast on:

1946	Bob Neal and Stan Gee (WGAR-AM 1220)
1947-49	Bob Neal and Bill Mayer (WGAR-AM 1220)
1950	Bob Neal and Don Cordray (WERE-AM 1300)
1951	Bob Neal and Phil McLean (WERE-AM 1300)
1952-53	Ken Coleman and Bob Bousma (WTAM-AM 1100)
1954	Bill McColgan and Bill Mayer (WGAR-AM 1220)
1955	Bill McColgan and Jim Graner (WTAM-AM 1100)
1956-60	Bill McColgan and Jim Graner (WGAR-AM 1220)
1961	Gib Shanley and Les Clark (WGAR-AM 1220)
1962	Gib Shanley and Ray Tannehill (WERE-AM 1300)
1963-67	Gib Shanley and Jim Graner (WERE-AM 1300)
1968-74	Gib Shanley and Jim Graner (WHK-AM 1420)
1975-84	Gib Shanley and Jim Mueller (WHK-AM 1420)
1985	Nev Chandler, Doug Dieken, and Jim Mueller (WHK-AM 1420)
1986-89	Nev Chandler, Doug Dieken, and Jim Mueller (WWWE-AM 1100, WDOK-FM 102.1)
1990-93	Nev Chandler, Doug Dieken, and Jim Mueller (WHK-AM 1420, WMMS-FM 100.7)
1994-95	Casey Coleman, Doug Dieken, and Jim Mueller (WKNR-AM 1220, WDOK-FM 102.1)
1999-2012	Jim Donovan and Doug Dieken (WMJI-FM 105.7, WTAM-AM 1100)
2013-	Jim Donovan and Doug Dieken (WKRK-FM 92.3, WNCX-FM 98.5, WKNR-AM 850)

BROADCASTS, TELEVISION

The following are the Browns' television broadcasters and the network/stations Browns road games have been broadcast on:

1948	Bob Neal and Stan Gee (Dumont Network)
1949-51	Bob Neal and Bill Mayer (Dumont Network)
1952	Don Wattrick and Lou Saban (WXEL-Channel 9)
1953	Bill McColgan and John Fitzgerald (WXEL-Channel 9)
1954-55	Ken Coleman (WJW-Channel 8)
1956	Ken Coleman and Otto Graham (WJW-Channel 8)
1957-60	Ken Coleman and Jimmy Dudley (WJW-Channel 8)
1961-62	Ken Coleman and Cliff Lewis (WJW-Channel 8)
1963-65	Ken Coleman and Warren Lahr (WJW-Channel 8)
1966-67	Frank Glieber and Warren Lahr (WJW-Channel 8)

In 1968, CBS began broadcasting NFL games on a regional and national basis, until it lost its NFL package in 1994 to FOX. FOX, like CBS from 1970-93, broadcasts Browns Sunday afternoon home games when their opponent is an NFC team. From 1970-95, NBC beamed Browns games on Sunday afternoon and selected Saturday afternoon and Thanksgiving games when they were on the road or at home against a fellow AFC team. ABC started its *Monday Night Football* package in 1970 with the very first game in Cleveland against Joe Namath and the New York Jets on September 21. The *Monday Night Football* package also included special edition games on other nights, of which the Browns appeared on Thursday and Sunday. ESPN joined the fray in 1987 with a Sunday night package on which the Browns have appeared, including special edition games on Thursday and Saturday, and took over the Monday night games from ABC in 2006, on which the Browns have also appeared. NBC has had its *Football Night in America* since that same year of 2006, on which the Browns have appeared.

BROOKLYN DODGERS

The Brooklyn Dodgers were Browns opponents in the AAFC from 1946-48. They were blown out at home by the Browns 66-14 on December 8, 1946, the largest point total ever for the Browns. The Dodgers were the Browns' first-ever exhibition opponents, when on August 30, 1946, they lost to Cleveland 35-20 in the Rubber Bowl in Akron, Ohio. The Dodgers merged with the New York Yankees following the 1948 season. Brooklyn's all-time record against the Browns was 0-6, 0-3 at home and 0-3 on the road.

BROOKLYN-NEW YORK YANKEES

The Brooklyn-New York Yankees were opponents of the Browns in the AAFC in 1949. The team was the result of a merger by the New York Yankees and the Brooklyn Dodgers of the AAFC. Their all-time record against Cleveland was 0-2, 0-1 at home and 0-1 on the road.

BROWN BLUES, THE

The Brown Blues was a half-hour program hosted by Jerry Sherk and Brian Sipe that originally aired on WKYC TV-3 in 1996, not long after the final game in Cleveland Stadium. The show was a retrospective about the two ex-Browns' days with the team in the Stadium.

BROWN, COURTNEY

Courtney Brown was a defensive end for Cleveland from 2000-04. He was the first overall selection by the Browns that year out of Penn State University. He had a career-high six sacks in 2003 and totaled 19 as a Brown. He returned a fumble 25 yards for a touchdown in a 27-21 overtime defeat in Chicago on November 4, 2001.

BROWN, JIM

Jim Brown was a Cleveland running back from 1957-65. He was a first-round draft choice of the Browns in 1957 out of Syracuse University. He rushed for 942 yards his rookie year while leading the Browns back to the NFL title game after their first losing season ever the year before. Included was his first 100-yard game when he gained 109 in a 21-17 victory over Washington on November 3 in Cleveland Municipal Stadium, a game in which he also scored two touchdowns rushing. Three weeks later, he set an NFL record that was not broken until fourteen years later, when he rushed for 237 yards in a 45-31 triumph over Los Angeles at home. He rushed for four touchdowns in that game, including an early 69-yarder.

Brown rushed for 1,527 yards in 1958, including nine 100-yard games, in leading the Browns to an Eastern Conference Playoff against the New York Giants. He rushed for 1,329 yards in 1959, including five rushing touchdowns that helped the Browns to a 38-31 victory at Baltimore on November 1. He rushed for 1,257 yards in 1960, including a 71-yard touchdown run against the Eagles on November 23. He gained 1,403 yards in 1961 and matched his

237-yard performance from four years earlier when he did it on November 19 in a 45-24 home win over Philadelphia, a game in which he scored four touchdowns rushing.

Brown had a "down" year in 1962 when he gained "just" 996 yards on the ground, the only year he failed to lead the league. He rebounded big time in 1963 under a more wide-open offense with new head coach Blanton Collier, scorching opposing defenses for 1,863 yards—an NFL record until O.J. Simpson broke it ten years later. In the season opener at home against Washington on September 15, he had quite a day, scoring on an 83-yard play off a short pass from Frank Ryan, a 10-yard run, and an 80-yard run en route to a 37-14 victory. One week later, on September 22, he scored on a 71-yard run in a victory over the Cowboys in Dallas.

A year later, on October 18, 1964, Brown had another 71-yard run in another victory over the Cowboys in Dallas. That year, he gained 1,446 yards and in 1965 he gained 1,544 in leading the Browns to consecutive NFL title-game appearances, the first of which they won (defeating the Colts in '64).

Brown retired in the summer of 1966 to pursue an acting career in the movies. All seven of his 1,000-yard rushing seasons rank in the top eight all-time in Browns history. He was the team leader in rushing yards every year and rushed for a team record 12,312 yards overall, an astonishing 5.2-yards per game average, also a team record. He averaged a remarkable 104.3 yards per game. He scored 106 rushing touchdowns, another team mark. He also holds four of the top six spots in team history for most rushing yards in one game (the two 237-yard performances are tied for second). He also had 262 receptions for 2,499 yards and 20 touchdown catches in his career. His 756 points are fourth in team history, and his 15,459 combined net yards rank first (######) in team history.

In addition, Brown holds four of the top 10 spots in Browns history for most combined net yards in one season, including the number three spot with 2,131 in 1963. He holds the top spot in club annals for most points scored in one season with 126 in 1965. His 114 rushing yards in the Browns' 27-0 victory over Baltimore in the 1964 NFL Championship game rank as the fourth most in team history.

Brown's awards include: NFL Player of the Year in 1957 (AP), NFL Rookie of the Year in 1957 (AP, UP), NFL Most Valuable Player in 1958 (NEA, UPI), NFL Most Valuable Player in 1963 (MAX, UPI), NFL co-Most Valuable Player with New York Giants quarterback Y.A. Tittle in 1963 (NEA), NFL Player of the Year in 1965 (AP), NFL Most Valuable Player in 1965 (NEA, SN, and UPI). Brown was named to All-NFL offensive teams in 1957 (AP, NYN, NEA,

Jim Brown in action against the Cowboys in 1964. Photo courtesy of the Cleveland Press Collection.

and UP) and from 1958-61 and 1963-65 (AP, NYN, NEA, and UPI). He was a Pro Bowl pick from 1957-65. His uniform No. 32 is retired by the Browns. He was inducted into the Pro Football Hall of Fame in 1971.

BROWN, ORLANDO

Orlando Brown was an offensive tackle with Cleveland from 1994-95 and in 1999. He was a South Carolina State University product obtained by the team as a free agent on May 13, 1993. He spent the 1993 season on injured reserve with a shoulder problem. He signed with Cleveland as a free agent again on February 28, 1994, again on July 19, 1995, and finally on February 17, 1999.

Brown was the center attraction in one of the more unusual plays in NFL history when he was hit in his open right eye with a penalty flag thrown by referee Jeff Triplett. This happened during the second quarter of a home game against Jacksonville on December 19 in the second-to-last game of the season. After much confusion as to whether or not he should have left the game for a play, Brown returned to the field and shoved Triplett to the ground. He was kicked out of the game and suspended indefinitely by the NFL.

The suspension eventually was shortened to one game—that year's season finale. Brown's eye suffered direct trauma that affected his vision and could develop into glaucoma. He never played again and was cut by the Browns in September 2000. At the time, he had a six-year, $27 million contract from which he collected a $7.5 million signing bonus. He filed a $200 million lawsuit against the NFL. U.S. District Judge Gerard E. Lynch ruled on March 18, 2002, that the NFL could not force the lawsuit into arbitration by saying that a union contract governs a player's claim that his career was ruined. The case was moved from federal to state court and is still pending.

BROWN, PAUL

Paul Brown was Cleveland's first head coach. He held the position from 1946-62. His surname is the reason behind the team's nickname, and he is the only pro football coach for whom a team has been named. Brown led Cleveland to four straight championships in the AAFC from 1946-49 and six straight title-game appearances in the NFL from 1950-55, three of which his team won (1950, '54, and '55).

Brown was an innovator when it came to the game of football, as he was the first head coach to hire a full-time coaching staff, utilize classroom study to such a broad extent, use intelligence tests, grade his players from individual film clips, and develop a messenger-guard system so he could call plays from the sideline. He had much to do in inventing, or improving, plays such as the screen pass, draw play, and trap plays. He also invented the first single-bar facemask.

Brown's days as head football coach and athletic officer at the Great Lakes Naval Training Center had much to do with his firing by Browns majority owner

Paul Brown (left) and Lou Groza. Photo courtesy of the Cleveland Press Collection.

Art Modell on January 9, 1963. Toward the end of his reign as head coach, many players were growing tired of his military-like approach to dealing with them. They also believed the game was passing him by, that his play-calling had become too conservative for the changing times. He was constantly in disagreement with Modell over how the team should be run.

Brown was voted AAFC Coach of the Year in 1947 (PFI), in 1948 (NYN), and in 1949 (NYN and SN). He won NFL Coach of the Year honors in 1951 and 1953 (NYN), in 1954 (UP), and in 1957 (NYN and UP). He was inducted into the Pro Football Hall of Fame in 1967, two months before he and his family were awarded an AFL franchise that would turn out to be the Cincinnati Bengals (the Bengals would later become bitter rivals of the Browns in the NFL). Brown's all-time record as Cleveland head coach was 158-48-8, 81-24-2 at home and 77-24-6 on the road. His all-time postseason record as Browns head coach was 9-5, 7-1 at home and 2-4 on the road.

BROWN, SHELDON

Sheldon Brown was a Browns cornerback from 2010-12. A product of the University of South Carolina, he was traded to Cleveland from Philadelphia on April 2, 2010. He tied for the team lead in interceptions in 2012 with three, the first of which was a 19-yard return off an Andy Dalton pass for a touchdown that pretty much sealed what turned out to be a 34-24 Browns victory over the visiting Bengals.

BROWNIE ELF

The Brownie Elf was a character used to represent the Browns that surfaced in advertisements, game programs, and on the back of players' parkas, among other places.

BROWNS BACKERS WORLDWIDE

Browns Backers Worldwide is the official Browns fan club that surfaced in March 1984. It is one of the largest organized fan clubs in all of professional sports. There are members and clubs throughout the world. Browns Backers Worldwide grew with the help of *Browns News/Illustrated,* a publication from 1981-2001 that received letters from transplanted Browns fans throughout the country requesting other Browns fans in their locales to contact them.

BROWNS NEWS/ILLUSTRATED

Browns News/Illustrated was a publication from 1981-2001 that offered news, views, features, and many other things regarding the Browns.

BRYANT, ANTONIO

Antonio Bryant was a Browns wide receiver from 2004-05. He was acquired by the Browns in a trade with the Dallas Cowboys after five games of the 2004 season. In 10 games in '04, he had 42 receptions for 546 yards and tied for second on the Browns with four touchdowns receptions. In 2005 he led the team with 69 receptions (tied for ninth in team history) for 1,009 yards (ninth in team annals) and four TD catches.

BRYANT, DESMOND

Desmond Bryant has been a Browns defensive lineman since 2013. A product of Harvard University, he signed with Cleveland as an unrestricted free agent on March 12, 2013. He had 3.5 sacks in 2013 and five sacks in 2014, the latter which ranked second on the team.

BUFFALO BILLS (CURRENT)

The Buffalo Bills were opponents of the Browns in the NFL from 1970-95 and have been since 1999. The most memorable game between the two teams occurred in the postseason, when on January 6, 1990, the Browns won a 34-30 barnburner in an AFC Divisional Playoff in Cleveland Stadium. Buffalo's all-time record against Cleveland is 8-11, 4-5 at home and 4-6 on the road. The Bills' all-time postseason record against Cleveland is 0-1 (road game).

BUFFALO BISONS/BILLS (ORIGINAL)

The original Buffalo Bisons/Bills were Browns opponents in the AAFC from 1946-49. The team's nickname was changed from "Bisons" to "Bills" (no relation to the current Buffalo Bills) in 1947. They lost both postseason matchups in Cleveland—49-7 in the AAFC Championship game on December 19, 1948, and 31-21 in an AAFC First-Round Playoff on December 4, 1949. Buffalo's all-time record against the Browns was 0-6-2, 0-3-1 at home and 0-3-1 on the road. Its all-time postseason record against Cleveland was 0-2 (road games).

BURNETT, ROB

Rob Burnett was a defensive end for the Browns from 1990-95. He was a fifth-round draft choice of the Browns in 1990 out of Syracuse University. He had a team-high 10 sacks in 1994 and nine in both 1992 and '93, the former tying Clay Matthews for the team lead and the latter leading the team. Burnett's 40.5 sacks all-time are third most in Browns history. He was a Pro Bowl pick in 1994.

BURRELL, CLINTON

Clinton Burrell was a Browns defensive back from 1979-84. He was a sixth-round draft choice of Cleveland's in 1979 out of Louisiana State University. He was second on the team with five interceptions in 1980. He returned a Ken Anderson pass 14 yards for the Browns' only touchdown in a 23-10 defeat to the Bengals on December 12, 1982, in Cincinnati.

Clinton Burrell sends Buffalo's Dan Fulton (a future teammate of Burrell's with the Browns) to the ground during a scrimmage in 1979. Photo courtesy of the Cleveland Press Collection.

BUSH, DEVIN

Devin Bush was a Browns free safety from 2001–2002. A product of Florida State University, he returned an Elvis Grbac pass 43 yards for a touchdown on November 18, 2001 to give the Browns a 17-0 lead en route to a 27-17 upset of the Ravens in Baltimore.

BYNER, EARNEST

Earnest Byner was a Browns running back from 1984-88 and '94-95. He was a 10th-round draft choice by Cleveland in 1984 out of East Carolina University. He was part of one of the worst trades in franchise history when he was shipped to Washington for Mike Oliphant on draft day 1989. Byner went on to lead the Redskins in rushing yards for three straight years, including two 1,000-yard seasons and a 998-yard season, respectively, and helped them to the 1991 NFL Championship. Meanwhile, Oliphant gained 188 combined net yards in three seasons with the Browns, with all of the yardage coming in 1989. Byner was re-acquired by the Browns on May 5, 1994, as a free agent.

One highlight of Byner's rookie year occurred on November 4, 1984, when he recovered a fumble and raced 55 yards for a touchdown in a 13-10 victory at Buffalo. Another highlight happened on December 16 of the same year when he rushed for 188 yards (tied for 10th in Browns history) in a 27-20 triumph at Houston in the season finale.

In 1985, Byner became part of only the third running-back tandem in NFL history in which both backs rushed for 1,000 yards in the same season (he totaled 1,002, while Kevin Mack had 1,104). He set a Browns record for most rushing yards in a postseason game, with 161 in an AFC Divisional Playoff loss at Miami on January 4, 1986. He also holds the No. 3 spot in the same category with his 122-yard performance against the Indianapolis Colts on January 9, 1988.

Byner was injured for most of the 1986 season. His crucial fumble in the 1987 AFC Championship game in Denver—"The Fumble"—will always offset his titanic performance leading up to it, including the fifth-highest receiving yardage total (120) in one playoff game (####) in team history. His seven catches in the Broncos game are tied for second in team history (#####). He is seventh on the Browns' all-time rushing yardage list with 3,364. His 36 postseason points are tied with Otto Graham for third in team history. He ranks second all-time for the Browns with 480 postseason rushing yards (#).

C

CAMERON, JORDAN

Jordan Cameron was a Browns tight end from 2011-14. He was a fourth-round draft pick of the Browns in 2011 out of the University of Southern California. Cameron's best year with the Browns was in 2013 when he was voted to the Pro Bowl due to his 80 receptions for 917 yards and seven touchdowns. His receptions total that year is tied for seventh in Browns history.

CAMP, REGGIE

Reggie Camp was a Cleveland defensive end from 1983–1987. He was a third-round draft choice of the Browns in 1983 out of the University of California, Berkeley. He had 14 sacks in 1984, a Browns record. Camp's 35 sacks all-time rank fifth in team history.

CAMPBELL, MARK

Mark Campbell was a Browns tight end from 1999-2000 and in 2002. He was signed by Cleveland in 1999 as an undrafted free agent out of the University of Michigan. His bet year with the Browns was in 2002 when he had 25 receptions for 179 yards and three touchdowns.

CAROLINA PANTHERS

The Carolina Panthers were opponents of the Browns in the NFL in 1995 and have been since 1999. Their all-time record against the Browns is 4-1, 2-0 at home and 2-1 on the road

CARPENTER, KEN

Ken Carpenter was a Browns running back from 1950-53. He was a first-round draft choice of Cleveland's in 1950 out of Oregon State University. He was picked for the Pro Bowl in 1951.

CARSON, BUD

Bud Carson was the Browns' head coach from 1989-90. He was fired after nine games in 1990. He coached the Browns to an appearance in the 1989 AFC Championship Game. His all-time record as Browns head coach was 11-13-1, 6-5-1 at home and 5-8 on the road. His all-time postseason record with Cleveland was 1-1, 1-0 at home and 0-1 on the road.

CBS TELEVISION NETWORK

The CBS television network broadcast Browns games from 1968-69 and Sunday afternoon home games when their opponent was an NFC team from 1970-93.

CENTRAL DIVISION

The Central Division was Cleveland's home from 1970-95 and '99-2001. The division was formed in 1970 when the NFL and AFL merged to become one National Football League consisting of 26 teams. The Central Division was one of three divisions in the AFC that consisted of the Cincinnati Bengals, Houston Oilers, and Pittsburgh Steelers from its inception through 1994. It was joined in 1995 by the expansion Jacksonville Jaguars and in 1996 by the Baltimore Ravens (former relocated Browns team). Houston relocated to Tennessee in 1997 and became known as the Titans in 1999. The Browns won the division six times—in 1971, '80, from '85-87, and in '89.

CENTURY DIVISION

The Century Division was home to the Browns from 1967 to 1969. It was formed in 1967 when the NFL's Eastern Conference split into two divisions (the other was the Capitol). It lasted through 1969 as the NFL merged with the AFL the following season. The Century was won by the Browns all three years. They finished 9-5, 10-4, and 10-3-1, respectively. The division was also made up of the New York Giants, Pittsburgh Steelers, and St. Louis Cardinals in 1967 and '69 and the New Orleans Saints, Pittsburgh, and St. Louis in 1968.

CHANDLER, NEV

Nev Chandler was the Browns' radio play-by-play man from 1985-93.

CHICAGO BEARS

The Chicago Bears were opponents of the Browns in the NFL from 1950–1995 and have been since 1999. Four of the more memorable games between the two teams occurred on November 25, 1951, September 7, 1986, October 23, 1989, and November 4, 2001. The Browns won the 1951 game in Cleveland 42-21 as Dub Jones set a Cleveland record, and tied an NFL mark, by scoring six touchdowns. NFL single-game records were set that day for most penalties against both teams (37) and most yards penalized against both teams (374). Several players had to be helped off the field, and Browns quarterback Otto Graham suffered a broken nose.

The Bears escaped the 1986 game in Chicago with a wild 41-31 victory in a contest that left the Browns looking like a MASH unit. The game also marked the first time in NFL history a team had a play reviewed by instant replay when, on the third play of the game, Al Gross appeared to recover an errant Chicago snap in the Bears' end zone. The debate was whether Gross gained possession of the ball before sliding across the end line. After a review, referees ruled that Gross did indeed gain possession of the ball in time for a touchdown and a 7-0 Browns lead.

The Browns won the 1989 game 27-7 in Cleveland on *Monday Night Football* as they shook off recent offensive doldrums. The key play was a 97-yard touch-down strike from Bernie Kosar to Webster Slaughter, the second-longest pass play in team history. The Bears won the 2001 game 27-21 in overtime at Chicago in miracle fashion. The Bears trailed 21-7 but scored a touchdown, recovered an onside kick, and scored another touchdown (on a Hail Mary play) in the final 28 seconds of regulation before Mike Brown returned a batted interception of a Tim Couch pass 16 yards for the winning score on Cleveland's third play from scrimmage in overtime.

Chicago's all-time record against Cleveland is 6-9, 4-2 at home and 2-7 on the road.

CHICAGO COLLEGE ALL-STAR GAME

The College All-Star Game was an annual summer exhibition contest matching the previous season's NFL Champion and the college all-star team. The Browns participated four times, and won each time—33-0 in 1951, 30-27 in 1955, 26-0 in 1956, and 24-16 in 1965. Each of those four games was played in Soldier Field in Chicago.

CHICAGO ROCKETS

The Chicago Rockets were opponents of the Browns in the AAFC from 1946-49. Their all-time record against the Browns was 0-8, 0-4 at home and 0-5 on the road.

CINCINNATI BENGALS

The Cincinnati Bengals were Browns opponents in the NFL from 1970-95 and have been since 1999. The Bengals were rivals of the Browns in the AFC Central Division from 1970-95 and '99-2001 and have been rivals in the AFC North Division since 2002. The "Interstate 71" rivalry was fueled by bad blood between former Browns head coach Paul Brown and majority owner Art Modell. Brown was fired by Modell on January 9, 1963, after seventeen years as head coach of the Browns. With Brown then head coach of the Bengals, Cincinnati lost its first meeting with the Browns 30-27 on October 11, 1970, in Cleveland. The Bengals beat the Browns for the first time 14-10 in Cincinnati on November 15 of the same season.

Another memorable Browns win against the Bengals came on November 23, 1975, in Cleveland, a game the Bengals entered with an 8-1 record to the Browns' 0-9 mark. The Browns upset the Bengals 35-23.

The Bengals administered a 10-7 setback to the Browns on November 6, 1977, in Cleveland that brought the first-place Browns back to earth and headed them towards their final destination of the basement of the AFC Central.

The Bengals beat the Browns 12-9 on October 21, 1984, in Cincinnati on a last-second field goal in a battle of 1-6 teams that cost Browns head coach Sam Rutigliano his job.

Browns head coach Blanton Collier (left) shakes hands with his former mentor and the man he replaced seven years earlier, Cincinnati Bengals head coach Paul Brown, prior to the start of the first meeting between the Browns and the Bengals on October 11, 1970. Photo courtesy of the Cleveland Press Collection.

Greg Pruitt tries to elude a Bengals defender on October 13, 1974. Photo courtesy of the Cleveland Press Collection.

The Browns annihilated Cincinnati 34-3 on December 14, 1986, in Cincinnati, a game in which the Bengals were favored despite a 9-5 record to the Browns' 10-4 mark. The Bengals' loss that afternoon not only gave the Browns the AFC Central Division title but also ultimately kept them from qualifying for the postseason.

The Bengals won 23-21 on November 3, 1991, in Cincinnati in a game in which the Browns handed them their first win of the year in nine games, wasting numerous scoring opportunities and committing mistakes galore, the last of which was Matt Stover's 34-yard field goal try that was blocked as time expired.

In the 1994 season opener on September 4 in Cincinnati, Randy Baldwin and Eric Metcalf led the way to a 28-20 victory over the Bengals with some second-quarter magic. Baldwin returned a kickoff 85 yards for a touchdown, and some three minutes later Metcalf raced 92 yards for a score off a punt return. It was the first time the Browns had both a kickoff return and punt return for touchdowns in the same game since Bobby Mitchell had one of each in a victory over the Eagles on November 23, 1958. It was the first time any team accomplished the feat since the Lions' Eddie Payton did both against the Vikings on December 17, 1977 (ironically, Payton had played for the Browns earlier that year).

The Bengals lost to the Browns 26-10 on December 17, 1995, in the final game in Cleveland Stadium on a day where emotions on and off the field ran high on the Browns' side, due to the fact that many believed it to be the final home game in franchise history because of the Browns' impending move to Baltimore.

Two memorable—and high-scoring—games between the two teams took place in 2004 and 2007. On November 28, 2004, the Bengals outscored the visiting Browns 58-48 in what is the second-highest-scoring game in NFL history. Three years later, on September 16, 2007, Derek Anderson led the Browns to a 51-45 triumph over the visiting Bengals in what is the seventh-highest-scoring games in league annals.

The Bengals' all-time record against the Browns is 44-39, 27-15 at home and 17-24 on the road.

CLARK, LES

Les Clark was a Browns radio broadcaster in 1961.

CLARK, MONTE

Monte Clark was a Browns offensive tackle from 1963-69. He was a University of Southern California product acquired by Cleveland on April 30, 1963, in a trade with Dallas for Jim Ray Smith.

CLEVELAND BROWNS FOUNDATION

The Cleveland Browns Foundation has existed since 1999. It was founded by Browns majority owner Al Lerner. It is dedicated to taking a solution-based, holistic approach to ensure Northeast Ohio youth receive the tools they need for a foundation for independence and success.

CLEVELAND BROWNS TRUST

The Cleveland Browns Trust kept the Browns organization afloat during the three seasons absent of Browns football from 1996-98. It originated on July 1, 1996, and undertook numerous tasks, including helping plan Cleveland Browns Stadium, organizing alumni events, and producing television and radio programs. Its president was Bill Futterer.

CLEVELAND INDIANS

The Cleveland Indians were the Major League Baseball team that shared the use of Cleveland Municipal/Cleveland Stadium with the Browns from 1947–1995.

CLEVELAND MUNICIPAL/CLEVELAND STADIUM

Cleveland Municipal/Cleveland Stadium was home to the Browns from 1946-95. Its name changed from "Cleveland Municipal Stadium" to

"Cleveland Stadium" in 1978. Its seating capacity was exactly 80,000 in 1946. The seating capacity then fluctuated for years before reaching a high of 80,385 from 1978-80. In the Browns' last four seasons there, capacity was 78,512.

CLEVELAND MUNICIPAL/CLEVELAND STADIUM SEATING CAPACITIES

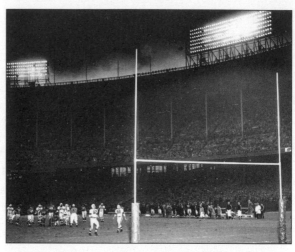

1946	80,000
1947	77,563
1948-51	77,707
1952-61	78,207
1962-64	78,166
1965	77,096
1966	77,124
1967-74	79,282
1975-76	80,165
1977	80,233
1978-80	80,385
1981-82	80,322
1983-91	80,098
1992-95	78,512

The bright lights of Cleveland Municipal Stadium shine down on action on the field in 1951. Photo courtesy of the Cleveland Press Collection.

CLEVELANDBROWNS.COM

Clevelanbrowns.com is the official Browns website. It features several interactive elements for fans, updated information before each game, and is updated with activity from both on and off the field.

COACH OF THE YEAR

Various news organizations voted for Coach of the Year designations. Those organizations that voted are denoted after the coach's names. *Please see the abbreviations key.*

1947   Paul Brown (AAFC by PFI)
1948   Paul Brown (AAFC by NYN)

1949   Paul Brown (AAFC by NYN, SN)
1951   Paul Brown (NFL by NYN)
1953   Paul Brown (NFL by NYN)
1954   Paul Brown (NFL by UP)
1957   Paul Brown (NFL by NYN, UP)
1976   Forrest Gregg (AFC by AP)
1979   Sam Rutigliano (AFC by UPI)
1980   Sam Rutigliano (AFC by UPI)
1986   Marty Schottenheimer (AFC by FWA, UPI)

COACHES, HEAD AND ASSISTANT

For a complete list of head coaches and assistant coaches, please see Coaches and Assistant Coaches on page 213 for a full list of assistant coaches.

COCKROFT, DON

Don Cockroft was a Browns kicker/punter from 1968-80. He was a third-round draft choice of Cleveland's in 1967 out of Adams State College. He spent the '67 season on the practice squad before beating out veteran Lou Groza for the kicking position in the 1968 training camp. He ranks second all-time in Browns history in scoring with 1,080 points. He was the team's leading scorer each season from 1969-80. His longest field goal was a 57-yarder in Denver on October 29, 1972. He kicked a 51-yarder in a 38-20 victory in St. Louis on October 28, 1979.

One game Cockroft might like to forget happened on January 4, 1981, when his two missed field goals and failed extra point had much to do with the Browns' 14-12 defeat to the Oakland Raiders in an AFC Divisional Playoff in a frozen Cleveland Stadium. Twice, he had punts that traveled 71 yards on November 22, 1970, against Houston and on December 2, 1973, against Kansas City. Cockroft's 3,643 punting yards in 1974 rank eighth it team history. He is number one all time in punting yards for the Browns with 26,262. His 965 postseason punting yards rank second in team history. He was named to the All-AFC defensive team in 1972 by NEA.

COLELLA, TOM

Tom Colella was a punter/defensive back with the Browns from 1946-48. He was a Canisius College product acquired by the team as a free agent.

His 10 interceptions in 1946 are tied with two other players for the most in one Browns season. He also returned punts and scored on an 82-yard return on September 12, 1947, in a 55-7 Browns victory against the Dodgers in Brooklyn.

COLEMAN, CASEY

Casey Coleman was a Browns radio broadcaster from 1994-95. He is the son of Ken Coleman, another Browns broadcaster who did television and radio.

COLEMAN, COSEY

Cosey Coleman was a Browns guard from 2005-06. He attended the University of Tennessee.

COLEMAN, KEN

Ken Coleman was a Browns radio broadcaster from 1952-53 and television broadcaster from 1954-65. He was also the father of Casey Coleman, another Browns broadcaster who did radio.

COLEMAN, KENYON

Kenyon Coleman was a Browns defensive end from 2009-10. A product of UCLA, he was obtained by Cleveland on April 25, 2009, in a trade with the New York Jets.

COLLIER, BLANTON

Blanton Collier was the Browns' head coach from 1963-70. He led the Browns to the 1964 NFL Championship. His all-time record as Browns head coach was 76-34-2, 40-14-2 at home and 36-20 on the road. His all-time postseason record as head coach of the team was 3-4, 2-1 at home and 1-3 on the road. Collier was also a Browns assistant coach from 1946-53, and in 1962, '75, and '76.

COLLINS, GARY

Gary Collins was a wide receiver for Cleveland from 1962-71. He was a first-round draft pick by the Browns in 1962 out of the University of Maryland.

He ranks fifth in team all-time receiving yards with 5,299 and fourth in team all-time receptions with 331. His highest receptions and receiving yards totals came in 1966 when his 56 catches went for 946 yards.

Collins will always be remembered for his performance in the 1964 NFL title game at home against heavily-favored Baltimore. After a scoreless first half, he was on the receiving end of three scoring strikes from Frank Ryan for 18, 42, and 51 yards en route to a 27-0 upset. His 18 points in that game are tied for first all-time, and his 130 receiving yards against the Colts are the second-most ever by a Browns player in a postseason game (####).

Collins also punted and holds the Browns' all-time record for highest average yards per punt for one season with 46.7 in 1965. His 420 all-time points rank eighth in team history, and his 30 postseason points are tied for fifth in team history. His 13,764 punting yards rank fourth all-time for the Browns, and his 595 postseason punting yards rank fourth in team history. He had a 73-yard punt against the Steelers on October 5, 1963, and a 71-yarder against the Eagles on October 2, 1965. He was named to All-NFL offensive teams in 1965 by NYN and UPI and in 1969 by AP and UPI, and was selected for the Pro Bowl in 1965 and '66.

COLO, DON

Don Colo was a Cleveland defensive tackle from 1953-58. A Brown University product, Colo was acquired by the team on March 26, 1953, as part of a 15-player deal with Baltimore. He was voted to All-NFL defensive teams in 1955 by NEA and UP and in 1957 by NYN and NEA. He was a Pro Bowl selection in 1954, '55, and '58.

COMBINED NET YARDS LEADERS

Please see Individual Statistics on page 225.

COMPOSITE WON-LOST-TIED RECORDS

Please see Team Statistics on page 248.

CONFERENCE CHAMPIONSHIP GAMES (NFL)

Dallas 52, Cleveland 14 (Eastern Conference, Dec. 24, 1967, at Dal.)
Cleveland 31, Dallas 20 (Eastern Conference, Dec. 21, 1968, at Cle.)
Cleveland 38, Dallas 14 (Eastern Conference, Dec. 28, 1969, at Dal.)

Denver 23, Cleveland 20 (OT) (AFC, Jan. 11, 1987, at Cle.)
Denver 38, Cleveland 33 (AFC, Jan. 17, 1988, at Den.)
Denver 37, Cleveland 21 (AFC, Jan. 14, 1990, at Den.)

Overall – 2-4 (.333)
Home – 1-1 (.500)
Away – 1-3 (.250)

CORDRAY, DON

Don Cordray was a Browns radio broadcaster in 1950.

CORNER BROTHERS

Browns cornerbacks Hanford Dixon and Frank Minnifield were known as the "Corner Brothers." They teamed up to stifle opposing wide receivers as the Browns' starters together from 1985-89. "Top Dawg" Dixon played on the right side from 1981-89. "Mighty Minnie" Minnifield played on the left side from 1984-92. One of the Corner Brothers' finest performances came in the Browns' 24-21 loss to the Miami Dolphins in the AFC Divisional Playoffs on January 4, 1986, in South Florida. Dixon and Minnifield held the "Marks Brothers," Miami's vaunted wide receivers duo of Mark Clayton and Mark Duper, to one catch between the two.

COSTELLO, VINCE

Vince Costello was a Browns linebacker from 1957-66. He was an Ohio University product acquired by the Browns as a free agent in 1956 after he had toiled in baseball's minor leagues for awhile. He was out of action in '56 due to a pulled muscle. He intercepted 18 passes in his Browns career with a high of seven in 1963 when he tied for the team lead with Larry Benz.

COUCH, TIM

Tim Couch was Browns quarterback from 1999-2003. He was a first-round draft pick—the first overall selection—of Cleveland's in 1999 out of the University of Kentucky. Couch established all-time Browns rookie records and led all NFL rookie quarterbacks in completions, pass attempts, yards passing, touch-down passes, and quarterback rating. He completed 223 of 399 passes for 2,447 yards, 15 touchdown passes, and 13 interceptions that year, becoming just the sixth rookie quarterback in the NFL since 1952 to have more touchdown passes than interceptions. He replaced starter Ty Detmer in the fourth quarter of the Browns' season-opening 43-0 loss at home to Pittsburgh on September 12, 1999.

Couch gave the Browns their first victory of the "new era" when he completed a 56-yard Hail Mary bomb with no time left that was tipped into the hands of Kevin Johnson as the Browns beat New Orleans in the Superdome 21-16. He left the December 19 home game against Jacksonville in the second quarter with an ankle sprain, causing him to miss the final game of the season the next week against the Colts. Couch got off to a fine start in 2000 with 259 yards passing in a win over the Bengals and 316 yards through the air in a win over Pittsburgh. In the Steelers game he connected with Johnson on a 79-yard pass play. He completed a 67-yarder to Johnson on November 26 against Baltimore. However, Couch played in just seven games that season due to a fractured right thumb suffered in a practice session during the season.

Couch came back strong in 2001 by passing for 3,040 yards on 272-for-454 and a 59.9 completion percentage. He had 17 touchdown passes and 21 interceptions that year, a year in which the Browns improved to 7-9 and were thinking playoffs into December after 2-14 and 3-13 seasons in 1999 and 2000, respectively. He directed three fourth-quarter comeback wins in 2001, including a thriller at Tennessee on December 30 in which he threw for a career-high 336 yards on 20-for-27, including a 78-yarder to Quincy Morgan.

In 2002 Couch missed the first two games due to injury, but when he returned he led the Browns to eight wins—including a handful of late-game comebacks—in 14 games as the starter but played only part of the finale at home against the Falcons due to injury once again. The Browns qualified for the playoffs, but his injury kept him out of their 36-33 loss to the Steelers in Pittsburgh in a wild card game in which he was replaced by Kelly Holcomb. Couch and Holcomb played musical quarterbacks during a 2003 season in which the Browns won just five games. One of Couch's best games ever was on October 5 of that year when he went 20-for-25 for 208 yards, two touchdowns, an interception, and a passer rating of 111.3 in leading the Browns to a 33-13 upset of the Steelers in Pittsburgh.

Most Browns fans would be shocked to learn that Couch possesses the highest career completion percentage in team history at 59.8 (minimum 750 attempts). His 11,131 career passing yards rank fifth in club annals, and his 1,025 career completions rank fourth.

COUSINEAU, TOM

Tom Cousineau was a Browns linebacker from 1982-85. He was an Ohio State University product acquired by Cleveland on April 23, 1982, in a trade with the Bills for a first-round draft choice in 1983, a third-round pick in '84, and fifth-round pick in '85. He was the overall number one pick in the 1979 draft by the Bills, for whom he never played (he spent three years in the CFL). Cousineau led the Browns with four interceptions in 1983 and was voted to All-AFC defensive teams both that year and in 1984 by UPI.

COWHER, BILL

Bill Cowher was a Browns linebacker from 1980-82. He was a North Carolina State University product acquired in 1980 by Cleveland as a free agent. He was an assistant coach from 1985-88. As special teams coach in 1985, Cowher was a major factor in the Browns going from worst to first in the NFL in kickoff coverage.

COX, STEVE

Steve Cox was a punter/kicker for the Browns from 1981-84. He was a fifth-round draft choice of Cleveland's in 1981 out of the University of Arkansas. He ranks 10th all-time for the Browns in punting yards with 7,984. He also holds the top two spots in the category of longest field goal in team history—a 60-yarder in Cincinnati on October 21, 1984, and a 58-yarder in Denver on December 4, 1983. Cox's 291 yards punting in a 27-10 loss to the Raiders in Los Angeles in an AFC First-Round Playoff game on January 8, 1983, rank fifth in team history.

CRIBBS, JOSH

Josh Cribbs was a Cleveland kickoff and punt returner from 2005-12. Cribbs, who played quarterback for Kent State University, was signed by the Browns as an undrafted free agent on April 29, 2005. He led the Browns in kickoff returns and kickoff return yards every season he was with the Browns from 2005-12 and in punt returns and punt return yards from 2007-12. His 1,809 kickoff return yards in 2007 rank first in Browns history. He also holds the numbers two through six spots in that category. He holds four of the top eight spots for punt return yards in one season in team history. Cribbs returned eight kickoffs and three punts for touchdowns as a Brown, including two kickoff returns against the Chiefs in Kansas City on December 20, 2009—a 100-yarder and a 103-yarder—in helping the Browns to a 41-34 victory. For the game, he returned six kickoffs for 269 yards.

Cribbs also played wide receiver for Cleveland. His best year at that position was in 2011 when he had 41 receptions for 518 yards and four touchdowns. He made First-Team All-NFL by the AP in 2009 and was a three-time Pro Bowler (2007, '09, '12).

CROCKER, CHRIS

Chris Crocker was a Browns defensive back from 2003-05. He was a third-round draft pick of the Browns in 2003 out of Marshall University. He returned a Ben Roethlisberger pass 20 yards for a first-quarter touchdown on October 10, 2004, in Pittsburgh. His pick-six tied the game at seven, but the Browns wound up losing 34-23.

CROWELL, ISAIAH

Isaiah Crowell has been a Browns running back since 2014. A product of Alabama State University, he was signed by the Browns as an undrafted free agent on May 10, 2014. He was second on the Browns with 607 rushing yards and was tops on the team with eight rushing touchdowns in '14. He also had nine receptions for 87 yards.

CUNDIFF, BILLY

Billy Cundiff was a Browns kicker in 2009 and from 2013-14. A product of Drake University, he was first signed by Cleveland on September 26, 2009, after an injury to Phil Dawson. He was waived on November 3, 2009. He returned to the Browns, signing with them on September 3, 2013. He kicked three field goals of 50 yards or more in his second stint with the Browns.

CURTIS, ISAAC

Isaac Curtis was a Cincinnati Bengals wide receiver from 1973-84. He not only caused havoc on Browns defensive backs throughout his career but also on the team's front office. Cleveland had a chance to draft Curtis from San Diego State University in 1973 but instead opted for wide receiver Steve Holden from Arizona State University. Holden played with the Browns until 1976 and ended his career with 62 receptions for 927 yards and four touchdowns. Curtis wound up with 416 catches for 7,101 yards and 53 touchdowns in a career that lasted through 1984.

D

DALLAS COWBOYS

The Dallas Cowboys were Browns opponents in the NFL from 1960-95 and have been since 1999. They were co-members of the Eastern Conference from 1960-69. Dallas lost 11 of its first 12 meetings with the Browns. One of the more memorable contests between the Cowboys and Browns occurred on December 12, 1970, in Cleveland Municipal Stadium when the Cowboys won a mud fest 6-2, severely denting the Browns' AFC Central Division title hopes.

Another memorable game between the two teams was a 26-7 Browns victory on September 24, 1979, on *Monday Night Football* in front of 80,123 crazed fans in Cleveland Stadium. Yet another was a 19-14 Browns upset win on December 10, 1994, in Dallas that was finalized when Cowboys tight end Jay Novacek slipped and fell inside the Browns' one-yard line after a short reception from Troy Aikman with no time left on the clock.

The Browns defend against the Cowboys at Cleveland Municipal Stadium on December 12, 1970. Photo courtesy of the Cleveland Press Collection.

The Browns and Cowboys played three times in the postseason in the Eastern Conference Championship game from 1967-69. Dallas blew the Browns out of the Cotton Bowl 52-14 on December 24, 1967. However, the Browns came back to win the next two games 31-20 on December 21, 1968, in Cleveland and 38-14 on December 28, 1969, in Dallas.

The Cowboys' all-time record against the Browns is 12-15, 8-6 at home and 4-9 on the road. Their all-time postseason record against Cleveland is 1-2, 1-1 at home and 0-1 on the road.

DANIELSON, GARY

Gary Danielson was a Browns quarterback in 1985 and from '87-88. He was a product of Purdue University obtained by Cleveland May 1, 1985, in a trade with Detroit for a third-round draft pick in 1986. He was on the injured reserve list in 1986 after sustaining a fractured left ankle in the final preseason game on August 28. He was acquired to stand in for Bernie Kosar until the rookie was ready to take over.

Danielson directed the Browns to a 2-2 start in '85 before suffering a severe right shoulder injury at home against New England on October 6. He returned to action against the Bengals on November 24 and hooked up with Clarence Weathers for a perfect 72-yard pass play that went for a touchdown, the Browns' only pass of the entire second half, in a key 24-6 victory. The next week against the Giants in the Meadowlands Danielson re-injured his shoulder, but was gutsy in leading two late drives that were major factors in a thrilling upset of New York 35-33. The win was the impetus for Cleveland's AFC Central Division title. The Giants game was Danielson's last action of the season. He ended his Browns career with 1,879 yards passing on 153 completions out of 248 attempts, 12 touchdown passes, and seven interceptions.

DANSBY, KARLOS

Karlos Dansby has been a Browns linebacker since 2014. An Auburn University product, he signed with Cleveland on March 11, 2014. He had three sacks and an interception in '14.

DARDEN, THOM

Thom Darden was a Browns defensive back from 1972-74 and 1976-81. He was a first-round draft choice of Cleveland's in 1972 from the University of Michigan. He missed the entire 1975 season due to preseason knee surgery. He is the Browns' all-time interceptions leader with 45. His 10 picks in 1978 led the league and tie him with Tom Colella (1946) and Anthony Henry (2001) for Cleveland's all-time single-season record. His eight thefts in 1974 are tied for eighth all-time in team history. His 45 career interceptions is tops in team annals. Darden was named to All-AFC defensive teams in 1978 by NEA, PFW, FWA, SN and UPI, and in 1979 by PFW. He was a Pro Bowl selection in 1978.

DAVIS, ANDRA

Andra Davis was a Browns linebacker from 2002-08. He was a fifth-round draft choice of the Browns in 2002 out of the University of Florida. He was second on the team with three interceptions in 2004. He had five sacks in 2003.

DAVIS, ANDRE

Andre Davis was a Browns wide receiver from 2002-04. He was a second-round draft pick of Cleveland's in 2002 out of Virginia Tech University. He had six touchdown receptions in 2002 and led the Browns with five TD catches in 2003. He was on the receiving end of a 99-yard touchdown pass from Jeff Garcia—his only catch of the day—on October 17, 2004, that jumpstarted the Browns to a 34-17 victory over the Bengals in Cleveland that is tied for the longest pass play in Browns history. For his Browns career, Davis totaled 93 receptions for 1,412 yards and 13 touchdowns. He also returned kickoffs and punts for the Browns. He led the team in kickoff returns and kickoff return yards from 2002-03 and ranks sixth all-time for the Browns with 1,871 kickoff return yards.

DAVIS, BEN

Ben Davis was a Cleveland defensive back from 1967-68 and '70-73. He was a 17th-round draft choice of the Browns in 1967 from Defiance College. He missed the 1969 season because of two knee operations from an injury in a pre-season game on August 23 in San Diego. Davis's eight interceptions in 1968 are tied for eighth in team history. He returned punts and kickoffs early in his career and led the Browns in punt returns, punt return yards, kickoff returns, and kickoff return yards in 1967.

DAVIS, BUTCH

Butch Davis was head coach of the Browns from 2001-04. He led the Browns to more victories (seven) in 2001 than they had in 1999 and 2000 combined (five). The next year he led the team to its last playoff berth with a 9-7 record. The Browns blew a 24-7 third-quarter lead and fell 36-33 to the Steelers in Pittsburgh in an AFC Wild Card Game. Davis resigned after 11 games in 2004. His all-time record as Browns head coach was 24-35, 12-18 at home and 12-17 on the road. His postseason record was 0-1 (away game).

DAVIS, ERNIE

Ernie Davis was acquired by the Browns on December 14, 1961, in a trade with Washington for running back Bobby Mitchell and the rights to 1962 first-round draft pick Leroy Jackson, a defensive back. He was the Redskins' first-round—and the first overall—pick in that draft. He had speed and power as a running back that helped him break most of legendary Browns running back Jim Brown's records at Syracuse University, where he won the 1961 Heisman Trophy. Davis contracted leukemia, however, and never played a down for the Browns. He died on May 18, 1963. His uniform number 45 is retired by the Browns.

DAWG POUND, THE

The Dawg Pound was the name originally given to the Cleveland Stadium bleachers section in 1984 that lasted through the Browns' last season there in 1995. The Dawg Pound has been the official name of the FirstEnergy Stadium bleachers section since the stadium opened in 1999. The Dawg Pound originated from the antics of cornerbacks Hanford Dixon and Frank Minnifield, and linebacker Eddie Johnson, when they began barking at fans in the bleachers of Cleveland Stadium late in the 1984 season. Johnson was actually barking at teammates who made big defensive plays during training camp, but this led to the crazy canine antics of fans in the bleachers such as woofing, wearing dog masks, painting their faces brown, orange, and white and even eating dog biscuits. Fans became a little too enthusiastic at times, as some would hurl objects such as biscuits, batteries, and eggs at opposing players. Born at a time when the Browns were starting to win again after some down years, The Dawg Pound was a nice complement to the success of the team in the late 1980s and remained in force during the down times of the early 1990s.

DAWSON, LEN

Len Dawson was a Browns quarterback from 1960-61. A product of Purdue University, he was obtained by Cleveland on December 31, 1959, in a trade with the Pittsburgh Steelers as part of a four-player deal. Dawson attempted just 28 passes, completing 15 before jumping to the AFL's Dallas Texans (who became the Kansas City Chiefs in 1963) and enjoying a Hall of Fame career there.

DAWSON, PHIL

Phil Dawson was a kicker for the Browns from 1999-2012. He was a product of the University of Texas acquired by the team on March 25, 1999, as a free agent. He was one of the few bright spots for the Browns in some very down times. He converted on 305 of 363 field-goal attempts as a Brown, an 84 percent success rate. He also was successful on 24 or 34 treys from at least 50 yards with Cleveland. Dawson's 1,271 points ranks second in team history. Dawson was a Pro bowler in 2012.

DECEMBER
-2, 1946

The Browns game in Miami against the Seahawks was postponed until the next day due to heavy rain. The Browns won 34-0.

-22, 1946

Cleveland beat the New York Yankees 14-9 on a 16-yard pass from Otto Graham to Dante Lavelli late in the AAFC Championship Game in Cleveland.

-19, 1948

The Browns routed the Buffalo Bills 49-7 in the AAFC Championship Game in Cleveland.

-11, 1949

The Browns defeated the San Francisco 49ers 21-7 in the AAFC Championship Game in Cleveland.

-17, 1950

Cleveland defeated the New York Giants 8-3 in an American Conference Playoff in Cleveland.

-24, 1950

The Browns defeated the Los Angeles Rams 30-28 on Lou Groza's late 16-yard field goal in the NFL Championship Game in Cleveland.

-26, 1954

The Browns routed the Detroit Lions 56-10 in the NFL Championship Game in Cleveland.

-26, 1955

The Browns defeated the Los Angeles Rams 38-14 in the NFL Championship Game in Los Angeles.

-27, 1964

The Browns upset the Baltimore Colts 27-0 in the NFL Championship Game in Cleveland.

-29, 1968

The Browns were obliterated by the Baltimore Colts 34-0 in the NFL Championship Game in Cleveland.

-14, 1980

The Browns lost to the Vikings 28-23 in Minnesota when Ahmad Rashad caught a game-winning 46-yard Hail Mary touchdown pass from Tommy Kramer with no time showing on the clock. The heartbreaking defeat kept the Browns from clinching their first playoff berth in eight years.

-17, 1995

Cleveland defeated Cincinnati 26-10 in Cleveland in the final home game before the Browns relocated to Baltimore, where they became the Ravens.

-24, 1995

The Browns fell to the Jacksonville Jaguars 24-21 in Jacksonville in Cleveland's final game prior to its relocation to Baltimore.

-8, 2002

Tim Couch's 50-yard Hail Mary touchdown pass to Quincy Morgan with no time left gives the Browns a 21-20 win over the Jaguars in Jacksonville to keep realistic playoff hopes alive.

-16, 2007

The Browns beat the Buffalo Bills 8-0 in a blizzard at Cleveland Browns Stadium to improve to 9-5 as they looked to be on their way to the playoffs.

-20, 2009

Josh Cribbs returned two kickoffs for touchdowns—for 100 and 103 yards—and Jerome Harrison rushed for a team-record 286 yards as the Browns defeated the Chiefs in Kansas City 41-34.

DEFENSIVE BACKS

Notable Browns defensive backs include Cliff Lewis, Tommy James, Warren Lahr, Ken Konz, Don Paul, Junior Wren, Jim Shofner, Bernie Parrish, Ross Fichtner, Don Fleming, Bobby Franklin, Larry Benz, Erich Barnes, Mike Howell, Ernie Kellerman, Ben Davis, Walt Sumner, Clarence Scott, Thom Darden, Tony Peters, Ron Bolton, Clinton Burrell, Hanford Dixon, Al Gross, Frank Minnifield, Don Rogers, Felix Wright, Ray Ellis, Thane Gash, Eric Turner, Stevon Moore, Antonio Langham, Earl Little, Daylon McCutcheon, Anthony Henry, Leigh Bodden, Brodney Pool, Sean Jones, Eric Wright, Mike Adams, T.J. Ward, Sheldon Brown, Joe Haden, Buster Skrine, Tashaun Gipson, and Donte Whitner.

DEFENSIVE LINEMEN

Notable Browns defensive linemen include Bill Willis, Len Ford, John Kissell, Don Colo, Willie Davis, Bob Gain, Paul Wiggin, Bill Glass, Walter Johnson, Jim Kanicki, Jerry Sherk, Bob Golic, Reggie Camp, Carl Hairston, Michael Dean Perry, Rob Burnett, Anthony Pleasant, Courtney Brown, Gerard Warren, Orpheus Roye, Kenard Lang, Mark Word, Alvin McKinley, Ebenezer Ekuban, Ahtyba Rubin, Jabaal Sheard, and Desmond Bryant.

DEFENSIVE MOST VALUABLE PLAYER

1989 – Michael Dean Perry (AFC by UPI)

DEFENSIVE PLAYER OF THE YEAR

1976 – Jerry Sherk (NFL by NEA)

DEFENSIVE ROOKIE OF THE YEAR

1982 – Chip Banks (NFL by AP, PFW)

DELAMIELLEURE, JOE

Joe DeLamielleure was a Browns guard from 1980-84. A product of Michigan State University, DeLamielleure was acquired by Cleveland on September 1, 1980, in a trade with the Buffalo Bills for a second-round draft choice in 1981 and third-round pick in 1982. PFW, FWA, SN, and UPI named him to All-AFC offensive teams in 1980. He was also voted to the Pro Bowl in 1980.

DELEONE, TOM

Tom DeLeone was a Browns center from 1974-84. A product of Ohio State University, he was obtained by the team in 1974 as a free agent. He was a Pro Bowl selection in 1979 and '80.

DEMARCO, BOB

Bob DeMarco was a Browns center from 1972-74. He was a product of the University of Dayton. Cleveland acquired him in a trade with the Dolphins in

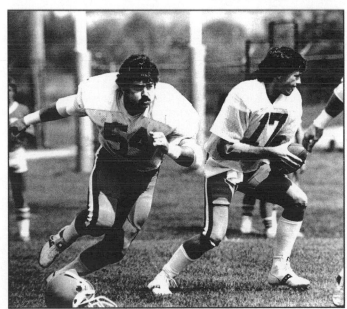

Tom DeLeone (left) and Brian Sipe run through a play in practice in 1980. Photo courtesy of the Cleveland Press Collection.

late September 1972 in exchange for a draft choice after starter Jim Copeland went down with a dislocated hip.

DEMARIE, JOHN

John DeMarie (left) and Blanton Collier. Photo courtesy of the Cleveland Press Collection.

John DeMarie was a Browns guard and offensive tackle from 1967-75. He was a Browns sixth-round draft choice in 1967 out of Louisiana State University.

DENVER BRONCOS

The Denver Broncos were Browns opponents in the NFL from 1970-95 and have been since 1999. The Broncos lost three of their first four games against the Browns before winning the next eight games. The streak was broken on October 1, 1989, in thrilling fashion when the Browns finally beat the Denver 16-13 on a last-second 48-yard field goal by Matt Bahr. Cleveland followed that up with an equally—and possibly more—exciting win the next season on October 8 when Bernie Kosar led a remarkable comeback from nine points down late to a 30-29 triumph on Jerry Kauric's last-second field goal.

The most memorable aspect of the Browns-Broncos rivalry has come in the postseason in the form of three AFC title games in a four-year period. Denver won each time, 23-20 in overtime in 1986 in Cleveland (*please see Drive, The*), 38-33 in 1987 in Denver (see *Fumble, The*), and 37-21 in 1989 in Denver.

The Broncos' all-time record against the Browns is 19-5, 10-3 at home and 9-2 on the road. Their all-time postseason record against them is 3-0, 2-0 at home and 1-0 on the road.

Action from the NFL Championship Game between the Browns and the Detroit Lions on December 29, 1957. Photo courtesy of the Cleveland Press Collection.

DETROIT LIONS

The Detroit Lions were a Browns opponent in the NFL from 1950-95 and have been since 1999. The Lions played the Browns four times in six years from 1952-57 in the NFL Championship Game, winning three. They won 17-7 at home on December 28, 1952, and 17-16 at home on December 27, 1953, before getting trashed 56-10 in Cleveland on December 26, 1954. Detroit won the fourth game in a blowout of their own 59-14 in Detroit on December 29, 1957. Detroit's all-time record against the Browns is 15-4, 9-1 at home and 6-3 on the road. The Lions' all-time postseason record against the Browns is 3-1, 2-0 at home and 1-1 on the road.

DIEKEN, DOUG

Doug Dieken was a Browns offensive tackle from 1971-84. A sixth-round draft choice of Cleveland's in 1971 from the University of Illinois, Dieken carried on the fine tradition of Browns left tackles when he replaced veteran

Dick Schafrath during the 1971 season. One of Dieken's more memorable moments actually came as a receiver when, on October 30, 1983, at home against Houston, he caught a short touchdown pass from Paul McDonald on a fake field goal late in the first half that tied score at 10. It was the only touchdown of his career. He was selected to play in the Pro Bowl in 1980. He was a Browns radio broadcaster from 1985-95 and has been since 1999.

DILFER, TRENT

Trent Dilfer was a Browns quarterback in 2005. A product of Fresno State University, he was traded to Cleveland from the Seattle Seahawks in March 2005. His best game that year was on September 18 when he led the Browns to a 26-24 upset of the Packers in Green Bay. In that game, he outplayed Brett Favre in going 21-for-32 for 336 yards, three touchdowns—including an 80-yarder to Braylon Edwards and a 62-yarder to Steve Heiden—and no interceptions. Dilfer completed 199 of 333 passes for 2,321 yards, 11 touchdowns, and 12 interceptions that season.

DIVISIONAL PLAYOFF GAMES

Baltimore 20, Cleveland 3 (AFC, Dec. 26, 1971, at Cle.)
Miami 20, Cleveland 14 (AFC, Dec. 24, 1972, at Mia.)
Oakland 14, Cleveland 12 (AFC, Jan. 4, 1981, at Cle.)
Miami 24, Cleveland 21 (AFC, Jan. 4, 1986, at Mia.)
Cleveland 23, N.Y. Jets 20 (2OT) (AFC, Jan. 3, 1987, at Cle.)
Cleveland 38, Indianapolis 21 (AFC, Jan. 9, 1988, at Cle.)
Cleveland 34, Buffalo 30 (AFC, Jan. 6, 1990, at Cle.)
Pittsburgh 29, Cleveland 9 (AFC, Jan. 7, 1995, at Pit.)

Overall – 3-5 (.375)
Home – 3-2 (.600)
Away – 0-3 (.000)

DIXON, HANFORD

Hanford Dixon was a Cleveland cornerback from 1981-89. A first-round draft choice of the Browns in 1981 from the University of Southern Mississippi, he teamed with Frank Minnifield to form the "Corner Brothers" duo in the mid- to late-1980s. Dixon is tied with Felix Wright for 10th on the all-time Browns interceptions list with 26. One of his finest games came on December 19, 1982, when he picked off three Terry Bradshaw passes in a 10-9 victory over visiting Pittsburgh. He was named to All-AFC defensive teams in 1986 and 1987 by AP, NEA, PFW, FWA, SN, and UPI. He was picked for the Pro Bowl from 1986-88.

DOMES RECORD

When playing in domes, the Browns are 34-39. *For a complete list of scores, please see Team Statistics on page 248.*

DONOVAN, JIM

Jim Donovan has been a Browns radio broadcaster since 1999.

DOUBLEHEADERS

Erich Barnes (left) and Joe Jones (right) defend against the Vikings in preseason action and the second game of a doubleheader on September 5, 1970. Photo courtesy of the Cleveland Press Collection.

Doubleheaders were held in Cleveland Municipal Stadium once each preseason from 1962-71 with the Browns playing an opponent after a game between two other teams. The first doubleheader was held on August 18, 1962, when the Browns beat the Pittsburgh Steelers 33-10 after the Detroit Lions defeated the Dallas Cowboys 35-24. The last twin bill was held on September 4, 1971, when the Browns topped the New York Giants 30-7 following the Steelers' 35-21 victory over the New York Jets.

DRAFT CHOICES BY COLLEGE (REGULAR DRAFTS) (TOP TEN)

1.	Ohio State University	38
2.	Purdue University	23
3.	University of Michigan	22
4.	Michigan State University	20
5.	Baylor University	18
	University of Illinois	18
7.	University of Notre Dame	17
	University of Southern California	17

9.   University of Nebraska   16
10. University of Colorado   15
     University of Maryland   15
     University of Oklahoma   15

DRAFTS

The Browns took part in the AAFC college player draft from 1947-49 and the NFL college player draft from 1950-95 and have taken part in it since 1999. *Please see First-Round Draft Choices.*

DRIVE, THE

The Drive was a 98-yard march that Denver quarterback John Elway led late in the 1986 AFC Championship game against the Browns in Cleveland. The Drive began with the Broncos trailing 20-13 with 5:43 left. The final salvo of the long march was Elway's five-yard scoring strike to wide receiver Mark Jackson with 37 seconds left to tie the score. The key play of The Drive was when Elway connected with Jackson on a 20-yard pass play on third-and-18. Denver won in overtime 23-20.

DROUGHNS, REUBEN

Reuben Droughns was a Browns running back from 2005-06. A product of the University of Oregon, Droughns was traded to Cleveland from the Denver Broncos on March 30, 2005. In 2005 he rushed for 1,232 yards in becoming the first Browns player to gain 1,000 yards on the ground in two decades. He also had 39 receptions for 369 yards that year. In 2006 Droughns rushed for 758 yards and a team-leading four touchdowns.

DUDLEY, JIMMY

Jimmy Dudley was a Browns television broadcaster from 1957-60.

DUMONT TV NETWORK

The Dumont TV Network broadcast Browns road games from 1948-51.

E

EASTERN CONFERENCE

The Eastern Conference was home to the Browns from 1953-69. The conference was renamed in 1953 after being known as the American Conference from 1950-52. The Eastern Conference was won by the Browns from 1953-55 and in 1957. The Browns tied the Giants in 1958 as both teams finished 9-3. The Browns lost to New York in a playoff 10-0 on December 21 in Yankee Stadium.

From 1959-63, Cleveland finished in the upper echelon of the conference but failed to win it. The Browns came back, however, to claim titles in 1964 and '65. In 1966, they tied Philadelphia for second place at 9-5 behind the 10-3-1 Cowboys.

The conference was divided into two divisions in 1967 – the Capitol and Century. The Browns were placed in the Century with the Giants, Pittsburgh Steelers, and St. Louis Cardinals (the New Orleans Saints replaced the Giants in 1968, and the Giants took the Saints' place in the Capitol that year). The Browns won the conference in 1968 and '69 as they defeated the Cowboys in the title games.

EDWARDS, BRAYLON

Braylon Edwards was a Browns wide receiver from 2005-09. He was a first-round selection—the third overall pick—of Cleveland's out of the University of Michigan in the 2005 NFL Draft. Edwards's best season—and his only Pro Bowl year—came in 2007 when he had 80 receptions for both a team-leading 1,289 yards and 16 touchdowns. He also led the team in receiving yards in 2006 (884) and '08 (873) and led the club in receptions (55) in '08.

EIGHTY THOUSAND FANS

The attendance mark has been at least 80,000 for 53 Browns home games, the largest being 85,703 in the first *Monday Night Football* game on September

21, 1970, against the New York Jets. Twice the Browns had home attendance marks of at least 80,000 in the postseason, both in 1968. Once, the Browns played in front of a crowd of at least 80,000 in a postseason game on the road, in the 1955 NFL Championship Game against the Los Angeles Rams.

EKUBAN, EBENEZER

Ebenezer Ekuban was a Browns defensive end in 2004. A product of the University of North Carolina, he signed with the Browns as a free agent in 2004. He led the Browns with eight sacks that season.

ELAM, ABRAM

Abram Elam was a Browns safety from 2009-10. A product of Kent State University, he was traded to Cleveland from the Jets on April 25, 2009. He had two interceptions in 2010.

ELWAY, JOHN

John Elway was the Denver Broncos' quarterback who caused havoc on the Browns throughout a 16-year career that lasted from 1983-98. He led the Broncos to seven wins in nine games against Cleveland. Even in the two games the Browns won, it took last-second field goals to do it. Elway's coming-out party—at least in the regular season—occurred on December 4, 1983, when he completed 16 of 24 passes for 284 yards and two touchdowns in a 27-6 romp over the Browns in a crucial contest.

Elway shined even more in the postseason when he really gave the Browns headaches. He directed Denver to three AFC Championship game victories in four years—in 1986, '87, and '89, the first one in Cleveland. In 1986 he led the Broncos on The Drive in which his team trailed by seven points with possession of the ball at its own two-yard line with 5:43 remaining. Denver traveled 98 yards with the help of several remarkable passing and running plays by Elway to the tying touchdown with 37 seconds left. The Broncos won 23-20 in overtime. Elway passed for three touchdowns in a 38-33 win in the 1987 game in which the Browns rallied from an 18-point, third-quarter deficit to tie the game, but Elway drove his team to the winning touchdown once again. Earnest Byner's fumble deep in Broncos territory on the Browns' ensuing drive sealed his team's fate. Elway passed for 385 yards and three touchdowns en route to a 37-21 Denver triumph in the 1989 title game.

ESPN

ESPN broadcast five Browns prime-time games from 1987-95 and has since 1999. They are the following:

San Francisco 38, Cleveland 24 (Sunday, Nov. 29, 1987, at S.F.)
Cleveland 24, Houston 20 (Saturday, Dec. 23, 1989, at Hou.)
Houston 28, Cleveland 24 (Sunday, Nov. 17, 1991, at Hou.)
Cleveland 11, Houston 8 (Thursday, Oct. 13, 1994, at Hou.)
Pittsburgh 43, Cleveland 0 (Sunday, Sept. 12, 1999, at Cle.)
Baltimore 26, Cleveland 21 (Sunday, Oct. 6, 2002, at Cle.)
Cleveland 33, Pittsburgh 13 (Sunday, Oct. 5, 2003, at Pit.)
Baltimore 27, Cleveland 13 (Sunday, Nov. 7, 2004, at Bal.)
Miami 10, Cleveland 7 (Sunday, Dec. 26, 2004, at Mia.)
Pittsburgh 34, Cleveland 21 (Sunday, Nov. 13, 2005, at Pit.)
Cleveland 35, New York Giants 14 (Monday, Oct. 13, 2008, at Cle.)
Cleveland 29, Buffalo 27 (Monday, Nov. 17, 2008, at Buf.)
Philadelphia 30, Cleveland 10 (Monday, Dec. 15, 2008, at Phi.)
Baltimore 16, Cleveland 0 (Monday, Nov. 16, 2009, at Cle.)

Overall – 5-9 (.357)
Home – 1-3 (.250)
Away – 4-6 (.400)

EVANS, JOHNNY

Johnny Evans was a Browns punter from 1978-80. He was a second-round draft choice of the Browns in 1978 from North Carolina State University. His 8,463 punting yards rank ninth all-time for the Browns.

EVERITT, STEVE

Steve Everitt was a Cleveland center from 1993-95. He was a Browns first-round draft choice in 1993 from the University of Michigan.

FAINE, JEFF

Jeff Faine was a Browns center from 2003-05. He was a first-round draft pick of Cleveland's in 2003 out of the University of Notre Dame.

FARREN, PAUL

Paul Farren was a Cleveland offensive tackle from 1983-91. He was a Browns 12th-round draft choice in 1983 from Boston University.

FAST FACTS

For fascinating facts on Browns history, please see Browns Trivia on page 205.

FEACHER, RICKY

Ricky Feacher was a Browns wide receiver from 1976-84. He was a product of Mississippi Valley State University acquired by Cleveland in October 1976 as a free agent. One of Feacher's finest performances came on December 21, 1980, in the season-ending AFC Central Division-clinching 27-24 triumph over the Bengals in which he caught two long touchdown passes from Brian Sipe. He tied with Ozzie Newsome for the team lead in touchdown catches in 1982 with three. His 124 receiving yards in a 27-10 loss to the Raiders in an AFC First-Round Playoff game in Los Angeles on January 8, 1983, rank third all-time for the Browns

FICHTNER, ROSS

Ross Fichtner was a defensive back for the Browns from 1960-67. A third-round draft selection of the Browns in 1960 from Purdue University, he had a team-leading seven interceptions in 1962. His eight picks in 1966 tied for the team lead and are tied for eighth in team history. His four interceptions in 1967 tied for the team lead. On October 1 that year he took a lateral from Erich Barnes, who had intercepted the ball, and raced 88 yards deep into New Orleans territory en route to a 42-7 rout of the Saints. It was the Browns' first win of the year after two defeats. Fichtner's 27 career interceptions are tied for eighth in Browns history.

FIKE, DAN

Dan Fike was a Browns guard from 1985-92. He was a product of the University of Florida obtained by Cleveland as a free agent in 1985.

FINALES

For a listing of the scores of the season finales, please see Team Statistics on page 248.

FIRST-ROUND DRAFT CHOICES

1947	Dick Hoerner (University of Iowa)
1948	Jeff Durkota (Penn State University)
1949	Jack Mitchell (University of Oklahoma)
1950	Ken Carpenter (Oregon State University)
1951	Ken Konz (Louisiana State University)
1952	Bert Rechichar (University of Tennessee)
	Harry Agganis (Boston University)
1953	Doug Atkins (University of Tennessee)
1954	Bobby Garrett (Stanford University)
	John Bauer (University of Illinois)
1955	Kurt Burris (University of Oklahoma)
1956	Preston Carpenter (University of Arkansas)
1957	Jim Brown (Syracuse University)
1958	Jim Shofner (Texas Christian University)
1959	Rich Kreitling (University of Illinois)
1960	Jim Houston (Ohio State University)
1961	Bobby Crespino (University of Mississippi)
1962	Gary Collins (University of Maryland)
	Leroy Jackson (Western Illinois University)
1963	Tom Hutchinson (University of Kentucky)
1964	Paul Warfield (Ohio State University)

1966   Milt Morin (University of Massachusetts)
1967   Bob Matheson (Duke University)
1968   Marvin Upshaw (Trinity University)
1969   Ron Johnson (University of Michigan)
1970   Mike Phipps (Purdue University)
        Bob McKay (University of Texas)
1971   Clarence Scott (Kansas State University)
1972   Thorn Darden (University of Michigan)
1973   Steve Holden (Arizona State University)
        Pete Adams (University of Southern California)
1975   Mack Mitchell (University of Houston)
1976   Mike Pruitt (Purdue University)
1977   Robert L. Jackson (Texas A&M University)
1978   Clay Matthews (University of Southern California)
        Ozzie Newsome (University of Alabama)
1979   Willis Adams (University of Houston)
1980   Charles White (University of Southern California)
1981   Hanford Dixon (Southern Mississippi University)
1982   Chip Banks (University of Southern California)
1984   Don Rogers (UCLA)
1987   Mike Junkin (Duke University)
1988   Clifford Charlton (University of Florida)
1989   Eric Metcalf (University of Texas)
1991   Eric Turner (UCLA)
1992   Tommy Vardell (Stanford University)
1993   Steve Everitt (University of Michigan)
1994   Antonio Langham (University of Alabama)
        Derrick Alexander (University of Michigan)
1995   Craig Powell (Ohio State University)
1999   Tim Couch (University of Kentucky)
2000   Courtney Brown (Penn State University)
2001   Gerard Warren (University of Florida)
2002   William Green (Boston College)
2003   Jeff Faine (University of Notre Dame)
2004   Kellen Winslow, Jr. (University of Miami)
2005   (Braylon Edwards (University of Michigan)
2006   Kamerion Wimbley (Florida State University)
2007   Joe Thomas (University of Wisconsin)
        Brady Quinn (University of Notre Dame)

2009   Alex Mack (University of California)
2010   Joe Haden (University of Florida)
2011   Phil Taylor (Baylor University)
2012   Trent Richardson (University of Alabama)
        Brandon Weeden (Oklahoma State University)
2013   Barkevious Mingo (Louisiana State University)
2014   Justin Gilbert (Oklahoma State University)
        Johnny Manziel (Texas A&M University)

FIRSTENERGY STADIUM

FirstEnergy Stadium, originally Cleveland Browns Stadium, has been home to the Browns since 1999. The name change occurred on January 15, 2013. The stadium was built on the site of old Cleveland Stadium. It had a seating capacity of 73,200 through 2013. Since 2014, its capacity has been 67,407.

FIRSTS

* Denotes only time

Majority owner – Arthur "Mickey" McBride
Head coach – Paul Brown
Training camp site – Bowling Green State University in Bowling Green, Ohio
Player signed to a contract – Otto Graham
Draft choice – Dick Hoerner
Preseason opponent – Brooklyn Dodgers
Opponent – Miami Seahawks
Road opponent – Chicago Rockets
Opponent the Browns lost to – San Francisco 49ers
Postseason opponent – New York Yankees
Postseason road opponent – New York Yankees
Starting quarterback – Cliff Lewis
Points scored by – Mac Speedie
Field goal by – Lou Groza
ABC Monday Night Football opponent – New York Jets
ABC Monday Night Football road opponent – Houston Oilers
Overtime opponent – New England Patriots
Overtime opponent the Browns lost to – Pittsburgh Steelers

Season the Browns missed the postseason – 1956
Season with a losing record – 1956
Player to rush for 1,000 yards in one season – Jim Brown
Player to pass for 3,000 yards in one season – Brian Sipe
*Player to pass for 4,000 yards in one season – Brian Sipe
Player to total 1,000 yards receiving in one season – Mac Speedie
Players selected for the Pro Bowl – Tony Adamle, Otto Graham, Lou Groza, Weldon Humble, Marion Motley, Mac Speedie, Bill Willis
Most Valuable Player – Otto Graham
Rookie of the Year – Jim Brown
Coach of the Year – Paul Brown
Player of the Year – Jim Brown

FISS, GALEN

Galen Fiss was a Cleveland linebacker from 1956-66. He was a 13th-round Browns draft choice in 1953 from the University of Kansas. He spent 1953-55 in the military. He was a Pro Bowl selection from 1962-63.

FITZGERALD, JOHN

John Fitzgerald was a Browns television broadcaster in 1953.

FLEMING, DON

Don Fleming was a Browns defensive back from 1960-62. He was a University of Florida product obtained by Cleveland on May 12, 1960, in a trade with the St. Louis Cardinals. He intercepted 10 passes for 160 yards in his Cleveland career. Fleming was killed in the spring of 1963 when electrocuted on a construction project in Florida. His uniform number 46 is retired by the Browns.

FONTENOT, HERMAN

Herman Fontenot was a Browns running back from 1985-88. A product of Louisiana State University, he was obtained by Cleveland on May 4, 1985, as a free agent. His most productive season came in 1986 when he was second on the team with 47 receptions, for 559 yards including a 72-yard catch-and-run from Bernie Kosar that went for a touchdown in a 24-9 win in Indianapolis on November 2. He scored the first points in both playoff games that year—on a

37-yard reception from Kosar in the first quarter that tied the AFC Divisional Playoff at home against the Jets on January 3, 1987, and on a six-yard pass from Kosar that gave Cleveland a 7-0 first-quarter lead over the Broncos in the AFC Championship Game on January 11, also in Cleveland.

Fontenot's seven receptions in the Broncos game are tied for second all-time for the Browns (#####). He also returned kickoffs, totaling 879 yards. He had kickoff returns of 81 and 84 yards, respectively—the first one at home against Houston on December 15, 1985, and the second one at home against Cincinnati on October 30, 1988.

FORD, LEN

Len Ford was a Browns defensive end from 1950-57. A product of the University of Michigan, he was an early-round choice of Cleveland's in the 1950 special allocation draft that consisted of players (other than those from the New York Yankees, who were split among the New York Giants and New York Bulldogs) from the folded AAFC. He returned a fumble 54 yards in a 33-17 loss to the Eagles in Philadelphia on November 13, 1955. Ford was named to All-NFL defensive teams from 1951-54 by AP, NYN, and UP and in 1955 by NYN, NEA, and UP. He played in the Pro Bowl from 1951-54 and was inducted into the Pro Football Hall of Fame in 1976.

FOUR-THOUSAND-YARD PASSER

Brian Sipe is the only Browns quarterback to pass for 4,000 yards in a single season. He totaled 4,132 in 1980.

FOX TELEVISION NETWORK

The FOX television network broadcast Browns Sunday afternoon home games when their opponent was an NFC team from 1994-95 and since '99.

FRALEY, HANK

Hank Fraley was a Browns center from 2006-08. A product of Robert Morris University, Fraley was traded to the Browns from the Eagles on September 2, 2006.

FRANKLIN, BOBBY

Bobby Franklin was a Cleveland defensive back from 1960-66. An 11th-round draft choice of the Browns in 1960 from the University of

Mississippi, Franklin had eight interceptions in his rookie year that tied for the team lead and also are tied for eighth most in one season for the Browns.

FRIDAY NIGHT GAMES

(Local starting times of 5 p.m. or later)

Cleveland 44, Miami 0 (Sept. 6, 1946, at Cle.)
Cleveland 20, Chicago 6 (Sept. 13, 1946, at Chi.)
Cleveland 30, Buffalo 14 (Sept. 5, 1947, at Cle.)
Cleveland 55, Brooklyn 7 (Sept. 12, 1947, at Bro.)
Cleveland 41, Chicago 21 (Sept. 26, 1947, at Chi.)
Cleveland 19, Los Angeles 14 (Sept. 3, 1948, at Cle.)
Cleveland 28, Chicago 7 (Sept. 17, 1948, at Chi.)
Cleveland 61, Los Angeles 14 (Oct. 14, 1949, at L.A.)

Overall – 8-0 (1.000)
Home – 3-0 (1.000)
Away – 5-0 (1.000)

FRYE, CHARLIE

Charlie Frye was a Browns quarterback from 2005-07. He was a third-round draft pick by Cleveland in 2005 out of the University of Akron. He backed up Trent Dilfer for most of his 2005 rookie season but was the starter when the 2006 season opened. That year he completed 252 of 392 passes for 2,454 yards, 10 touchdowns, and 17 interceptions. Once again Frye was the opening-day starter in 2007, but his atrocious performance in a 34-7 home loss to Pittsburgh resulted in him getting traded—yes, traded!—to Seattle two days later.

FUJITA, SCOTT

Scott Fujita was a Browns linebacker from 2010-12. A product of the University of California, Berkeley, he signed with Cleveland as a free agent on March 7, 2010. He had 3.5 sacks in 2010.

FUMBLE, THE

The Fumble occurred during the AFC title game against the Denver Broncos in Mile High Stadium on January 17, 1988. Earnest Byner was headed for the end zone late in the fourth quarter with the Browns trailing 38-31. The play began at the Broncos' eight-yard line. Byner, bursting off left tackle, was stripped of the football by cornerback Jeremiah Castille, who then fell on the ball at the three-yard line. Denver deliberately took a safety and won 38-33.

FULLER, COREY

Corey Fuller was a Browns defensive back from 1999-2002. A Florida State University product, he led the team in interceptions in 2000 with three. Fuller had his only pick-six as a Brown on December 9, 2001, in New England when he returned a Tom Brady pass 49 yards late in the first quarter to give his team a 10-3 lead in a game they would lose 27-16.

G

GABRIEL, TAYLOR

Taylor Gabriel has been a Browns wide receiver since 2014. A product of Abilene Christian University, he signed with the Browns as an undrafted free agent in 2014. In '14 Gabriel had 36 receptions for 621 yards and a touchdown, the yardage total ranking second on the team.

GAIN, BOB

Bob Gain was a Browns defensive tackle in 1952 and from 1954-64. A product of the University of Kentucky, Gain was acquired by Cleveland on September 20, 1951, in a trade with Green Bay for four players. He played in the CFL in 1951. After spending the 1953 season and most of the '54 campaign in the military, he re-joined the Browns in time for the last two games and the 1954 NFL title game. He was voted to the All-NFL defensive team in 1958 by NEA. He was picked for the Pro Bowl from 1957-59 and in 1961 and '62.

GAMES IN WHICH BOTH TEAMS SCORED FEWER THAN 10 POINTS

Please see Team Statistics on page 248.

GARCIA, JEFF

Jeff Garcia was a Browns quarterback in 2004. A product of San Jose State University, he signed with Cleveland on March 9, 2004. In his one season with the Browns he completed 144 of 252 passes for 1,731 yards, 10 touchdowns, and nine interceptions. He connected with Andre Davis for a 99-yard touchdown pass—tied for the longest pass play in team annals—to give the Browns a 7-0 first-quarter lead over the visiting Cincinnati Bengals on October 17 en route to a 34-17 Browns victory.

GARDOCKI, CHRIS

Chris Gardocki was a Browns punter from 1999-2003. He was a product of Clemson University acquired by Cleveland on February 16, 1999, as a free agent. He set a Browns record for most punting yards in one season with 4,645 in 1999. He broke it a year later with 4,919. He had 4,249 punting yards in 2001, which rank third in team history. Gardocki's 20,220 career punting yards rank third in Browns history. He holds the NFL record for most consecutive punts without being blocked with a streak of 1,177 that dates to his rookie year of 1991 with the Bears through his last season in 2006 with the Steelers.

GARLINGTON, JOHN

John Garlington was a Browns linebacker from 1968-77. He was a second-round draft choice of the Browns in 1968 from Louisiana State University.

GATSKI, FRANK

Frank Gatski was a Browns center from 1946-56. He was a product of Marshall University acquired by Cleveland as a free agent. He was voted to All-NFL offensive teams in 1951 by NYN and UP; in 1952 by AP and NYN; in 1953 by AP, NYN, and UP; and in 1955 by AP, NYN, NEA, and UP. He was picked to play in the Pro Bowl in 1954 and was enshrined into the Pro Football Hall of Fame in 1985.

Joe Jones (left) and John Garlington chase Dallas's Bob Hayes in the end zone for a safety. It was the Browns' only score in a 6-2 home loss on December 12, 1970. Photo courtesy of the Cleveland Press Collection.

GEE, STAN

Stan Gee was a Browns radio broadcaster in 1946 and television broadcaster in 1948.

GIBRON, ABE

Abe Gibron was a Browns guard from 1950-56. A product of Purdue University, he was obtained by Cleveland prior to the 1950 season as one of three players in a merger deal with the folded AAFC's Buffalo Bills. He was voted to All-NFL offensive teams in 1953 by NYN and in 1955 by NYN, NEA, and UP. He was a Pro Bowl selection from 1952-55.

GILLOM, HORACE

Horace Gillom was a punter and wide receiver for the Browns from 1947-56. He was a product of the University of Nevada obtained by Cleveland as a free agent. He ranks second all-time for the Browns in punting yards with 21,206. He holds the Browns' all-time postseason record for most punting yards with 1,943. He holds the team record for most punting yards in a postseason game with 363 against the Giants on December 17, 1950, in New York. He had a 74-yard punt on September 21, 1947, against Baltimore; a 75-yarder on October 29, 1950, against Pittsburgh; a 73-yarder on October 26, 1952, against the Redskins; and an 80-yarder against New York on November 28, 1954. Gillom was a Pro Bowl pick in 1952.

GIPSON, TASHAUN

Tashaun Gipson has been a Cleveland free safety since 2012. A product of the University of Wyoming, he was signed by the Browns as an undrafted free agent in 2012. He led the Browns in interceptions with five in 2013 and six in 2014 despite missing the final five games of the '14 season due to an injury. A Pro Bowl selection in '14 (even though the injury kept him out of the game), Gipson has had two pick-sixes—a 44-yarder off of Jay Cutler in a 38-31 loss to the visiting Bears on December 15, 2013, and a 62-yarder off of Drew Brees in a 26-24 upset of the visiting Saints on September 14, 2014.

GLASS, BILL

Bill Glass was a Browns defensive end from 1962-68. A product of Baylor University, he was acquired by Cleveland on March 28, 1962, as part of a six-player trade with the Detroit Lions. He was a Pro Bowler from 1962-64 and in 1967.

GLIEBER, FRANK

Frank Glieber was a Browns television broadcaster in 1966 and '67.

GOCONG, CHRIS

Chris Gocong was a Browns linebacker from 2010-12. A product of Cal Poly—San Luis Obispo, he was traded to Cleveland from the Eagles on April 2, 2010. He had 3.5 sacks in 2011.

GOLIC, BOB

Bob Golic was a Browns nose tackle from 1982-88. He was a product of the University of Notre Dame acquired by Cleveland via waivers on September 2, 1982. He returned a Lynn Dickey dead-duck pass seven yards for a touchdown on November 6, 1983, in a 35-21 loss to the Packers in Milwaukee. He was voted to the All-AFC Defensive Team in 1985 by SN. He was selected to the Pro Bowl from 1985-87.

GORDON, JOSH

Josh Gordon has been a Cleveland wide receiver since 2012. He was a second-round selection by the Browns in the 2012 NFL Supplemental Draft. He had 50 receptions for both a team-leading 805 yards and five touchdowns in his rookie year of '12. Despite missing the first two games the next year due to off-the-field issues, Gordon was the team leader in receptions (87), receiving yards (1,646), and TD receptions (9). His yardage total that year was tops in the entire NFL. He was voted to the Pro Bowl and was First-Team All-Pro. The off-the-field problems resurfaced and caused him to miss 11 games in 2014 and got him suspended for the entire 2015 season.

GORGAL, KEN

Ken Gorgal was a Cleveland defensive back in 1950 and from '53-54. He was a sixth-round draft choice of the Browns in 1950 from Purdue University. After two years in the Army,

Ken Gorgal attempts to tackle the Chicago Cardinals' John Olszweski during the Browns' 31-7 victory on October 10, 1954. Photo courtesy of the Cleveland Press Collection.

he re-joined the team in 1953 and was voted to All-NFL defensive teams that year by NYN and UP.

GOSSETT, JEFF

Jeff Gossett was a Browns punter in 1983 and from 1985-87. An Eastern Illinois University product, Gossett was acquired by the Browns via waivers on August 31, 1983. After two years in the USFL, he was re-acquired as a free agent in 1985. His 10,307 punting yards rank sixth all-time for the Browns, and his 792 career postseason punting yards rank third in team history. His 310 punting yards in Cleveland's 23-20 double overtime victory over the Jets in an AFC Divisional Playoff on January 3, 1987, in Cleveland also rank third all-time for the Browns.

GRAHAM, OTTO

Otto Graham was a Browns quarterback from 1946-55. A product of Northwestern University, Graham was acquired by Cleveland as a free agent and was the first player to be signed by the Browns. He led Cleveland to every AAFC Championship from 1946-49. In 1946 he had 17 touchdown passes and just five interceptions; in 1947 he had 25 touchdown passes and 11 interceptions; in 1948 he had 25 touchdown passes and 15 interceptions; and in 1949 he had 19 touchdown passes and 10 interceptions. Overall from 1946-49 he totaled 86 touchdown passes and 41 interceptions.

Graham led the Browns to three NFL Championships from 1950-55. He announced prior to the 1954 season that the '54 campaign would be his last. The Browns won the NFL title that year. He changed his mind and returned for one more season, and led the Browns to their second straight NFL title in 1955 with a 38-14 destruction of the Rams in Los Angeles on December 26.

Graham ranks second behind Brian Sipe in Browns all-time passing yards with 23,584 and third all-time in team history in pass completions with 1,464. He holds two of the top nine rankings for most passing yards in one game in team history. His highest total was 401 yards in a 21-20 win at Pittsburgh on October 4, 1952. His longest completion was a screen pass to Mac Speedie that turned into a 99-yard touchdown against the Buffalo Bills on November 2, 1947, that is tied for the longest pass play in Browns history.

Graham made more notable connections, including a 70-yard touchdown pass to Speedie on September 26, 1947, against the Chicago Rockets and a 78-yard touchdown pass to Speedie on November 3, 1946, against the

Los Angeles Dons. He hit Dante Lavelli on a 72-yard touchdown strike on November 9, 1947, in Brooklyn, Speedie for an 82-yard pass in a 28-28 tie with the New York Yankees two weeks later on November 23, and Lewis Mayne for a 69-yard scoring strike that helped beat the Dons in Los Angeles four days later on Thanksgiving day. Graham hooked up with Bob Cowan on a 68-yard scoring strike in a 35-7 win over the Yankees on October 24, 1948. He connected with Bill Boedecker on a 79-yard pass play for a touchdown in a 42-7 rout of Los Angeles on October 2, 1949, in Cleveland. Graham also connected with Dub Jones on an 81-yard pass play for a score on September 30, 1951, against the 49ers.

Graham passed for a team-record six touchdowns in a 61-14 destruction of the Dons on October 14, 1949, in Los Angeles. He ranks first in all-time Browns postseason passing yards with 2,001 and pass completions with 159. He ranks fifth in all-time Browns postseason rushing yards with 247 (#). He is tied for most points scored in one postseason game with 18 against Detroit on December 26, 1954, and is tied for fourth in the same category with 12 points against the Rams in the 1955 NFL title game. Graham holds the fourth- and fifth-place rankings both for most passing yards in one Browns postseason game and most pass completions a postseason affair. He is tied for third in team history with 36 postseason points.

Graham was voted AAFC Most Valuable Player in 1947 and '49 by OFF and in '48 by UP. He was named AAFC co-Most Valuable Player with San Francisco 49ers quarterback Frankie Albert in 1948 by OFF. He was voted NFL Most Valuable Player in 1953 by UP and in '55 by SN and UP. He was voted to All-AAFC teams in 1946 by OFF and UP; in '47 by AP, C&O, NYN, OFF, and SP; in '48 by AP, OFF, and UP; and in '49 by AP, NYN, OFF, and UP. INS voted Graham to the All-AAFC offensive team in 1949. He was voted to All-NFL offensive teams in 1951 by AP, NYN, and UP; in '52 by NYN and UP; in '53 by AP, NYN, and UP; in '54 by AP, NYN, SN, and UP; and in '55 by AP, NYN, and UP.

Graham was a Pro Bowl selection from 1950-54. His uniform number 14 is retired by the Browns (he also wore No. 60). He was inducted into the Pro Football Hall of Fame in 1965. He was a Browns television broadcaster in 1956.

GRANER, JIM

Jim Graner was a Browns radio broadcaster from 1955-60 and '63-74.

GRAYSON, DAVID

David Grayson was a Browns linebacker from 1987-90. A product of Fresno State University, Grayson was acquired by Cleveland as a free agent during the 1987 players' strike. He returned a fumble 28 yards for a touchdown and returned an interception 14 yards for a score in the Browns' 51-0 opening-day rout of the Steelers in Pittsburgh on September 10, 1989.

GRECO, JOHN

John Greco has been a Cleveland offensive lineman since 2011. A product of the University of Toledo, he was traded to the Browns from the St. Louis Rams in 2011.

GREEN, BOYCE

Boyce Green was a Cleveland running back from 1983-85. He was an 11th-round draft choice of the Browns in 1983 from Carson-Newman College. Green was the Browns' rushing yards leader in 1984 with 673. On November 4 of that year, he rushed for a career-high 156 yards in the Browns' 13-10 victory over the Bills in Buffalo. A year earlier in his rookie season on October 16, he rushed for 137 yards despite the Browns' crushing 44-17 loss the Steelers in Pittsburgh in a battle for first place, becoming the first running back to top the century mark against the Steelers in Three Rivers Stadium in six years.

GREEN, ERNIE

Ernie Green was a Cleveland running back from 1962-68. He was a product of the University of Louisville obtained by the Browns on August 13, 1962, in a trade with the Green Bay Packers for a seventh-round draft choice in 1963. His longest rush was a 73-yarder in a 38-10 loss in Detroit on December 8, 1963. He was second on the team in rushing yards behind Jim Brown from 1963-65 and Leroy Kelly from 1966-67. He was second on the team in touchdowns rushing from 1964-67 and also was tops on the team with 39 receptions in 1967. Green returned kickoffs and punts, too, and had team highs of 13 and 18 kickoff returns in 1962 and '63, respectively. Green's 3,204 career rushing yards rank eighth in team history. He was selected to play in the Pro Bowl in 1966 and '67.

GREEN, WILLIAM

William Green was a Browns running back from 2002-05. He was a first-round draft choice of the Browns in 2002 out of Boston College. His rookie season was his best as he rushed for both a team-leading 887 yards and six touchdowns. The majority of his success that year came in the final seven games when he accumulated 726 of his rushing yards. There is no doubt that Green's most memorable moment came in the finale that year at home against the Atlanta Falcons. With the Browns' playoff hopes alive and well, he broke free for a 64-yard touchdown run that upped the Browns' lead to 24-16, which turned out to be the final score. With sold-out Cleveland Browns Stadium in an uproar as Green was running toward the end zone, Browns radio play-by-play man Jim Donovan's "Run, William, Run!" will be ingrained in the minds of those who listened forever. Green also led the Browns in rushing yards in 2003. Off-the-field issues unfortunately led to his career lasting only four seasons.

GREEN BAY PACKERS

The Green Bay Packers were a Browns' opponent in the NFL from 1950-95 and have been since 1999. The Packers handed the Browns one of their two most lopsided defeats 55-7 on November 12, 1967, in Milwaukee. One memorable Browns-Packers game was on October 19, 1980, when Brian Sipe hit Dave Logan for a 46-yard touchdown with little time left to give Cleveland a heart-stopping 26-21 victory. Another memorable game between the two teams came on September 18, 2005, when the Browns upset the Packers 26-24 in Green Bay.

The Browns and Packers have met once in the postseason, a 23-12 Packers win in the 1965 NFL title game in Lambeau Field. Green Bay's all-time record against Cleveland is 11-7, 5-3 at home and 6-4 on the road. They are 1-0 against the Browns all-time in the postseason (home game).

GREGG, FORREST

Forrest Gregg was Cleveland's head coach from 1975-77. He began his first season 0-9 en route to a 3-11 finish. The Browns improved to 9-5 in 1976, barely missing the playoffs. The team started the 1977 season 5-2 but lost six of its last seven to finish 6-8 and in last place. Gregg was fired with one game left that season, although his departure was announced publicly as a resignation. Defensive coordinator Dick Modzelewski coached the final game in Seattle.

Forrest Gregg watches the game as Mike Phipps hangs his head in the background in 1975. Photo courtesy of the Cleveland Press Collection.

Gregg was voted AFC Coach of the Year in 1976 by AP. His all-time record as Browns head coach was 18-23, 11-10 at home and 7-13 on the road. He was a Browns assistant coach in 1974.

GREGORY, JACK

Jack Gregory was a Browns defensive end from 1967-71 and in 1979. He was a ninth-round draft choice of Cleveland's in 1966 from Delta State University while he still had college eligibility left. He was traded to the Giants on June 15, 1972, and then re-acquired on August 1, 1979, in another trade with New York for a 1980 draft choice. Gregory was a Pro Bowl pick in 1969.

GRIFFITH, ROBERT

Robert Griffith was a Browns strong safety from 2002-04. A product of San Diego State University, he signed with Cleveland in 2002 as a free agent. He had six interceptions as a Brown.

GROSS, AL

Al Gross was a Browns safety from 1983-87. A product of the University of Arizona, Gross was acquired by the Browns on August 3, 1983, off waivers. He intercepted five passes in both 1984 and '85, tying for the team lead in '84 and leading the team outright in '85. He returned a 37-yard pass for a touchdown that was instrumental in Cleveland's 35-33 upset of the Giants on December 1, 1985, in the Meadowlands. Gross also has the distinction of being the first player in NFL history to have a play reviewed by instant replay.

On the third play of a game between the Browns and Chicago Bears in Soldier Field on September 7, 1986, he recovered a bad snap by Chicago center Jay Hilgenberg in the Chicago end zone. The officials on the field said the play might have been was a touchdown, and the man in the replay booth said it was definitely a touchdown.

GROZA, LOU

Lou Groza was a Cleveland offensive tackle and kicker from 1946-59 and '61-67. A product of Ohio State University, Groza was acquired by the Browns as a free agent. He retired for one season—1960—due to a back injury during training camp. Upon his return in 1961, he focused solely on his kicking duties, leaving his left tackle position in the hands of Dick Schafrath.

Groza is the Browns' all-time leading scorer with 1,608 points. His 115 points in 1964 rank fifth in team history, and his 108 points in 1953 are tied for eighth. He led the Browns in scoring every year from 1950-57 and in 1961 and '64. He ended his career with 810 extra points and 264 field goals

Lou Groza in action against the Rams on September 28, 1958. Photo courtesy of the Cleveland Press Collection.

in 481 attempts. His 83 postseason points rank first all-time for the Browns. He kicked a 53-yard field goal on October 10, 1948, against the Brooklyn Dodgers. He nailed 52-yarders against the Rams in the NFL Championship Game on December 23, 1951, and against the Giants on October 12, 1952. He connected on 51-yarders against the Chicago Rockets on November 17, 1946, the Los Angeles Dons on September 3, 1948, the Chicago Cardinals on December 16, 1956, and the Steelers on October 28, 1962.

Groza was voted NFL Most Valuable Player in 1954 by SN. He was named to All-NFL offensive teams in 1951 by NYN and UP; in '53 by AP, NYN, and UP; in '54 by AP, NYN, SN, and UP; in '55 by AP, NYN, NEA, and UP; and in '57 by NYN and UP. He was voted First-Team All-Pro in 1952. Groza was picked for the Pro Bowl from 1950-55 and '57-59. His uniform number 76 is retired by the Browns (he also wore number 46). He was voted into the Pro Football Hall of Fame in 1974.

H

HADEN, JOE

Joe Haden has been a Browns cornerback since 2010. He was a first-round draft choice—the seventh overall pick—of Cleveland's in 2010 out of the University of Florida. He had a career-high six interceptions in his rookie year of 2010. He tied for the team lead with three picks in 2012, he had four in 2013 and three in 2014. One of his picks in 2013 was a 29-yard return off an Andy Dalton pass for a touchdown that gave the Browns a 13-0 first-quarter that turned out to be a 41-20 defeat in a crucial contest on November 17 in Cincinnati. Haden was a Pro Bowler from 2013-14.

HAIRSTON, CARL

Carl Hairston was a Cleveland defensive end from 1984-89. A product of the University of Maryland Eastern Shore, Hairston was obtained by the Browns on February 9, 1984, in a trade with the Eagles for an undisclosed draft choice. His 37.5 sacks are fourth all-time in Browns history. Hairston was part of one of the most memorable plays in Browns history on December 13, 1987, against the Bengals in Cleveland Stadium. With the Browns leading 21-3 in the second quarter, he was on the receiving end of a lateral from Clay Matthews following Matthews's interception of a Boomer Esiason pass at the Browns' four-yard line. When Matthews got to the Browns' 40, he threw the ball to Hairston, who was the only Brown in the vicinity. The big guy lumbered 40 yards before he was taken down at the Bengals' 20-yard-line.

HALL, CHARLIE

Charlie Hall was a Browns linebacker from 1971-80. He was a Browns third-round draft choice in 1971 from the University of Houston. He tied for the team lead in interceptions in 1975. One memorable pick by Hall occurred on November 4, 1979, when he picked off a Ron Jaworski pass with no time left and Philadelphia at the Cleveland one-yard line, thus preserving the Browns' 24-19 win.

HALL, DINO

Dino Hall was mainly a Browns kickoff and punt returner from 1979-83. He played a little at running back. A product of Glassboro State College, Hall was acquired by Cleveland as a free agent on June 14, 1979. He was released on August 21, 1979, and then resigned on October 2, 1979, when Keith Wright injured a knee in Week 5. Hall led the Browns in kickoff returns and kickoff return yardage every year from 1979-82. He also led the team in punt returns and punt return yardage in 1979, '81, and '83. His 1,014 kickoff return yards in 1979 rank 10th for the Browns in one season. His 295 punt return yards in 1979 rank ninth for the most in one Browns season. His 3,185 career kickoff return yards rank second in team history, and his 901 all-time punt return yards rank sixth.

HALL OF FAME GAME

The Browns have played in the Hall of Fame Game, the annual exhibition contest in Canton, Ohio, five times. The following are the results:

Pittsburgh 16, Cleveland 7 (Sept. 8, 1963)
Philadelphia 28, Cleveland 13 (Aug. 5, 1967)
Cleveland 24, Atlanta 10 (Aug. 1, 1981)
Chicago 13, Cleveland 0 (Aug. 4, 1990)
Cleveland 20, Dallas 17 (OT) (Aug. 9, 1999)

Overall – 2-3 (.400)

HALL OF FAMERS

Sixteen Browns have been inducted into the Hall of Fame. The year the individuals were inducted is in parentheses.

Otto Graham (1965)
Paul Brown (1967)
Marion Motley (1968)
Jim Brown (1971)
Lou Groza (1974)
Dante Lavelli (1975)

Len Ford (1976)
Bill Willis (1977)
Bobby Mitchell (1983)
Paul Warfield (1983)
Mike McCormack (1984)
Frank Gatski (1985)
Leroy Kelly (1994)
Ozzie Newsome (1999)
Joe DeLamielleure (2003)
Gene Hickerson (2007)

HANSEN, BRIAN

Brian Hansen was a Browns punter from 1991-93. A product of the University of Sioux Falls, he was acquired by Cleveland on April 1, 1991, as a free agent. He had punts of 73 yards on September 27, 1992, at home against Denver and 72 yards on October 17, 1993, in Cincinnati. His 3,632 punting yards in 1993 rank ninth in Browns history. Hansen ranks seventh in team history with 10,112 career punting yards.

HARRISON, JEROME

Jerome Harrison was a Browns running back from 2006-10. He was drafted by the Browns in the fifth round of the 2006 NFL Draft out of Washington State University. His best year was in 2009 when he rushed for both a team-leading 862 yards and five touchdowns. He rushed for 561 of his yards in the Browns' last three games, including a team record 286 in a 41-34 victory at Kansas City on December 20. Harrison also tied for the team lead with 34 receptions for 220 yards and two TDs. Harrison also led the Browns with seven total touchdowns.

HAWKINS, ANDREW

Andrew Hawkins had been a Browns wide receiver since 2014. A University of Toledo product, he signed with Cleveland in 2014. He led the Browns both with 63 receptions and 824 receiving yards plus tied for the team lead in touchdown receptions.

HEAD COACHES

Please see Coaches and Assistant Coaches on page 213 for a full list of head coaches.

HEAD COACHES' COMPOSITE
WON-LOST-TIED RECORDS

Paul Brown – 158-48-8 (.757)
Blanton Collier – 76-34-2 (.688)
Nick Skorich – 30-24-2 (.554)
Forrest Gregg – 18-23 (.439)
Dick Modzelewski – 0-1 (.000)
Sam Rutigliano – 47-50 (.485)
Marty Schottenheimer – 44-27 (.620)
Bud Carson – 11-13-1 (.460)
Jim Shofner – 1-6 (.143)
Bill Belichick – 36-44 (.450)
Chris Palmer – 5-27 (.156)
Butch Davis – 24-35 (.407)
Romeo Crennel – 24-40 (.375)
Eric Mangini – 10-22 (.313)
Pat Shurmur – 9-23 (.281)
Rob Chudzinski – 4-12 (.250)
Mike Pettine – 7-9 (.438)

HEIDEN, STEVE

Steve Heiden was a Cleveland tight end from 2002-09. A product of South Dakota State University, he was traded to the Browns by the San Diego Chargers on August 31, 2002. He led the Browns with five touchdown receptions in 2004. His best year was in 2005 when he caught 43 balls for 401 yards. For his Browns career, Heiden had 187 receptions for 1,602 yards.

HEISMAN TROPHY WINNERS

The following winners of the Heisman Trophy in college went on to play for the Browns:

Howard Cassady
Les Horvath
Vinny Testaverde
Charles White
Johnny Manziel

HELMET TOSS, THE

With less than 10 seconds left and the Browns leading the Kansas City Chiefs 39-37 in the season opener on September 8, 2002, in Cleveland, Chiefs quarterback Trent Green dropped back to pass. It looked like Browns linebacker Dwayne Rudd sacked Green as time expired. However, Green lateraled the ball to tackle John Tait just before he went down. Rudd did not see this and, thinking the game was over, he took off his helmet and threw it in the air in celebration of what he thought was a Browns victory. Tait lumbered to the Browns' 26-yard line where he was knocked out of bounds. That would have been the end of the game, but Rudd's premature helmet toss resulted in an unsportsmanlike conduct penalty, and a game cannot end on a defensive penalty. Thus Kansas City got to run an untimed play, and the ball was moved to the 13-yard line (half the distance to the goal line from the end of Tait's run due to the penalty). Morten Andersen then booted a 30-yard field goal to give the Chiefs an unbelievable 40-39 victory.

HENRY, ANTHONY

Anthony Henry was been a Browns defensive back from 2001-04. A fourth-round draft choice by Cleveland in 2001 from the University of South Florida, he intercepted 10 passes in 2001, tying him with Tom Colella's 1946 total and Thom Darden's 1978 total for the all-time team record. He led the AFC in interceptions, and tied for first in the NFL, becoming the first NFL rookie to lead the league in picks since 1995.

Henry became the first Browns player to have a pair of three-interception games in the same season, the first player in the NFL to accomplish the feat since 1989, and the first rookie to do so since 1962. His three-pick games came on September 23, 2001, at home against Detroit and on November 18 at Baltimore. His 97-yard interception return for a touchdown late in the third quarter against Jacksonville at home that year on December 16 kept the Browns within striking distance in what turned out to be a harrowing loss (*please see Bottlegate*). Henry also led the Browns in interceptions in 2004 with four.

HICKERSON, GENE

Gene Hickerson was a Browns guard from 1958-60 and '62-73. He was Cleveland's seventh-round draft choice in 1957 from the University of Mississippi with one year of eligibility in school left. He missed the 1961 season due to a broken leg suffered in the first preseason game at Detroit on

August 11. He fractured the leg again late in the season while watching a game from the sideline. Hickerson was voted to All-NFL offensive teams in 1966 by NEA; in '67 by AP, NYN, NEA, and UPI; in '68 by AP, NYN, NEA, PFW, FWA, and UPI; and in '69 by AP, NYN, OFF, PFW, FWA, SI, and UPI. He was voted to All-AFC offensive teams in 1970 by FWA and UPI. He was selected to play in the Pro Bowl from 1965-70.

HIGHEST-SCORING GAMES

The highest-scoring game for the Browns occurred in 1946 when they stomped Brooklyn 66-14. *For more highest-scoring games by the Browns and Browns' opponents, please see Team Statistics on page 248.*

HILL, CALVIN

Calvin Hill was a Browns running back from 1978-81. A Yale University product, he was acquired by Cleveland four weeks into the 1978 season as a free agent. He was used mostly as a receiver out of the backfield. He had 25 receptions for 334 yards and six touchdowns in 1978, 38 catches for 381 yards and a pair of touchdowns in 1979, and 27 receptions for 383 yards and a team-leading six touchdowns in 1980.

HILLIS, PEYTON

Peyton Hillis was a Browns running back from 2010-11. A product of the University of Arkansas, he was traded to Cleveland from the Broncos on March 15, 2010. He came out of nowhere to rush for both a team-leading 1,177 yards and 11 touchdowns in 2010, becoming a fan favorite due to his powerful style of running the ball. He also caught 61 passes for 477 yards and two TDs. The next year, off-the-field issues contributed to Hillis's numbers taking a dive—587 yards rushing for three touchdowns (both of which still led the team) and just 22 receptions for 130 yards.

HIRAM COLLEGE

Hiram College acted as the Browns' training camp site from 1952-74.

HOAGLIN, FRED

Fred Hoaglin was a Cleveland center from 1966-72. He was a Browns sixth-round draft choice in 1966 from the University of Pittsburgh. He was picked to play in the Pro Bowl in 1969.

HOARD, LEROY

Leroy Hoard was a Cleveland running back from 1990-95. He was a second-round draft choice by the Browns in 1990 from the University of Michigan. He had a team-leading 11 touchdowns in 1991—nine receiving and two rushing—with several of his TD catches in spectacular fashion. He was tops for the Browns in rushing yards in 1994 with 890 and 1995 with 547. His '94 rushing yards total was the highest for a Browns player in nine years. Hoard was a Pro Bowl selection in 1994.

HODGES, REGGIE

Reggie Hodges was a Browns punter from 2009-12. A product of Ball State University, he signed with Cleveland on November 15, 2009. His 3,766 punting yards in 2012 rank sixth in Browns history. His 8,979 career punting yards rank eighth in team annals.

HOLCOMB, KELLY

Kelly Holcomb was a Browns quarterback from 2001-04. He started the first two games 2002 season after Tim Couch got injured. He put up impressive numbers in those two games, against the Chiefs and Bengals—a combined 44-of-69 for 524 yards, five touchdown passes, and no interceptions. He replaced an injured Couch once again during that season's finale and helped the Browns to a win over the visiting Atlanta Falcons that, in the end, put them in the playoffs. In a wild 36-33 wild card loss at Pittsburgh, Holcomb went 26-for-43 for 429 yards, three TD passes, and an interception. His yardage total is the seventh most in a postseason game in NFL history.

When Holcomb was named the starter for the 2003 season opener, he just was not consistent enough to hang on to the job. He and Couch each started eight games that year, and neither could really get much going during a 5-11 season. Holcomb did have his moments, though, in his last two seasons with the Browns, passing for 392 yards in a 44-6 rout of the Arizona Cardinals on November 16, 2003, and passing for 413 yards in a 58-48 loss in Cincinnati on November 28, 2004.

HOLLY, DAVEN

Daven Holly was a Browns cornerback from 2006-07. A product of the University of Cincinnati, he was signed as a free agent by Cleveland on

July 13, 2006. He tied for the team lead in 2006 with five interceptions, including one off Ben Roethlisberger on November 19 that he returned 57 yards for a touchdown in a 24-20 home loss to the Pittsburgh Steelers. He had another pick off Roethlisberger later in the quarter. Later that season he also returned a fumble 40 yards for a score in a 22-7 Christmas Eve home defeat to Tampa Bay.

HOME WON-LOST-TIED RECORDS

Please see Team Statistics on page 248.

HOOKER, FAIR

Fair Hooker was a Browns wide receiver from 1969-74. Cleveland's fifth-round draft choice in 1969 from Arizona State University, Hooker led the team in receptions (45) and receiving yards (649) in 1971. He totaled 129 catches for 1,845 yards and eight touchdown catches in his Browns career. He was on the receiving end of a 27-yard TD pass from Mike Phipps that gave the Browns a surprising 14-13 lead over the undefeated Miami Dolphins late in an AFC Divisional Playoff on Christmas Eve 1972 in the Orange Bowl. The Browns eventually lost 20-14. Hooker had three catches for 53 yards that day.

HORVATH, LES

Les Horvath was a Cleveland running back in 1949. He was a product of Ohio State University. He returned a fumble 84 yards for a touchdown that gave the Browns their winning touchdown in a 14-3 victory over the New York Yankees on September 18, 1949, in Cleveland.

HOUSTON, JIM

Jim Houston was a Browns defensive end and linebacker from 1960-72. A first-round draft choice by Cleveland in 1960 from Ohio State University, he was the younger brother of Lin Houston, who was a Cleveland guard from 1946-53. Houston returned an interception 44 yards for a touchdown in the Browns' 38-24 victory over visiting Philadelphia on November 29, 1964. He returned a Fran Tarkenton pass 79 yards for a score on December 3, 1967, in a 24-14 win over the visiting Giants, and a week later returned a Jim Hart pass 18 yards for Cleveland's final score in a key 20-16 victory over the Cardinals in St. Louis. Houston was named to All-NFL defensive teams in 1964 by NEA and in 1965 by UPI. He was selected to play in the Pro Bowl in 1964, '65, '69, and '70.

HOUSTON, LIN

Lin Houston was a guard for the Browns from 1946-53. He was a product of Ohio State University obtained by the Browns as a free agent. He was the older brother of Jim Houston, a defensive end and linebacker for the Browns from 1960-72.

HOWELL, MIKE

Mike Howell was a Browns defensive back from 1965-72. Cleveland's eighth-round draft choice in 1965 from Grambling State University, Howell had eight interceptions in 1966 that tied for the team lead and for eighth all-time in team history. His six picks in 1969 were tops on the team. He returned a Billy Kilmer pass 68 yards in the Browns' season-ending 20-13 triumph in Washington on December 19, 1971. Howell's 27 career interceptions are tied for eighth in Browns history.

HOYER, BRIAN

Brian Hoyer was a Browns quarterback from 2013-14. A product of Michigan State University, the North Olmsted native signed with Cleveland on May 16, 2013. Hoyer took over for the struggling Brandon Weeden in Week 3 of the '13 season in which he led the Browns to a 31-27 comeback win over the Vikings in Minnesota on a seven-yard touchdown pass to Jordan Cameron with 51 seconds to go. He then directed the Browns to a solid 17-6 win over the visiting Bengals before tearing an ACL in the early stages of a Thursday night home game against Buffalo that ended his season. Hoyer led the Browns to seven wins in their first 11 games in 2014, but he had begun to struggle and was replaced as the starter by Johnny Manziel, who was even worse than Hoyer. Hoyer returned to start once more, but the Browns lost their last five games.

HUFF, SAM

Sam Huff was a linebacker for the New York Giants from 1956-63 and the Washington Redskins from 1964-69. Memorable were his hard-hitting confrontations with Jim Brown, especially during his days with the Giants.

HUMBLE, WELDON

Weldon Humble was a Cleveland linebacker from 1947-50. A product of Rice University, Humble was acquired by the Browns on August 14, 1947, in a trade with the Baltimore Colts for four players. He was a Pro Bowl pick in 1950.

HUNTER, ART

Art Hunter was a center for the Browns from 1956-59. He was a product of the University of Notre Dame acquired by the Browns on September 8, 1955, in a trade with Green Bay for two players. He was in the military in 1955 and for the first month of the 1956 season. He was a Pro Bowler in 1959.

I

INDIANAPOLIS COLTS

The Indianapolis Colts were NFL opponents of the Browns from 1953-95 and have been since 1999. The team was located in Baltimore from 1953-83 as a holding of the defunct Dallas Texans (no relation to the future AFL Dallas Texans). One of the more memorable Browns victories against the Colts was on November 1, 1959, in Baltimore when Jim Brown rushed for a team-record five touchdowns in a 38-31 win.

Another notable Cleveland victory came at home on October 25, 1981, when the team defeated Baltimore 42-28 as Brian Sipe passed for a team-record 444 yards. The Browns and Colts played an exciting game on December 26, 1999, in snowy Cleveland that was not decided until Mike Vanderjagt's 21-yard field goal with four seconds left gave Indianapolis a 29-28 victory. Another memorable game between the two teams was on December 15, 2002, in Cleveland when Tim Couch, the top overall draft pick in 1999 and Peyton Manning, the top overall draft pick in 1998, went head-to-head for the first—and only—time in the pros. The two QBs' statistics that day were eerily similar—Couch was 21-of-35 for 287 yards with two touchdowns, and Manning was

Bobby Franklin defends as Baltimore's R. C. Owens catches a pass on the goal line during the Colts' 36-14 rout of the Browns in Cleveland on October 14, 1962. Photo courtesy of the Cleveland Press Collection.

20-of-34 for 277 yards with two TDs and an interception. The Browns led the entire game until the fourth quarter when the Colts took the lead and won the crucial contest 28-23.

The Colts and Browns have clashed four times in the postseason, all in Cleveland. Each team has won twice—once in the NFL Championship Game and once in the AFC Divisional Playoffs. The heavily-favored Colts were upset by the Browns 27-0 in the 1964 NFL Championship Game. Baltimore destroyed Cleveland 34-0 in the 1968 NFL title game. Baltimore defeated the Browns 20-3 in a 1971 AFC Divisional Playoff, and the Browns won 38-21 in a 1987 AFC Divisional Playoff.

The Colts' all-time record against Cleveland is 14-15, 6-10 at home and 8-5 on the road. Their all-time postseason record against the Browns is 2-2 (away games).

INDIVIDUAL TOP FIVES (POSTSEASON)

Please see Individual Statistics on page 225.

INDIVIDUAL TOP TENS

Please see Individual Statistics on page 225.

INTERCEPTIONS LEADERS

Please see Individual Statistics on page 225.

J

JACKSON, D'QWELL

D'Qwell Jackson was a Browns linebacker from 2006-09 and '11-13. A product of the University of Maryland, he was traded to Cleveland from the New Orleans Saints on April 29, 2006. Jackson was the steadying force on a defense that showed promise at times. He suffered a shoulder injury during a loss at Pittsburgh in the sixth game of the 2009 season that would cause him to miss the rest of '09 and the entire 2010 season. Jackson had 11.5 career sacks. On September 9, 2012, in the season opener, he intercepted a Michael Vick pass and returned it 27 yards for a touchdown to give the Browns a 16-10 fourth-quarter lead in a game they would eventually lose 17-16.

JACKSON, JAMES

James Jackson was a Browns running back from 2001-04. He was a third-round draft pick of Cleveland's in 2001 out of the University of Miami. He led the Browns with 554 rushing yards in '01 and led the team with three rushing touchdowns in 2003.

JACKSON, MICHAEL

Michael Jackson was a Browns wide receiver from 1991-95. He was a sixth-round draft choice of the Browns in 1991 from the University of Southern Mississippi. He tied Eric Metcalf for the Browns' lead in receptions in 1992 with 47. He was also the team leader that year in receiving yards (755) and touchdown receptions (seven). He also led the Browns in receiving yards and touchdown catches in 1993 (756, eight) and '95 (714, nine). Jackson's 122 receiving yards in Cleveland's 20-13 win over New England at home in an AFC Wild Card Playoff game on January 1, 1995, rank fourth in Browns history. His seven receptions in the Patriots game are tied for second all-time.

JACKSON, ROBERT E.

Robert E. Jackson was a Browns guard from 1975-85. He was a product of Duke University acquired by Cleveland as a free agent in 1975.

JACKSON, ROBERT L.

Robert L. Jackson was a Browns linebacker from 1978-81. He was a first-round draft pick of Cleveland's from Texas A&M University in 1977. A serious knee injury suffered at the outset of training camp forced him to miss the entire 1977 season.

JACKSONVILLE JAGUARS

The Jacksonville Jaguars were Browns opponents in the NFL in 1995 and have been since 1999. They administered one of the Browns' most embarrassing losses in their 23-15 win on October 22, 1995, in Cleveland during Jacksonville's initial season. A memorable game in the series came on December 16, 2001, in Cleveland in a 15-10 Jaguars victory amid a frightening bottle-throwing episode by thousands of fans caused by a controversial call

Robert L. Jackson in 1978. Photo courtesy of the Cleveland Press Collection.

by the officials in the late stages of the game (*please see Bottlegate*). Another memorable game between the two teams occurred on December 8, 2002, in Jacksonville when Tim Couch connected with Quincy Morgan on a 50-yard Hail Mary touchdown pass with 0:00 on the clock to give the Browns a 21-20 victory in a crucial game for Cleveland. Jacksonville's all-time record against the Browns is 11-5, 5-3 at home and 6-2 on the road.

JAGADE, HARRY

Harry Jagade was a Browns running back from 1951-53. A product of Indiana University, he was acquired by Cleveland as a free agent in 1951.

He rushed for a team-high 104 yards on 15 carries and scored the Browns' only touchdown, a seven-yard run in the third quarter, during a 17-7 loss to the Lions in the 1952 NFL Championship Game in Cleveland. Remarkably, Jagade gave a repeat performance with the exact same rushing statistics in the 1953 NFL title game against the same Lions, but this time in the Motor City. Once again, he totaled 104 yards on 15 carries in the Browns' 17-16 loss. He even scored on a third-quarter run, but this time it was a nine-yard run, two yards longer than his touchdown the year before. He was picked for the Pro Bowl in 1953.

JAMES, TOMMY

Tommy James was a Browns defensive back from 1948-55. He was a product of Ohio State University obtained by the Browns as a free agent. His nine interceptions in 1950 led the Browns and are tied for fourth in team history. He ranks fourth all-time for the Browns in interceptions with 34 and was a Pro Bowl selection in 1953.

JANUARY
-9, 1963

Art Modell fired Paul Brown.

-2, 1966

The Browns fell to the Green Bay Packers 23-12 in the snow and mud of Lambeau Field in Green Bay in the NFL title game.

-4, 1970

Cleveland lost to the Minnesota Vikings 27-7 in the NFL Championship Game in Minnesota.

-26, 1970

The Browns traded sensational wide receiver Paul Warfield to Miami in exchange for the Dolphins' first-round pick—and third overall—in the next day's draft. The Browns did this in order to draft Purdue University quarterback Mike Phipps. Many believe this trade was the main reason behind the Browns' mediocrity in the mid-1970s.

-7, 1995

The Browns were obliterated by the Pittsburgh Steelers 29-9 in an AFC Divisional Playoff in Pittsburgh.

-5, 2003

The Browns blew a 24-7 third-quarter lead and lost 36-33 to the Steelers in Pittsburgh in an AFC Wild Card Game.

JOHNSON, EDDIE

Eddie Johnson was a Browns linebacker from 1981-90. He was a seventh-round draft choice by the team in 1981 from the University of Louisville. Johnson was partly responsible for the birth of the famous Dawg Pound due to his barking ways during the 1984 training camp when a defensive teammate would make a big play. *(Please see Dawg Pound, The.)*

JOHNSON, KEVIN

Kevin Johnson was a Browns wide receiver from 1999-2003. He was a second-round draft choice of Cleveland's in 1999 from Syracuse University. He led all NFL rookies in 1999 in receptions (66), receiving yards (986), and touchdown receptions (eight). He set Browns rookie records for receptions and receiving yards. In 2000 he was the Browns leader in receptions and receiving yards. In 2001 he led the team in receptions (84, which ranks fifth in team history), receiving yards (1,097, which ranks sixth in club annals), and touchdown catches (9), the latter which tied for third in the AFC and fifth in the NFL. In 2002 he led the team in receptions. Johnson was on the receiving end of a 56-yard Hail Mary pass from Tim Couch with no time left that gave the "new" Browns their very first victory on October 31, 1999, against the Saints in New Orleans. His 315 career receptions rank sixth in team history.

JOHNSON, MIKE

Mike Johnson was a Browns linebacker from 1986-93. He was a first-round supplemental draft choice of the Browns in 1984 from Virginia Tech University. He spent 1984 and '85 in the USFL. He returned an interception 64 yards for a touchdown on September 23, 1990, in a 24-14 home loss to the San Diego Chargers. Johnson was voted to All-AFC defensive teams in 1989 by PFW and UPI. He was selected to play in the Pro Bowl in 1989 and '90.

JOHNSON, PEPPER

Pepper Johnson was a Cleveland linebacker from 1993-95. He was an Ohio State University product acquired by the Browns as a free agent on September 2, 1993. He was selected to play in the Pro Bowl in 1994.

JOHNSON, WALTER

Walter Johnson was a Browns defensive tackle from 1965-76. He was a second-round draft choice by Cleveland in 1965 from California State University (Los Angeles). He was picked for the Pro Bowl from 1967-69.

JONES, DAVE

Dave Jones was Cleveland's majority owner from 1953-60.

JONES, DUB

Dub Jones was a Cleveland wide receiver from 1948-55. A Tulane University product, Jones was acquired by the Browns in 1948 in a trade with Brooklyn for that year's draft rights to University of Michigan All-American running back Bob Chappius. His most memorable game came on November 25, 1951, when he scored six touchdowns in Cleveland's 42-21 victory over the visiting Chicago Bears. Four of the touchdowns came on rushes and two on receptions. His feat set a Browns record and tied an NFL mark. On September 30 of that same year in a game against the 49ers, Jones was on

Dub Jones in preseason action, 1951. Photo courtesy of the Cleveland Press Collection.

the receiving end of an 81-yard pass play from Otto Graham that went for a touchdown. He was voted to All-NFL offensive teams in 1951 by AP, NYN, and UP. He was picked for the Pro Bowl in 1951. He was a Browns assistant coach from 1963-67.

JONES, EDGAR

Edgar Jones was a Browns running back from 1946-49. He was a product of the University of Pittsburgh obtained by Cleveland as a free agent. He returned a kickoff 96 yards for a touchdown in a 66-14 rout of the Brooklyn Dodgers in the 1946 season finale on December 8 in Brooklyn. Jones is tied for fourth in team history for most points scored in one postseason game with 12 against Buffalo on December 19, 1948. His 30 postseason points are tied for fifth all-time for the Browns.

JONES, HOMER

Homer Jones was a Browns kickoff returner in 1970. He was a Texas Southern University product obtained by the Browns on January 26, 1970, in a trade with the New York Giants for Ron Johnson, Jim Kanicki, and Wayne Meylan. He led the Browns in kickoff returns and kickoff return yards in 1970 with 29 and 739, respectively. Jones's most memorable moment came in Cleveland on September 21, 1970, in the NFL's first-ever ABC *Monday Night Football* game in which Jones returned the second-half kickoff 94 yards for a touchdown that helped the Browns defeat Joe Namath and the New York Jets 31-21.

JONES, JOE

Joe Jones was a Browns defensive end from 1970-71, in '73, and from 1975-78. He was a second-round draft pick of the team in 1970 from Tennessee State University. He missed the 1972 season due to knee surgery. He was traded to the Eagles on September 5, 1974, and then re-acquired via waivers on November 14, 1975. Jones was responsible for one of the more notable occurrences in Browns history, when early in the fourth quarter of an October 10, 1976, home game against Pittsburgh, he sacked quarterback Terry Bradshaw by lifting him up and slamming him head first to the ground, causing Bradshaw to miss the next two games due to back and neck injuries.

JONES, SEAN

Sean Jones was a Cleveland defensive back from 2005-08. He was a second-round draft choice of the Browns in 2004 out of the University of Georgia. He missed his entire rookie year of 2004 due to a knee injury he suffered before the start of the season. He spent most of 2005 playing on the special teams.

He tied for the team lead with five interceptions in 2006 and was second on the team with five picks in 2007 and four in '08. Jones was the AFC Defensive Player of the Week as he had two interceptions in helping the Browns to a 20-13 win over the New York Jets on October 29, 2006.

JONES, TONY

Tony Jones was a Browns offensive tackle from 1988-95. He was a Western Carolina University product obtained by Cleveland as a free agent on May 28, 1988. He was voted to the All-AFC defensive team in 1994 by PFW.

JUREVICIUS, JOE

Joe Jurevicius was a Browns wide receiver from 2006-07. A homegrown product of Lake Catholic High School, and also Penn State University, he signed with the team on March 11, 2006. Jurevicius had great hands. He had 40 receptions for 495 yards in 2006 and 50 receptions for 614 yards in 2007. He had three touchdown catches in each of those seasons.

K

KANICKI, JIM

Jim Kanicki was a Browns defensive tackle from 1963-69. He was a second-round draft choice by Cleveland in 1963 from Michigan State University.

KANSAS CITY CHIEFS

The Kansas City Chiefs were opponents of the Browns in the NFL from 1970-95 and have been since 1999. The last two Browns games to end in a tie came against the Chiefs. Both seasons in which these occurred, the Browns came away with seven wins and three losses. Following a 20-20 tie on December 2, 1973, in Kansas City Cleveland was 7-3-2, and after a 10-10 standoff at home on November 19, 1989, the Browns were 7-3-1. Kansas City's all-time record against Cleveland is 11-11-2, 8-3-1 at home and 3-8-1 on the road.

KARDIAC KIDS

The Kardiac Kids was the nickname attributed to the Browns early in the 1979 season and continued on throughout the 1980 season due to numerous games that were undecided until the final moments, most of which the Browns won.

KELLERMAN, ERNIE

Ernie Kellerman was a Cleveland defensive back from 1966-71. Kellerman was a Miami University product obtained by the Browns as a free agent in 1965. He spent that season on the practice squad. He tied for second on the team in 1967 with six interceptions.

KELLY, LEROY

Leroy Kelly was a Browns running back from 1964-73. He was an eighth-round draft pick of the Browns in 1964 from Morgan State University. He

Ernie Kellerman (24) or Mike Howell appear to have an interception on the Pittsburgh goal line on November 5, 1967. Photo courtesy of the Cleveland Press Collection.

led Cleveland in rushing yardage every season from 1966-72 and earned three straight 1,000-yard rushing seasons from 1966-68. His 1,141 yards rushing in 1966 ranked second in the NFL, 90 yards behind Chicago's Gale Sayers. He rushed for 1,205 yards in 1967 and 1,239 in 1968, the latter of which ranks 10th in Browns history.

Kelly caught a 46-yard touchdown pass from Bill Nelsen and scored on a 35-yard run in a 31-20 upset of the Dallas Cowboys on December 21, 1968, in the Eastern Conference Championship Game in Cleveland. He ranks second in all-time Browns rushing yardage with 7,274. His 540 points rank sixth in team history. His 120 points in 1968 rank second in Browns history. His 427 career postseason rushing yards rank third in team annals (#). His 12 points scored against Dallas in the 1968 Eastern Conference title game are tied for fourth all-time for the Browns.

Kelly was effective as a receiver, too, totaling 190 receptions for 2,281 yards (plus 18 for 190 in postseason play) in his career. He ranks third in team history in career combined net yards with 12,329 (######). He also returned

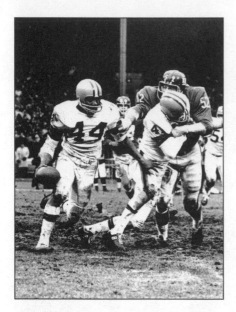

Leroy Kelly in action against the Giants on December 3, 1967. Photo courtesy of the Cleveland Press Collection.

punts and kickoffs on a regular basis early in his career. His 990 punt return yards rank fifth, and his 1,784 kickoff return yards rank seventh, in team history.

Kelly had three punt returns for touchdowns—a 68-yarder against the Giants on October 25, 1964, a 67-yarder on November 21, 1965, against the Cowboys, and a 56-yarder the very next week on November 28 against the Steelers. In addition, he returned a punt 74 yards in a home game against the Denver Broncos on October 24, 1971. His 2,014 combined net yards in 1966 rank fourth in Browns annals.

Kelly was named the NFL's Most Valuable Player in 1968 by MAX. He was voted to All-NFL offensive teams in 1966 and '67 by AP, NYN, NEA, and UPI; in '68 by AP, NYN, NEA, PFW, FWA, and UPI; and in '69 by NEA. He was voted to the All-AFC offensive team in 1971 by NEA and was a Pro Bowl selection from 1966-71. Kelly was inducted into the Pro Football Hall of Fame in 1994.

KENT STATE UNIVERSITY

Kent State University was the Browns' training-camp site from 1975-81. The school has had five players drafted by the Browns.

KICKERS

Notable kickers in Browns annals include Lou Groza, Don Cockroft, Matt Bahr, Matt Stover, and Phil Dawson.

KICKOFF LUNCHEON

The Browns kickoff luncheon was held annually before most seasons during the 1970s and '80s at various Cleveland hotels to acquaint players and coaches with the public. The luncheon was sponsored by the Cleveland Touchdown Club and Greater Cleveland Growth Association.

KICKOFF RETURN YARDS LEADERS

Please see Individual Statistics on page 225.

KICKOFF RETURNERS

Notable Browns kickoff returners include Edgar Jones, Marion Motley, Ken Carpenter, Bobby Mitchell, Walter Roberts, Ben Davis, Bo Scott, Homer Jones, Ken Brown, Greg Pruitt, Keith Wright, Dino Hall, Glen Young, Gerald McNeil, Eric Metcalf, Randy Baldwin, Andre Davis, and Josh Cribbs.

KICKOFF RETURNS LEADERS

Please Individual Statistics on page 225.

KIRKSEY, CHRISTIAN

Christian Kirksey has been a Browns linebacker since 2014. He was a third-round draft choice of the Browns in 2014 out of the University of Iowa. He had two sacks in '14.

KISSELL, JOHN

John Kissell was a Cleveland defensive tackle from 1950 52 and '54-56. He was a Boston College product acquired by the Browns prior to the 1950 season as part of a three-player merger with the Buffalo Bills of the folded AAFC. He played in the CFL in 1953.

KONZ, KEN

Ken Konz was a Cleveland defensive back from 1953-59. He was a first-round draft choice of the Browns in 1951 from Louisiana State University. He was in the military in 1951 and '52. He led the Browns in interceptions with seven in 1954 and tied for the team lead in 1953, '55, '57, and '58. He is tied for fifth in team history with 30 interceptions. He also returned punts, and ranks 10th in team annals with 556 return yards. Konz was selected to play in the Pro Bowl in 1955.

KOSAR, BERNIE

Bernie Kosar was a Browns quarterback from 1985-93. He was a first-round supplemental draft choice of the team in 1985 from the University of Miami. The Browns obtained the rights to choose him when they traded their first-and third-round draft choices in 1985 and first- and sixth-round picks in 1986 to Buffalo. Kosar went public with his desire to play for the Browns, the team he rooted for while growing up in nearby Boardman, Ohio.

Kosar fumbled his first snap in a home game against New England on October 6, 1985, after starter Gary Danielson went down with a severe right shoulder injury in the second quarter. He completed his first seven passes, though, and directed the Browns to a 24-20 triumph. He completed 124 of 248 passes for 1,578 yards with eight touchdowns and seven interceptions that year, sharing time with the oft-injured Danielson, as the Browns won their first AFC Central Division title in five years despite just an 8-8 record. In an AFC Divisional Playoff matchup with the Dolphins in Miami on January 4, 1986—a game the Browns eventually lost 24-21—Kosar threw a 16-yard touchdown pass to Ozzie Newsome that gave the Browns a 7-3 first-quarter lead.

Kosar became the starter once and for all the next year when Danielson went down with a season-ending injury—a fractured left ankle—in the final preseason game against the Raiders in Los Angeles on August 28. Kosar passed for 3,854 yards in 1986, completing 310 of 531 attempts in leading Cleveland to a 12-4 record and the Central Division title once again. That season, he had his only two 400-yard passing games—414 on November 23 at home against Pittsburgh and 401 two weeks earlier in a Monday night home game against Miami. In an AFC Divisional Playoff on January 3, 1987, in Cleveland, he passed for an NFL Playoff record 489 yards as the Browns fought back from a 20-10 deficit late in the fourth quarter to defeat the New York Jets 23-20 in double overtime. In the AFC Championship Game the next week—a 23-20 overtime loss to Denver at home—he completed 18 of 32 passes for 259 yards with two touchdown passes and two interceptions.

In 1987 Kosar led the AFC with a 95.4 quarterback rating. He completed 241 of 389 passes for 3,033 yards that year, with 22 touchdown passes and just nine interceptions as the Browns returned to the AFC title game but lost to the Broncos again—this time in Denver by a 38-33 count. His 356 yards through the air in the loss to the Broncos rank third in team history. He suffered an arm injury in the opening game in Kansas City the next season when Chiefs safety Lloyd Burruss blindsided him. He was out until Week 8 when he returned with flying colors by completing 25 of 43 passes for 314 yards and three touchdowns in a 29-21 victory over the Phoenix Cardinals. He injured his left knee on December 12 in a Monday night loss in Miami, which ended his season for good.

Kosar led the Browns back to their third meeting in four years with Denver in the conference championship game in 1989, but the Browns lost again 37-21 in Denver. On October 23 of that year, he completed a 97-yard touchdown pass to Webster Slaughter in a 27-7 Monday night victory over the Bears, the second-longest pass play in team history. He struggled along with the team in 1990 and was benched for a period during that horrible 3-13 season. He wound up completing 230 of 423 passes for 2,562 yards with 10 touchdown passes and 15 interceptions. His quarterback rating was only 65.7. However, Kosar rebounded in 1991, throwing for 3,487 yards, 18 touchdowns, and just nine interceptions while completing 307 passes in 494 attempts for a completion percentage of 62.1. He broke Bart Starr's twenty-six-year-old NFL record for most consecutive passes without an interception that actually dated back to the 1990 season. He was injured for part of 1992, splitting time with Mike Tomczak as the starter. He was released on November 8, 1993, after two months of playing musical quarterbacks with ex-college teammate Vinny Testaverde, who was acquired as a free agent in the off-season.

Kosar ranks third in all-time passing yards for the Browns with 21,904 and second in pass completions with 1,853. He holds three of the top 10 positions for most passing yards by a Browns quarterback in one season and three of the top five spots for most pass completions by a Browns quarterback in a season. His 1,860 career postseason passing yards and 146 career pass completions both rank second in team history. His 33 completions against the Jets on January 3, 1987, are the most by a Brown in a postseason game. His 26 completions in Denver on January 17, 1988, are tied for second. Kosar was voted to the Pro Bowl in 1987.

KRUGER, PAUL

Paul Kruger has been a Browns linebacker since 2013. A product of the University of Utah, he signed with Cleveland on March 12, 2013. He had 4.5 sacks in 2013 and was tops on the team with 11 sacks in 2014.

L

LAHR, WARREN

Warren Lahr was a Browns defensive back from 1948-59. A Case Western Reserve University product, Lahr was acquired by Cleveland as a free agent. He returned an interception 52 yards for a touchdown for Cleveland's final score in its 31-21 victory over the Bills in an AAFC First-Round Playoff Game on December 4, 1949, in Cleveland. His interception of a Joe Stydahar pass, his second pick of the day, with just seconds left in the 1950 NFL title game against the Rams preserved the Browns' 30-28 victory. His eight interceptions in 1950 are tied for eighth in team history. His 44 interceptions all-time rank second in Browns annals. He returned five interceptions for touchdowns in his Browns career. Lahr was named to All-NFL defensive teams in 1951 by NYN and UP. He was a Browns television broadcaster from 1963-67.

LAKELAND COMMUNITY COLLEGE

Lakeland Community College was the Browns' training-camp site from 1982-91.

LAMBERT, JACK

Jack Lambert was a Pittsburgh Steelers linebacker from 1974-84. Lambert was known for his ferocious play. He directed much of his energy toward Browns quarterback Brian Sipe, with whom he had some nasty encounters.

LANG, KENARD

Kenard Lang was a Browns defensive end and linebacker from 2002-05. He is a product of the University of Miami. Lang's eight sacks in 2003 were tops on the team. His seven sacks in 2004 were tied for second, and his 5.5 sacks in 2002 ranked second. His 22.5 career sacks are tied for 10th in team annals.

LANGHORNE, REGGIE

Reggie Langhorne was a Browns wide receiver from 1985-91. He was a seventh-round draft choice of Cleveland's in 1985 from Elizabeth City State University. He led the Browns in 1988 with 780 receiving yards and seven touchdown receptions. He concluded his Browns career with 261 receptions for 3,597 yards and 15 touchdown catches. He totaled 26 receptions (fourth all-time in Browns history) (###) for 370 yards (fifth all-time in team history) (##) and two touchdown catches in postseason play.

LANNING, SPENCER

Spencer Lanning has been a Cleveland punter since 2013. A product of the University of South Carolina, he signed with the Browns on May 2, 2012. Lanning's 3,679 punting yards in 2013 rank seventh in Browns history, and his 4,119 punting yards in 2014 rank fourth.

LAST TIME . . . , THE

Did you know that the last time a Browns player returned a punt for a touchdown was on October 3, 2013, when Travis Benjamin returned one by Shawn Powell 79 yards in a 37-24 victory over the Bills in Cleveland?
For more last times, please see Browns Trivia on page 205.

LAST TIME THE BROWNS BEAT (CURRENT TEAMS) . . . , THE

Please see Browns Trivia on page 205.

LAUVAO, SHAWN

Shawn Lauvao was a Browns guard from 2010-2013. He was a third-round draft pick of the team in 2010 out of Arizona State University.

LAVELLI, DANTE

Dante Lavelli was a wide receiver for the Browns from 1946-56. He was an Ohio State University product acquired by Cleveland as a free agent. He led the team in receptions in 1946 (40), '51 (43), '53 (45), and '54 (47). He led the Browns in receiving yards in 1946 (843), '50 (565), and '53 (783). He was the team leader in touchdown receptions in 1946 (eight), '47 (nine), '51 (six),

'53 (six), and '54 (seven), and the co-leader in touchdown catches in 1948 (five), '49 (seven), and '50 (five).

Lavelli ranks ninth all-time for the Browns in scoring with 372 points, second in receiving yards with 6,488, and second in receptions with 386. He caught a 72-yard touchdown pass from Otto Graham on November 9, 1947, in Brooklyn. He holds the fourth and eighth spots for most receiving yards in one game by a Browns player with 209 on October 14, 1949, on the road against the Los Angeles Dons and 183 on October 27, 1946, at home against the San Francisco 49ers (#######).

Lavelli is tied for fifth in Browns all-time scoring in the postseason with 30 points. His 526 career yards receiving in the postseason rank first in team history (##). His 30 career postseason receptions rank first in team annals (###). He caught 37- and 39-yard touchdown passes in Cleveland's 30-28 victory over the Rams in the 1950 NFL Championship Game in Cleveland. His 12 points in that game are tied for fourth in team history. Lavelli was voted to All-AAFC teams in 1946 by AP and OFF and in 1947 by OFF. He was named to All-NFL offensive teams in 1951 and '53 by NYN and UP and was selected to play in the Pro Bowl in 1951, '53, and '54. He was inducted into the Pro Football Hall of Fame in 1975.

Billy Lefear scores against the Redskins in preseason action at the Stadium on August 24, 1974. Photo courtesy of the Cleveland Press Collection.

LEFEAR, BILLY

Billy Lefear was a Browns kickoff returner mainly from 1972-75. A ninth-round draft choice of Cleveland's in 1972 from Henderson State University, Lefear led the Browns in 1974 with 26 returns and 574 yards, and led the team in 1975 with 412 return yards. His 92-yard return off the opening kickoff on November 23, 1975, sparked the winless Browns' upset of the red-hot Bengals in Cleveland. He totaled 1,461 career kickoff return yards for the Browns.

LERNER, AL

Al Lerner was Cleveland's majority owner from 1999 to October 23, 2002, when he passed away.

LEWIS, CLIFF

Cliff Lewis was a Browns defensive back from 1946-51. He was a Duke University product acquired by the Browns as a free agent. His nine interceptions in 1948 are tied for fourth in Browns history. He returned punts, too, and ranks seventh in team history with 710 career return yards. Lewis, believe it or not, was also the starting quarterback in the Browns' first-ever game on September 6, 1946, at home against the Miami Seahawks. He was a Browns television broadcaster in 1961 and '62.

LEWIS, JAMAL

Jamal Lewis was a Browns running back from 2007-09. A product of the University of Tennessee, he signed with Cleveland on March 7, 2007. After running roughshod over and through the Browns' defense for years—including 500 yards in two games in 2003—as a member of the Baltimore Ravens, Lewis rushed for both a team-leading 1,304 yards and nine touchdowns in 2007 in helping Cleveland finish 10-6 and barely miss the playoffs. He also had 30 receptions for two TDs that year. In 2008 he rushed for 1,002 yards and fourth touchdowns, again leading the team in both categories.

LINDSEY, DALE

Dale Lindsey was a Cleveland linebacker from 1965-72. He was a seventh-round draft choice of the Browns in 1965 out of Western Kentucky University. His 27-yard interception return gave the Browns a 17-10 lead en route to a 31-20 upset of Dallas in the 1968 Eastern Conference Championship Game. Lindsey was a Browns assistant coach in 1974.

LINEBACKERS

Notable Browns linebackers include Tommy Thompson, Walt Michaels, Chuck Noll, Galen Fiss, Vince Costello, Jim Houston, Dale Lindsey, Billy Andrews, Charlie Hall, Bob Babich, Dick Ambrose, Clay Matthews, Eddie Johnson, Chip Banks, Tom Cousineau, Mike Johnson, David Grayson, Davis Brandon, Pepper Johnson, Jamir Miller, Wali Rainer, Dwayne Rudd, Andra Davis, D'Qwell Jackson, Kamerion Wimbley, Willie McGinest, Chris Gocong, Scott Fujita, Craig Robertson, Paul Kruger, Karlos Dansby, Christian Kirksey, and Jabaal Sheard.

LITTLE, EARL

Earl Little was a Browns defensive back from 1999-2004. A product of the University of Miami, he was picked up by the Browns off waivers from the New Orleans Saints on October 26, 1999. He was second on the Browns with five interceptions in 2001. He led the team in picks in 2001 and '02 with four and six, respectively. Little totaled 18 career interceptions with the Browns.

LITTLE, GREG

Greg Little was a Browns wide receiver from 2011-13. He was a second-round draft choice of Cleveland's in 2011 out of the University of North Carolina. He led the Browns with 61 receptions and 709 receiving yards in his rookie season of 2011. He also led the Browns with 53 receptions in 2012.

Dave Logan celebrates after catching a touchdown pass from Brian Sipe in the Browns' 33-30 overtime loss in Pittsburgh on November 25, 1979. Photo courtesy of the Cleveland Press Collection.

LOGAN, DAVE

Dave Logan was a Browns wide receiver from 1976-83. He was a third-round draft choice of Cleveland's in 1976 from the University of Colorado. He was the team leader in receptions (59) and receiving yards (982) in 1979 and in receiving yards (822) in 1980. His 4,247 career receiving yards rank ninth in team history. Logan totaled 262 receptions and 24 touchdown catches during his Browns career.

LOS ANGELES DONS

The Los Angeles Dons were Browns opponents in the AAFC from 1946-49. The Browns amassed their fourth-highest point total in a 61-14 blowout of the Dons on October 14, 1949, in Los Angeles. The Dons' all-time record against the Browns was 2-6, 1-3 at home and 1-3 on the road.

LOWEST-SCORING GAMES BETWEEN BOTH TEAMS, REGULAR AND POSTSEASON

Please see Team Statistics on page 248.

M

MACK, ALEX

Alex Mack has been a Browns center since 2009. He was a first-round draft pick of the team in 2009 out of the University of California, Berkeley. He was a Pro Bowler in 2010 and '13.

MACK, KEVIN

Kevin Mack was a Browns running back from 1985-93. He was a first-round supplemental draft choice by Cleveland in 1984 from Clemson University. After one year in the USFL, he teamed with Earnest Byner in 1985 to become part of just the third running-back tandem in NFL history in which each back rushed for 1,000 yards in the same season. Mack led the team with 1,104 rushing yards that year. He was also tops on the team in rushing yards in 1986, '87, and from 1990-92. He was second on the team with seven rushing touchdowns in 1985 and led the Browns in the same category in 1986 (10), '90 (five), '91 (eight), and '92 (six).

Mack ranks fifth in rushing yards all-time for the Browns with 5,123. His 6,725 career combined net yards rank ninth in team history (######). His 424 postseason rushing yards rank fourth in Browns annals (#). He was voted AFC Rookie of the Year in 1985 by UPI. He was picked to play in the Pro Bowl that year and in 1987.

MAIAVA, KALUKA

Kaluka Maiava was a Browns linebacker from 2009-12. He was a Browns fourth-round draft choice in 2009 out of the University of Southern California.

MAJORITY OWNERS

Art McBride	1946-52
Dave Jones	1953-60

Art Modell   1961-95
Al Lerner   1999-2002
Randy Lerner   2002-12
Jimmy Haslam   2012-

MANZIEL, JOHNNY

Johnny Manziel has been a Browns quarterback since 2014. "Johnny Football," as he is known, was drafted by Cleveland in 2014 with the 22nd overall pick out of Texas A&M University, where he was outstanding and, as a redshirt freshman, won the Heisman Trophy in 2012, the first freshman to ever do so. He waited patiently on the bench in 2014 behind starter Brian Hoyer, who led the Browns to a 7-4 record but struggled as the team lost two straight games as their playoff hopes were dying a slow death. Manziel finally got his shot to start at home against Cincinnati on December 14. He was atrocious—10 of 18 for 80 yards and two interceptions—in a 30-0 loss. He started the next week at Carolina, where he was pulled in favor of Hoyer after going 3 for 8 for 32 yards in an eventual 17-13 defeat.

Manziel's off-the-field escapades landed him in rehab soon after the season. Browns fans can only hope Manziel gets his act together and gets back on the path that will lead him to becoming "Johnny Football" again.

MARSHALL, JIM

Jim Marshall was a Browns defensive end in 1960. He was a fourth-round draft choice of Cleveland's in 1960 from Ohio State University. He was traded to Minnesota as part of an eight-player deal on August 31, 1961, and enjoyed a successful career with the Vikings.

MASSAQUOI, MOHAMED

Mohamed Massaquoi was a Browns wide receiver from 2009-12. He was a second-round draft pick by the Browns in 2009 out of the University of Georgia. Massaquoi's 34 receptions in his rookie year of 2009 were tied for the team lead, and his 624 receiving yards and three touchdown receptions that year were both tops on the team. He totaled 118 career receptions for 1,745 yards.

MATTHEWS, CLAY

Clay Matthews was a Browns linebacker from 1978-93. He was a Cleveland first-round draft choice in 1978 from the University of Southern California.

His 12 sacks in 1984 ranked second on the team and are third most in one Browns season. His nine sacks in 1992 tied for the team lead and for 10th most in one Browns season. His 62 career sacks are the most in team annals. Matthews returned an interception 26 yards for a touchdown in the fourth quarter of the Browns' 34-10 rout of the Pittsburgh Steelers on September 20, 1987, in Cleveland Stadium. Two years later in the season opener against the same Steelers, but at Pittsburgh, he returned a fumble three yards for a score. Matthews was named to All-AFC defensive teams in 1984 by NEA, PFW, and SN. He was selected to play in the Pro Bowl in 1985 and from 1987-89.

MAYER, BILL

Bill Mayer was a Cleveland radio broadcaster from 1947-49 and in 1954 and a television broadcaster from 1949-51.

McBRIDE, ART

Art McBride was the Browns' majority owner from 1946-52. He was the team founder and known to almost everyone in Cleveland as "Mickey."

McCOLGAN, BILL

Bill McColgan was a Browns radio broadcaster from 1954-60 and television broadcaster in 1953.

McCORMACK, MIKE

Mike McCormack was a Browns offensive tackle from 1954-62. He was a University of Kansas product acquired by Cleveland on March 26, 1953, as part of a 15-player trade with the Baltimore Colts. He spent 1953 in the military. He was named to All-NFL offensive teams in 1955 by NYN and in 1957 by NEA. McCormack was picked for the Pro Bowl in 1956 and '57 and from 1960-62. He was inducted into the Pro Football Hall of Fame in 1984.

McCOY, COLT

Colt McCoy was a Browns quarterback from 2010-12. He was a third-round draft pick of Cleveland's in 2010 out of the University of Texas. McCoy's best year with the Browns was in 2011 when he completed 265 of 463 passes for 2,733 yards, 14 touchdown passes, and 11 interceptions.

McCUTCHEON, DAYLON

Daylon McCutcheon was a Browns cornerback from 1999-2005. He was chosen by Cleveland in the third round of the 1999 NFL Draft out of the University of Southern California. He had a career-high four interceptions in 2001, including one that he returned 32 yards for a touchdown off a Jonathan Quinn pass on September 30, 2001, with just 35 seconds left that, for all intents and purposes, clinched the Browns' 23-14 win at Jacksonville. He also had a pick-six on October 5, 2003, at Pittsburgh when he returned a Tommy Maddox pass 75 yards early in the third quarter that gave the Browns a 30-10 lead and basically put the nail in the coffin in their 33-13 rout of the Steelers on national television. McCutcheon had an even dozen interceptions in his career.

McDONALD, BRANDON

Brandon McDonald was a Browns defensive back from 2007-09. He was a fifth-round draft choice of Cleveland's in 2007 out of the University of Memphis. In 2008 he was both the team leader with five interceptions and 146 return yards. One of his picks in '08 was a 24-yard return of a Kevin Kolb pass that went for a touchdown—his second interception of the game—in the fourth quarter of a *Monday Night Football* game on December 15 in a 30-10 loss to the Eagles in Philadelphia.

McDONALD, PAUL

Paul McDonald was a Cleveland quarterback from 1980-85. He was a fourth-round draft choice of the Browns in 1980 from the University of Southern California. He backed up Brian Sipe for most of his first four seasons. He finished the 1982 campaign as the starter in the last three games and in an AFC First-Round Playoff Game in Los Angeles that resulted in a 27-10 loss to the Raiders. McDonald was the starter for the entire 1984 season, completing 271 of 493 attempts for 3,472 yards with 14 touchdown passes and 23 interceptions. Many of his picks in '84 were quite untimely. His 1984 yardage total ranks ninth in Browns history.

McGAHEE, WILLIS

Willis McGahee was a Browns running back in 2013. A University of Miami product, he signed with Cleveland in September 2013. That season, he led the Browns with 377 rushing yards and tied for the team lead with two rushing touchdowns.

McGINEST, WILLIE

Willie McGinest was a Browns linebacker from 2006-08. A product of the University of Southern California, he signed with the team on March 15, 2006. He totaled eight career sacks.

McKAY, BOB

Bob McKay was a Cleveland offensive tackle from 1970-75. He was a first-round draft choice of the Browns in 1970 from the University of Texas.

McKENZIE, KEITH

Keith McKenzie was a Browns defensive end from 2000-01. He is a Ball State University product who was acquired by the team on February 24, 2000, as a free agent. He was the team leader with eight sacks in 2000.

McKINLEY, ALVIN

Alvin McKinley was a Browns defensive lineman form 2001-06. He is a product of Mississippi State University. He tied for the team lead with five sacks in 2005.

McLEAN, PHIL

Phil McLean was a Browns radio broadcaster in 1951.

Bob McKay (left) and Garry Parris wrestle Pittsburgh's Joe Greene to the ground in a 42-6 loss in Cleveland on October 5, 1975. Photo courtesy of the Cleveland Press Collection.

McNEIL, GERALD

Gerald McNeil was mainly a Browns punt and kickoff returner from 1986-89. He was a first-round supplemental draft choice by Cleveland in 1984 from Baylor University. He played in the USFL in 1984 and '85 before joining the Browns. He led the team in kickoff returns and kickoff return yards in 1986. He led the Browns in punt returns and punt return yardage every season from 1986-89. His 496 punt return yards in 1989 are tops in team history, and his 386 in 1987 are ninth. His 1,545 career punt return yards rank third in team history.

McNeil returned a punt 84 yards for a touchdown in Cleveland's 24-21 home win over Detroit on September 28, 1986. A week later against the Steelers in Pittsburgh he helped end the Three Rivers Jinx by returning a kickoff 100 yards for a score in a 27-24 triumph, becoming the first NFL player to return a punt and kickoff for a touchdown in the same season since Washington Redskin Tony Green did so in 1978. McNeil was a Pro Bowl selection in 1987.

METCALF, ERIC

Eric Metcalf was a Browns running back and kickoff and punt returner from 1989-94. He was a first-round draft choice of the team from the University of Texas in 1989. He led Cleveland in rushing yards in his rookie year of 1989 with 633. He was also used as a receiver out of the backfield that year and turned several simple swing passes into long gains, including a spectacular one on *Monday Night Football* in which he jitterbugged his way into the end zone for a short touchdown on a pass from Bernie Kosar that completely faked out two Bengals defenders along the way.

Metcalf led the Browns in receptions in 1993 with 63. His 177 receiving yards in Cleveland's 28-16 win in Los Angeles against the Raiders on September 20, 1992, are tied for 10th in team history (#######). He scored all four of his team's touchdowns that day. His 297 career receptions rank 10th for the Browns.

Metcalf, however, enjoyed his greatest success as a kickoff and punt returner. He led the Browns in kickoff returns and kickoff return yardage every season from 1989-91 and returned two kickoffs for touchdowns in 1990—a 98-yarder on September 16 against the Jets and a 101-yarder on December 9 in Houston. He led Cleveland in punt returns and punt return yards every year from 1992-94. His 464 punt return yards in 1993 rank second all-time for the Browns, and his 429 rank sixth. His 1,052 kickoff return yards in 1990 rank eighth in team history. His 2,806 career kickoff return yards are third most in Browns history, and his 1,341 career punt return yards rank fourth.

Metcalf returned a kickoff 90 yards for a touchdown in the Browns' 34-30 AFC Divisional Playoff win over Buffalo at home on January 6, 1990, the only kickoff return for a score in Browns postseason history. His first punt return for a touchdown came on November 29, 1992, in a 27-14 victory over the Bears at home. His most memorable moment was when he became the first player in NFL history to return two punts of at least 75 yards for touchdowns in the same game. He did so on October 24, 1993, at home against the Steelers, returning a 91-yarder early in the game and a 75-yard late in the game that gave the Browns a 28-23 victory in a battle for first place.

Metcalf returned two punts for scores in 1994, both against the Bengals. The first was a 92-yarder in the season opener in Cincinnati and the second was a 73-yarder on October 23 in Cleveland. His 1,932 combined net yards in 1993 rank fifth in Browns annals. His 9,108 career combined net yards rank fifth in team history (######). He was voted to All-AFC offensive teams in 1993 by AP, PFW, SN, and UPI, and in 1994 by SN. He was named to the Pro Bowl in 1993 and '94.

MIAMI DOLPHINS

The Miami Dolphins were Browns opponents in the NFL from 1970-95 and have been since 1999. They were triumphant in two postseason games against the Browns, both in the AFC Divisional Playoffs at the Orange Bowl—a 20-14 conquest on December 24, 1972, and a 24-21 triumph on January 4, 1986. Miami's all-time record against Cleveland is 8-8, 3-2 at home and 5-6 on the road. The Dolphins' all-time record in the postseason against the Browns is 2-0 (home games).

MIAMI SEAHAWKS

The Miami Seahawks were opponents of the Browns in the AAFC in 1946. They were Cleveland's opponent in the team's first-ever game on September 6 of that year. The Seahawks franchise folded after that season. Miami's all-time record against Cleveland was 0-2, 0-1 at home and 0-1 on the road.

MICHAELS, WALT

Walt Michaels was a Browns linebacker from 1952-61. He was a seventh-round draft choice of Cleveland's in 1951 from Washington & Lee University. He was traded to Green Bay on August 20, 1951, and then re-acquired on

Walt Michaels tackles the Chicago Cardinals' (and future Browns teammate) Gern Nagler in the end zone after a 24-yard touchdown reception on October 12, 1958. Photo courtesy of the Cleveland Press Collection.

April 29, 1952, as part of a four-player deal with the Packers. Michaels was voted to the All-NFL defensive team in 1959 by NYN. He was selected to play in the Pro Bowl from 1956-59.

MILLER, CLEO

Cleo Miller was a Browns running back from 1975-82. An Arkansas AM&N College product, Miller was acquired by the Browns in November 1975 as a free agent. He tied Greg Pruitt for the lead in Browns rushing touchdowns in 1976 with four. His 613 rushing yards that year were second to Pruitt. In 1977 he gained 756 yards on the ground via 163 carries and once again rushed for a team-leading four touchdowns. Rushing for a pair of touchdowns and making a long run in the second half, he was a key figure in Cleveland's 17-14 upset of the Houston Oilers in a battle for first place in the AFC Central Division on November 30, 1980. Miller totaled 2,236 career rushing yards for the Browns.

MILLER, JAMIR

Jamir Miller was a Browns linebacker from 1999-2001. He was a UCLA product obtained by Cleveland on May 13, 1999, as a free agent. He ranked second on the Browns with 4.5 sacks in 1999 and five in 2000. He became the first Brown to lead the AFC in sacks with 13 in 2001, the second most in team history. His 22.5 career sacks are tied for 10th in team annals. Miller was voted to All-NFL teams in 2001 by AP, FD (first team), PFW, and SI. He was voted to the All-AFC defensive team by PFW in 2001 and was picked for the Pro Bowl that year, too.

MINGO, BARKEVIOUS

Barkevious Mingo has been a Browns linebacker since 2013. He was a first-round draft pick—the sixth overall selection—of Cleveland's in 2013 out of LSU. Mingo was second on the Browns in his rookie year of 2013 with five sacks.

MINNESOTA VIKINGS

The Minnesota Vikings were Browns opponents in the NFL from 1961-95 and have been since 1999. Two of their more memorable games with the Browns were victories in Metropolitan Stadium in Minnesota. The first was a 51-3 shellacking on November 9, 1969, in which they outgained the Browns more than three yards to one (454-151). That game is tied for the worst loss ever suffered by the Browns. The second game was a 28-23 triumph on December 14, 1980, when the Vikings rose from the dead after trailing 23-9 in the fourth quarter. Minnesota won when quarterback Tommy Kramer completed a 46-yard Hail Mary pass to Ahmad Rashad, who caught the ball after it was batted by defensive back Thom Darden and cradled it against his body as he backpedaled into the end zone with no time left.

The Vikings and Browns have met once in postseason play, a 27-7 Minnesota victory on January 4, 1970, in the NFL Championship Game at frigid Minnesota. The Vikings' all-time record against the Browns is 10-4, 6-2 at home and 4-2 on the road. Their all-time postseason record against Cleveland is 1-0 (home game).

MINNIFIELD, FRANK

Frank Minnifield was a Browns cornerback from 1984-92. He was a University of Louisville product acquired by the team as a free agent on April 3, 1984. He formed half of the famed "Corner Brothers" duo from 1985-89 (he started for part of the 1984 season) with Hanford Dixon. Minnifield tied Felix Wright for the team lead in interceptions in 1987 with four. He was second to Wright in the same category in 1988 with four. He returned an interception 48 yards for a touchdown as Cleveland's final score in the Browns' 38-21 AFC Divisional Playoff win over the Indianapolis Colts on January 9, 1988, in Cleveland. He was voted to All-AFC defensive teams in 1987 by PFW, FWA, SN, and UPI; in 1988 by AP, NEA, PFW, FWA, SN, and UPI; and in 1989 by UPI. He was selected to play in the Pro Bowl from 1986-89.

MITCHELL, BOBBY

Bobby Mitchell was a Browns running back from 1958-61. He was a seventh-round draft choice of Cleveland's in 1958 from the University of

Bobby Mitchell carries for a short gain and is stopped by several Eagles in the Browns' 28-14 victory on November 23, 1958. Photo courtesy of the Cleveland Press Collection.

Illinois. He complemented running back Jim Brown well, finishing second to him in rushing yards all four seasons. He gained 232 yards on the ground on November 15, 1959, against the Redskins, which are tied for fourth in team history. A 90-yard touchdown run was included in his total that afternoon. His 2,297 rushing yards rank 10th all-time for the Browns. He was the team leader in receptions (45) in 1960.

Mitchell also returned punts and kickoffs. He led the Browns in kickoff returns and kickoff return yards all four seasons (he was the co-leader in returns with Preston Powell his last year). His 1,550 kickoff return yards overall rank 10th in team annals. He returned three kickoffs for touchdowns—a 98-yarder against the Eagles on November 23, 1958, a 90-yarder against the Cowboys on October 16, 1960, and a 91-yarder against the Eagles again on November 19, 1961.

Mitchell totaled 607 career punt-return yards for the Browns that ranks ninth in team annals. He returned three punts for touchdowns—a 68-yarder at home against Philadelphia on November 23, 1958 (the same game in which he returned a kickoff 98 yards for a score), a 78-yarder against the Giants in New York on December 6, 1959, and a 64-yarder against the Redskins in Cleveland on October 8, 1961.

Mitchell was picked for the Pro Bowl in 1960. He was enshrined into the Pro Football Hall of Fame in 1983.

MODELL, ART

Art Modell was the Browns' majority owner from 1961-95.

MODZELEWSKI, DICK

Dick Modzelewski was a Cleveland defensive tackle from 1964-66. He was a University of Maryland product acquired by the Browns on March 4,

1964, in a trade with the New York Giants for wide receiver Bob Crespino. He was the younger brother of Browns running back Ed Modzelewski, who played for Cleveland from 1955-59. Modzelewski was selected to play in the Pro Bowl in 1964. He was the Browns' head coach in 1977 for one game, the season finale in Seattle on December 18, a 20-19 loss (Forrest Gregg had resigned on December 13). His all-time record as Browns head coach was 0-1 (away game). He was a Browns assistant coach from 1968-77.

MONDAY AFTERNOON GAMES

Buffalo 28, Cleveland 28 (Sept. 5, 1949, at Buf.)
Seattle 33, Cleveland 0 (Sept. 3, 1984, at Sea.)
Overall – 0-1-1 (.250) (away games)

MONDAY NIGHT FOOTBALL

Cleveland 31, N.Y. Jets 21 (Sept. 21, 1970, at Cle.)
Cleveland 21, Houston 10 (Dec. 7, 1970, at Hou.)
Oakland 34, Cleveland 20 (Oct. 4, 1971, at Cle.)
Cleveland 21, San Diego 17 (Nov. 13, 1972, at S.D.)
Miami 17, Cleveland 9 (Oct. 15, 1973, at Cle.)
Cleveland 30, New England 27 (OT) (Sept. 26, 1977, at Cle.)
Cleveland 26, Dallas 7 (Sept. 24, 1979, at Cle.)
Houston 16, Cleveland 7 (Sept. 15, 1980, at Cle.)
Cleveland 27, Chicago 21 (Nov. 3, 1980, at Cle.)
San Diego 44, Cleveland 14 (Sept. 7, 1981, at Cle.)
Cleveland 17, Pittsburgh 7 (Sept. 16, 1985, at Cle.)
Cleveland 26, Miami 16 (Nov. 10, 1986, at Cle.)
Cleveland 30, L.A. Rams 17 (Oct. 26, 1987, at Cle.)
Cleveland 23, Indianapolis 17 (Sept. 19, 1988, at Cle.)
Houston 24, Cleveland 17 (Nov. 7, 1988, at Hou.)
Miami 38, Cleveland 31 (Dec. 12, 1988, at Mia.)
Cincinnati 21, Cleveland 14 (Sept. 25, 1989, at Cin.)
Cleveland 27, Chicago 7 (Oct. 23, 1989, at Cle.)
Cleveland 30, Denver 29 (Oct. 8, 1990, at Den.)
Cincinnati 34, Cleveland 13 (Oct. 22, 1990, at Cle.)
Miami 27, Cleveland 23 (Sept. 14, 1992, at Cle.)
Cleveland 23, San Francisco 13 (Sept. 13, 1993, at Cle.)
Buffalo 22, Cleveland 19 (Oct. 2, 1995, at Cle.)
Pittsburgh 20, Cleveland 3 (Nov. 13, 1995, at Pit.)

St. Louis 26, Cleveland 20 (Dec. 8, 2003, at Cle.)
Cleveland 35, N.Y. Giants 14 (Oct. 13, 2008, at Cle.)
Cleveland 29, Buffalo 27 (Nov. 17, 2008, at Buf.)
Philadelphia 30, Cleveland 10 (Dec. 15, 2008, at Phi.)
Baltimore 16, Cleveland 0 (Nov. 16, 2009, at Cle.)

Overall – 15-14 (.542)
Home – 11-9 (.588)
Away – 4-5 (.429)

MOORE, EVAN

Evan Moore was a Browns tight end and wide receiver from 2009-11. He signed with the team on November 9, 2009. He had 16 receptions for 322 yards and a touchdown in 2010, and he had 34 receptions for 324 yards and four touchdowns in 2011. His TD catches total in '11 tied for the team lead.

MOORE, MARLON

Marlon Moore has been a Browns kickoff returner since 2014. A Fresno State University product, he signed with Cleveland on July 28, 2014. He led the Browns in both kickoff returns (13) and kickoff return yards (322) in '14.

MORGAN, QUINCY

Quincy Morgan was a Browns wide receiver from 2001-04. He was chosen by the Browns in the second round of the 2001 NFL Draft out of Kansas State University. He had 56 receptions for both a team-leading 964 yards and seven touchdowns in 2002. For his Browns career, he had 133 receptions for 2,056 yards and 15 touchdowns. He also returned kickoffs. Perhaps Morgan's most memorable moment came on December 8, 2002, when he was on the receiving end of a 50-yard, Hail Mary pass from Tim Couch with no time left that gave the Browns a crucial 21-20 victory over the Jaguars in Jacksonville.

MORIN, MILT

Milt Morin was a Browns tight end from 1966-75. A first-round draft choice of Cleveland's in 1966 from the University of Massachusetts, Morin was on the receiving end of an 87-yard pass play from Bill Nelsen on November 24, 1968, against Philadelphia. He was the team leader in receiving yards in 1973 with 417. He ranks 10th all-time for the Browns with 4,208 receiving yards. He was voted to All-AFC offensive teams in 1971 by AP and UPI and was voted to the Pro Bowl in 1967, '68, and '71.

MORRISON, FRED

Fred Morrison runs for 12 yards against the Redskins during a 62-3 home win on November 7, 1954. (The play was nullified, though, due to an offside penalty.) Photo courtesy of the Cleveland Press Collection.

Fred Morrison was a Cleveland running back from 1954-56. He was an Ohio State University product acquired by the Browns on July 7, 1954, in a trade with the Bears for the rights to Harry Jagade and a draft choice in 1955. He had a team high of 824 rushing yards in 1955 and was picked for the Pro Bowl that year.

MORROW, JOHN

John Morrow was a Browns center from 1960-66. He was a University of Michigan product acquired by Cleveland on March 14, 1960, in a trade with the Los Angeles Rams for Art Hunter. He was picked to play in the Pro Bowl in 1961 and '63.

MOSELEY, MARK

Mark Moseley was a Browns kicker in 1986. A Stephen F. Austin University product, Moseley was obtained by Cleveland on November 26, 1986, when regular kicker Matt Bahr went down with a season-ending injury. He kicked three field goals, including the game-winning 27-yarder 2:02 into the second extra period in the Browns' 23-20 double-overtime victory over the New York Jets in an AFC Divisional Playoff on January 3, 1987, in Cleveland.

MOST ONE-SIDED GAMES, REGULAR AND POSTSEASON

Please see Team Statistics on page 248.

MOST VALUABLE PLAYER

1947   Otto Graham (AAFC by OFF)
1948   Otto Graham (co-AAFC by OFF; AAFC by UP)
1949   Otto Graham (AAFC by OFF)
1953   Otto Graham (NFL by UP)
1954   Lou Groza (NFL by SN)
1955   Otto Graham (NFL by SN, UP)
1958   Jim Brown (NFL by NEA, UPI)
1963   Jim Brown (NFL by MAX, UPI; co-NFL by NEA)
1965   Jim Brown (NFL by NEA, SN, UPI)
1968   Leroy Kelly (NFL by MAX)
1980   Brian Sipe (NFL by FWA, SN; AFC by UPI)
1989   Michael Dean Perry (AFC Defensive by UPI)

MOTLEY, MARION

Marion Motley was a Browns running back from 1946-53. He was a product of the University of Nevada acquired by the team as a free agent. He led the Browns in rushing yards every season from 1946-50 and in 1952, totaling 601, 889, 964, 570, 810, and 444 yards, respectively. His 1946 total came on 73 carries for a remarkable average of 8.2 yards per attempt. He had 47- and 68-yard touchdown runs in the Browns' 31-14 victory over the visiting Los Angeles Dons on October 20, 1946. Later that season on November 24 he scored on a 76-yard run in a 42-17 romp over Buffalo at home. He rushed for 188 yards on October 29, 1950, against the Steelers, which is tied for 10th in Browns history.

Motley ranks sixth all-time for the Browns in rushing yards with 4,712. He is the all-time AAFC rushing yardage leader with 3,024. His 7,019 combined net yards rank eighth in team history (######). His 30 postseason points are tied for fifth in team history and his 512 rushing yards in the postseason rank first (#). His 18 points scored in the 1948 AAFC Championship Game against Buffalo are tied for most in team annals. He holds two of the top five spots for rushing yards in one postseason game—133 against Buffalo on December 19, 1948, in the AAFC Championship Game and 109 against New York on December 14, 1947, in the AAFC title game.

Motley retired in 1954 before attempting a comeback as a linebacker in 1955 for the Pittsburgh Steelers, to whom he had been traded on September 8 of that year. He was named to All-AAFC teams in 1946 by AP, NYN, OFF, and UP; in 1947 by AP, C&O, NYN, and OFF; in 1948 by AP, NYN, OFF, and SN; and in 1949 by NYN. He was voted to All-NFL offensive teams in 1950 by AP, NYN, and UP. Motley was picked for the Pro Bowl in 1950. He was inducted into the Pro Football Hall of Fame in 1968.

MUELLER, JIM

Jim Mueller was a Browns radio broadcaster from 1975-95.

MURPHY, LEO

Leo Murphy was the Browns' trainer from 1950-88 and emeritus trainer in 1989.

MUSTAFAA, NAJEE

Najee Mustafaa was a Browns cornerback in 1993. A product of Georgia Tech University, Mustafaa was acquired by the Browns as a free agent on March 17, 1993. He returned a Scott Mitchell pass 97 yards for a touchdown on October 10 that season that gave the Browns a 14-10 lead in what turned out to be a 24-14 loss to the Miami Dolphins at home. It was Mitchell's first pass of the game after replacing Dan Marino in the second quarter when Marino suffered a torn right Achilles tendon that ended his season.

N

NAGLER, GERN

Gern Nagler was a Cleveland wide receiver from 1960-61. He was a 14th-round draft choice of the Browns in 1953 from Santa Clara University but was traded to Baltimore. He wound up playing for the Chicago Cardinals from 1953-58 and the Pittsburgh Steelers in 1959. He was re-acquired by the Browns on December 31, 1959, as part of a four-player deal with the Steelers that included future Hall of Famer Len Dawson coming to the shores of Lake Erie for a short stay. Nagler led the Browns with 616 receiving yards in 1960, including a 177-yard performance on November 20 in Pittsburgh, which is tied for 10th all-time for Cleveland (#######).

NATIONAL FOOTBALL LEAGUE

The National Football League was home to the Browns from 1950-95 and has been since 1999.

NBC TELEVISION NETWORK

The NBC television network broadcast Browns afternoon home games when the Browns' opponent was an AFC team, as well as all afternoon road games, from 1970-95. The network has also broadcast Sunday night games beginning in 2006, including one Browns game—a 10-6 home loss to the Pittsburgh Steelers on September 14, 2008.

NEAL, BOB

Bob Neal was a Browns radio broadcaster from 1946-51 and television broadcaster from 1948-51.

NELSEN, BILL

Bill Nelsen was a Browns quarterback from 1968-72. A product of the University of Southern California, he was acquired by the Browns on May

14, 1968, as part of a five-player trade with the Pittsburgh Steelers. He was obtained when Frank Ryan began having arm troubles. Despite knee problems, Nelsen completed 152 of 293 passes for 2,366 yards, 19 touchdowns, and 10 interceptions in 1968. He started in place of the struggling Ryan on October 5 against the Steelers and led the Browns to a 31-24 triumph over his former club. He connected with Milt Morin on an 87-yard pass play against the Eagles on November 24 that year for his longest completion as a Brown. He hooked up with Paul Warfield for an 82-yard pass play that went for a touchdown in a 27-21 victory over the Cardinals in St. Louis on December 14, 1969

Nelsen directed Cleveland to appearances in the NFL title game in 1968 and '69. He ranks sixth in Browns annals with 9,725 passing yards and 689 completions. His 839 career postseason passing yards and 68 career postseason pass completions each rank third in team history. He was chosen to play in the Pro Bowl in 1969.

NEW ENGLAND PATRIOTS

The New England Patriots were opponents of the Browns in the NFL from 1970-95 and have been since 1999. Perhaps the most memorable game between the Browns and Patriots was Cleveland's 30-27 sudden-death victory on September 26, 1977, in Cleveland on *Monday Night Football*. In a crucial contest between possible AFC wild card qualifiers, the Browns hammered the Pats 30-0 in New England on November 20, 1983, becoming the second Browns team—and the first since 1951—to post consecutive shutouts (they beat the Buccaneers 20-0 the week before). The Patriots and Browns have met once in postseason play, with the Browns coming out on top 20-13 in an AFC Wild Card Game on New Year's Day 1995 in Cleveland. New England's all-time record against the Browns is 10-12, 6-5 at home and 4-7 on the road. Its all-time postseason record against Cleveland is 0-1 (away game).

NEW ORLEANS SAINTS

The New Orleans Saints were Browns opponents in the NFL from 1967-95 and have been since 1999. The Saints were the victims of the "new era" Browns' first win on October 31, 1999, in the Superdome in New Orleans. The Browns won 21-16 when Tim Couch completed a 56-yard Hail Mary pass to Kevin Johnson on the final play of the game. The Saints' all-time record against Cleveland is 4-12, 2-8 at home and 2-4 on the road.

NEW YORK GIANTS

The New York Giants were Browns opponents in the NFL from 1950-95 and have been since 1999. They were rivals of the Browns in the American Conference from 1950-52 and Eastern Conference from 1953-69. The two teams were rivals in the Century Division in 1967 and '69. They waged several titanic battles during the 1950s and '60s with Giants linebacker Sam Huff and Browns running back Jim Brown at the center of many of them. One memorable game between the teams occurred on December 1, 1985, in the Meadowlands when the Browns won a thriller 35-33 after trailing 33-21 late in the game. Giants kicker Eric Schubert missed a 34-yard field goal as time expired.

Pat Summerall boots the game-winning field goal that gives the New York Giants a 13-10 victory over the Browns in Cleveland on December 14, 1958. Photo courtesy of the Cleveland Press Collection.

The Giants and Browns have met twice in the postseason, splitting the pair. Both were defensive struggles. The Browns won at home 8-3 on December 17, 1950, in an American Conference playoff in 10-degree weather when Giants running back Eugene Roberts was tackled by Bill Willis from behind at the Browns' four-yard line late in the game. New York won 10-0 on December 21, 1958, in an Eastern Conference Playoff in New York. The week before, the Giants forced the playoff with a memorable 13-10 victory in Yankee Stadium on Pat Summerall's 49-yard field goal into the wind and through the driving snow little more than two minutes to play.

The Giants' all-time record against the Browns is 20-26-2, 10-12-2 at home and 10-14 on the road. Their all-time postseason record against the Browns is 1-1, 1-0 at home and 0-1 on the road.

NEW YORK JETS

The New York Jets were Browns opponents in the NFL from 1970-95 and have been since 1999. The Browns and Jets squared off in the first-ever *Monday Night Football* game on September 21, 1970, in Cleveland. The Browns won

31-21. Every game played between New York and Cleveland from 1978-84 went down to the wire, with those six games decided by a total of 17 points. Every game but the 1979 affair was played in Cleveland. The Browns won four of the games—37-34 in overtime on December 10, 1978, 25-22 in overtime on September 2, 1979, 17-14 on December 7, 1980, and 10-7 on October 9, 1983, on Matt Bahr's 43-yard field goal as time expired. The Jets won the other two games—14-13 on December 12, 1981, for their first-ever win against the Browns, and 24-20 on October 14, 1984, when three straight sacks, two by defensive end Mark Gastineau, stalled the Browns' final drive.

New York fell victim to one of the greatest comebacks in NFL history in the AFC Divisional Playoffs on January 3, 1987, in Cleveland when it blew a 20-10 lead late in the fourth quarter and lost 23-20 in double overtime. The Jets' all-time record against the Browns is 9-12, 3-4 at home and 6-8 on the road. New York's all-time record against Cleveland in the postseason is 0-1 (away game).

NEW YORK YANKEES

The New York Yankees were Browns opponents in the AAFC from 1946-48. They opposed the Browns in the 1946 and '47 AAFC Championship Games, losing both—14-9 in Cleveland and 14-3 in New York, respectively. They merged with their AAFC rival Brooklyn Dodgers to become the Brooklyn-New York Yankees in 1949, the last year the conference existed. The Yankees' all-time record against Cleveland was 0-5-1, 0-2-1 at home and 0-3 on the road. Their all-time record against the Browns in postseason play was 0-2, 0-1 at home and 0-1 on the road.

NEWSOME, OZZIE

Ozzie Newsome was a Browns tight end from 1978-90. He was a Browns first-round draft choice in 1978 from the University of Alabama. He had 38 receptions for 589 yards and two touchdown catches in his rookie year, 55 catches for 781 yards and nine touchdown receptions in 1979, and 51 catches for 594 yards and three touchdown catches in 1980. He led the team in receptions and receiving yards every season from 1981-85, and in touchdown receptions in 1979, '81, and from '83-85. He was the Browns' co-leader in touchdown catches in 1982.

Newsome's 1,002 yards receiving in 1981 were the most by a Brown in thirteen years and rank 10th in team history. His 69 catches that year

Ozzie Newsome makes a one-handed catch for a 14-yard touchdown as Miami's Norris Thomas hangs on. The Browns won the game in overtime 30-24 on November 18, 1979. Photo courtesy of the Cleveland Press Collection.

are tied for ninth in team history. In the strike-shortened 1982 season, he had 49 catches for 633 yards and three touchdowns. He totaled a team-record 89 catches (tied by Kellen Winslow in 2006) in both the 1983 and '84 seasons for 970 and 1,001 yards, respectively. His 191 receiving yards on October 14, 1984, at home against the Jets rank fifth in team history (#######). He caught 62 passes for 711 yards in 1985. His 662 career receptions rank first in Browns annals, as do his 7,980 career receiving yards. His 8,144 combined net yards rank seventh for the Browns all-time (######).

Newsome's 27 career postseason receptions are tied for second in Browns annals (###). His 373 career postseason receiving yards rank fourth in team history (##). He had 114 receiving yards in Cleveland's 23-20 double-overtime win over the Jets in the AFC Divisional Playoffs on January 3, 1987, in Cleveland. He was voted to All-AFC offensive teams in 1979 by FWA, SN, and UPI and in 1984 by AP, NEA, PFW, FWA, SN, and UPI. Newsome was selected to play in the Pro Bowl in 1981, '84, and '85 and was inducted into the Pro Football Hall of Fame in 1999.

NICKNAMES

The following are notable nicknames of Browns players:

Dick Ambrose	"Bam"	Bob Kolesar	"Doc"
Derek Anderson	"D.A."	Dante Lavelli	"Glue Fingers"
Al Baker	"Bubba"	Gerald McNeil	"The Ice Cube"
Johnny Brewer	"Tonto"	Frank Minnifield	"Minnie"
Darrell Brewster	"Pete"	Dick Modzelewski	"Little Mo"
Courtney Brown	"The Quiet Storm"	Ed Modzelewski	"Big Mo"
Orlando Brown	"Zeus"	Marion Motley	"The Train"
Howard Cassady	"Hopalong"	Ozzie Newsome	"The Wizard of Oz"
Don Cockroft	"Donny O"	Jim Ninowski	"Nino"
Johnny Davis	"B-1"	Vito Parilli	"Babe"
Doug Dieken	"Diek"	Don Phelps	"Dopey"
Hanford Dixon	"Top Dawg"	Frank Pitts	"Riddler"
Ross Fichtner	"Rocky"	Greg Pruitt	"Do It"
Frank Gatski	"Gunner"	Dave Puzzuoli	"Puz"
Otto Graham	"Automatic"	Andre Rison	"Full Moon"
Forrest Grigg	"Chubby"	Walter Roberts	"The Flea," "Mr. Rodgers"
Lou Groza	"The Toe"		
Carl Hairston	"Big Daddy"	Dick Schafrath	"Shaf"
Chet Hanulak	"The Jet"	Robert Scott	"Bo"
Kevin Johnson	"K.J."	Jerry Sherk	"The Sheik"
Michael Jackson	"Thriller"	Robert Sims	"Mickey"
Eddie Johnson	"The Assassin"	Matt Stover	"Stove Top"
Edgar Jones	"Special Delivery"	Eric Turner	"E-rock"
Joe Jones	"Turkey"	Tommy Vardell	"Touchdown"
Tony Jones	"T-Bone"	Gerard Warren	"Big Money"
William Jones	"Dub"	Kellen Winslow, Jr.	"K-2"
Jim Kanicki	"Smokey"	Lowell Wren	"Junior"

1999 EXPANSION DRAFT

The 1999 expansion draft was held on February 9 in Canton, Ohio. The expansion draft gave the "new" Browns an opportunity to stock up on players other teams believed were less important to their success and thus left "unprotected." The Browns selected 37 players. Their first choice was Jim Pyne, an offensive lineman from the Detroit Lions who played for the Browns from 1999-2000. Other notable selections were number two pick Hurvin McCormack, a defensive tackle from the Dallas Cowboys who was a member of the Browns in 1999; number three pick Scott Rehberg, an offensive lineman from the New England Patriots who was on the team in 1999; number six pick Tarek Saleh, a linebacker form the Carolina Panthers who was a Brown from 1999-2001; number 10 pick Lenoy Jones, a linebacker from the Tennessee Titans who played for the Browns from 1999-2002; and number 27 pick Orlando Bobo, an offensive lineman from the Minnesota Vikings who was a Brown in 1999.

NINOWSKI, JIM

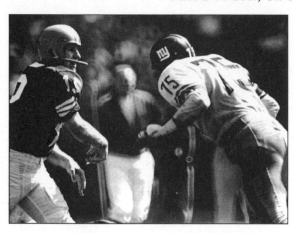

Jim Ninowski just gets his pass off while facing the onslaught of the New York Giants' Jim Katcavage in the season opener on September 16, 1962. Photo courtesy of the Cleveland Press Collection.

Jim Ninowski was a Cleveland quarterback from 1958-59 and from '62-66. He was a fourth-round draft choice of the Browns in 1958 from Michigan State University. He backed up Milt Plum before being traded to Detroit on July 12, 1960. He was re-acquired on March 28, 1962, in a trade with the Lions as part of a six-player deal. He backed up Frank Ryan from 1962-66.

NOLL, CHUCK

Chuck Noll was a Browns guard and linebacker from 1953-59. A hometown product of Cleveland Benedictine High School, and the University of Dayton, Noll was a 20th-round draft choice of Cleveland's in 1953. He tied for the team lead with five interceptions in 1955.

NORTHCUTT, DENNIS

Dennis Northcutt was a Browns wide receiver from 2000-06. He was a second-round draft pick of the Browns in 2000 out of the University of Arizona. He was the Browns' leader in receptions and receiving yards in 2003 and '04. He is unfortunately remembered for his fourth-quarter dropped pass form Kelly Holcomb that would have all but clinched a wild card win over the Steelers in Pittsburgh that instead turned out to be a 36-33 loss. He totaled 276 career receptions for 3,438 yards and 11 touchdowns as a Brown.

Northcutt also returned punts for the Browns and led the team in returns from 2000-06 and return yards in 2000 and from '02-06. His 2,149 career punt return yards rank second in Browns annals. He also returned three punts for touchdowns—a 74-yarder at Tennessee on September 22, 2002, an 87-yarder against Pittsburgh on November 3, 2002, and a 62-yarder against Baltimore on January 1, 2006.

NOVEMBER

-25, 1951

Browns wide receiver Dub Jones set a team record, and tied a league mark, for most touchdowns in one game by scoring six times in a 42-21 rout of the visiting Chicago Bears.

-20, 1983

The Browns blanked the New England Patriots 30-0 in New England in a crucial battle of AFC Wild Card contenders. Having shut out the Buccaneers 20-0 the week before, Cleveland became the first Browns team to post consecutive shutouts since 1951.

-4, 1990

The Browns were battered by the Buffalo Bills 42-0 in Cleveland in the team's second-worst shutout loss, and second-worst home defeat, ever. Head coach Bud Carson was fired the next day.

-8, 1993

The Browns released quarterback Bernie Kosar due to Kosar's ". . . lack of production and loss of physical skills," according to head coach Bill Belichick, as quoted from the Cleveland *Plain Dealer* on November 9, 1993.

-6, 1995

Browns majority owner Art Modell made the Browns' relocation to Baltimore official to the public with an announcement in Baltimore.

-4, 2001

Cleveland lost in overtime to the Chicago Bears 27-21 at Soldier Field in a game that the Browns were leading 21-7 with little more than 30 seconds remaining. The Bears cut their deficit to 21-14 with 28 seconds left and then recovered an onside kick at the Browns' 47-yard-line with 24 seconds left. Three plays later, quarterback Shane Matthews completed a 34-yard Hail Mary pass tipped by Browns defensive back Percy Ellsworth to running back James Allen with no time left. Mike Brown returned a Tim Couch pass batted by teammate Bryan Robinson 16 yards for the winning score on the Browns' first possession of the extra period.

-16, 2003

The Browns crushed the Arizona Cardinals 44-6 in Cleveland Browns Stadium. Browns quarterback Kelly Holcomb was 29-of-35 for 392 yards and three touchdowns.

-28, 2004

The Browns lost to the Cincinnati Bengals 58-48 in Paul Brown Stadium in the second-highest-scoring game in NFL history. Kelly Holcomb completed 30 of 39 passes for 413 yards and five touchdowns plus two interceptions.

-18, 2007

Cleveland beat the Baltimore Ravens 33-30 in overtime in the memorable "Ricochet" game in Baltimore (*please see Ricochet, The*).

-17, 2008

The Browns defeated the Buffalo Bills 29-27 in Buffalo on *Monday Night Football* on Phil Dawson's 56-yard field goal with 1:39 left.

-22, 2009

Cleveland fell 38-37 to the Lions in Detroit when Matthew Stafford completed a one-yard TD pass to Brandon Pettigrew with no time left.

-7, 2010

Behind Peyton Hillis's 184 yards on the ground and Colt McCoy's 14-of-19, 174-yard day, the Browns shocked the New England Patriots 34-14 in Cleveland.

-6, 2014

With solid performances from Brian Hoyer and rookie Terrance West, the Browns shined in the national spotlight when they methodically destroyed the Cincinnati Bengals 24-3 in Cincinnati on *Thursday Night Football*. The upset lifted the 6-3 Browns into a first-place tie with Pittsburgh in the AFC North.

NUMBERS ON HELMETS

Uniform numbers appeared on Browns players' helmets from 1957-59.

OAKLAND RAIDERS

The Oakland Raiders were opponents of the Browns in the NFL from 1970-95 and have been since 1999. They were located in Los Angeles from 1982-94. One memorable Raiders victory came in the first meeting between the teams on November 8, 1970, in Oakland, when George Blanda kicked a 53-yard field goal with seven seconds left in a 23-20 victory, one of four Raiders games in a month-long stretch that produced three miracle wins and a miracle tie when Blanda came through in the late stages. Two unforgettable Browns wins occurred in Los Angeles a year apart—on September 20, 1992, and September 19, 1993. In the '92 game, Eric Metcalf scored all four of Cleveland's touchdowns—three on receptions, one on a run—in a 28-16 triumph. In the '93 game, Metcalf was instrumental again, scoring on a one-yard sweep with no time left to give the Browns a 19-16 victory that capped a remarkable comeback from a 16-3 deficit late in the game.

The Raiders and Browns have met twice in the postseason, with the Raiders winning both. Most notable was their 14-12 triumph in an AFC Divisional Playoff on January 4, 1981, in frozen Cleveland Stadium when Browns quarterback Brian Sipe was picked off by Mike Davis in the end zone with less than a minute to play (*please see Red Right 88*).

Oakland's all-time record against Cleveland is 11-9, 7-7 at home and 4-2 on the road. The Raiders' all-time postseason record against the Browns is 2-0 (home games).

OCTOBER
-25, 1981

The Browns defeated the Baltimore Colts 42-28 in Cleveland as Brian Sipe set the Browns' single-game passing yards record by throwing for 444.

-21, 1984

The Browns lost to the Cincinnati Bengals 12-9 in Cincinnati on a 33-yard last-second field goal by Jim Breech in a battle of 1-6 teams. Browns head coach Sam Rutigliano was fired the following day.

-4-18, 1987

The Browns played three games during this period, but with a different twist. Replacement players (for the most part) represented the Browns (and the other teams) due to an NFL players' strike that actually canceled Cleveland's long-awaited Monday night rematch against the Denver Broncos that had been scheduled for September 28 (the Broncos had beaten the Browns in the AFC title game nearly nine months earlier). The "replacement" Browns won at New England 20-10 on October 4, lost at home to Houston 15-10 on October 11, and routed the Bengals 34-0 in Cincinnati on October 18 with help from a handful of regular players who returned to action early.

-24, 1993

Cleveland defeated Pittsburgh 28-23 in Cleveland as Eric Metcalf became the only player in NFL annals to return two punts for touchdowns for at least 75 yards in the same game. Metcalf's returns went for 91 and 75 yards—the second the game winner with 2:05 left.

-31, 1999

The Browns defeated the New Orleans Saints 21-16 in New Orleans as quarterback Tim Couch completed a Hail Mary 56-yard touchdown pass to Kevin Johnson as time expired for the "new era" Browns' first victory.

-27, 2002

The Browns recovered from a 21-3 second-quarter deficit to defeat the New York Jets 24-21 in the Meadowlands.

-5, 2003

Tim Couch had one of his finest performances in leading the Browns to a 33-13 rout of the Pittsburgh Steelers in Heinz Field on *Sunday Night Football*. Couch completed 20 of 25 passes for 208 yards, two touchdowns, and one interception.

-13, 2008

Behind strong games from Derek Anderson and Braylon Edwards, the Browns shocked the defending Super Bowl Champion New York Giants 35-14 in a rocking Cleveland Browns Stadium.

-24, 2010

Cleveland upset defending Super Bowl Champion New Orleans 30-17 in the Superdome. David Bowens led the way with two pick-sixes—a 30-yarder in the second quarter and a 64-yarder late in the fourth that was the icing on the cake.

OFFENSIVE LINEMEN

Notable offensive linemen for the Browns include Frank Gatski, Lou Groza, Lin Houston, Lou Rymkus, Abe Gibron, Mike McCormack, Jim Ray Smith, Gene Hickerson, Dick Schafrath, John Wooten, John Morrow, Monte Clark, Fred Hoaglin, John Demarie, Doug Dieken, Bob DeMarco, Tom DeLeone, Robert E. Jackson, Cody Risien, Joe DeLamielleure, Mike Baab, Paul Farren, Dan Fike, Tony Jones, Bob Dahl, Steve Everitt, Jim Pyne, Dave Wohlabaugh, Ross Verba, Shaun O'Hara, Ryan Tucker, Jeff Faine, Joe Thomas, Eric Steinbach, Kevin Shaffer, Alex Mack, and Mitchell Schwartz.

OFFENSIVE PLAYER OF THE YEAR

1980 Brian Sipe (NFL by PFW)

OGBONNAYA, CHRIS

Chris Ogbonnaya was a Browns running back from 2011-13. A product of the University of Texas, he signed with the Browns on October 18, 2011. Ogbonnaya's best year came in 2013 when he rushed for 240 yards and had 48 receptions for 343 yards and two touchdowns.

O'HARA, SHAUN

Shaun O'Hara was a Browns offensive lineman from 2000-03. He was acquired by the Browns in 2000 as an undrafted free agent.

ONE-THOUSAND-YARD RECEIVERS

Please see Individual Statistics on page 225.

ONE-THOUSAND-YARD RUSHERS

Please see Individual Statistics on page 225.

OPENERS

For a listing of the scores of the season openers, please see Team Statistics on page 248.

ORANGE AND BROWN REPORT, THE

The Orange and Brown Report was a magazine from 2006-15 that offered news, views, features, and many other things regarding the Browns.

ORANGE HELMETS

The Browns' helmets were orange from 1952-95 and have been since 1999.

ORANGE PANTS

The Browns wore orange pants for every game from 1975-83.

OVERTIME

The following are Browns overtime games:
* Denotes postseason

Cleveland 30, New England 27 (Sept. 26, 1977, at Cle.)
Cleveland 13, Cincinnati 10 (Sept. 10, 1978, at Cle.)
Pittsburgh 15, Cleveland 9 (Sept. 24, 1978, at Pit.)
Cleveland 37, N.Y. Jets 34 (Dec. 10, 1978, at Cle.)
Cleveland 25, N.Y. Jets 22 (Sept. 2, 1979, at N.Y.)
Cleveland 30, Miami 24 (Nov. 18, 1979, at Cle.)
Pittsburgh 33, Cleveland 30 (Nov. 25, 1979, at Pit.)
Denver 23, Cleveland 20 (Nov. 8, 1981, at Den.)
Cleveland 30, San Diego 24 (Sept. 25, 1983, at S.D.)
Cleveland 25, Houston 19 (Oct.30, 1983, at Cle.)
Cincinnati 20, Cleveland 17 (Dec. 2, 1984, at Cle.)
St. Louis 27, Cleveland 24 (Sept. 8, 1985, at Cle.)
Cleveland 37, Pittsburgh 31 (Nov. 23, 1986, at Cle.)
Cleveland 13, Houston 10 (Nov. 30, 1986, at Cle.)

*Cleveland 23, N.Y. Jets 20 (20T) (Jan. 3, 1987, at Cle.)
*Denver 23, Cleveland 20 (Jan. 11, 1987, at Cle.)
San Diego 27, Cleveland 24 (Nov. 1, 1987, at S.D.)
Miami 13, Cleveland 10 (Oct. 8, 1989, at Mia.)
Cleveland 10, Kansas City 10 (Nov. 19, 1989, at Cle.)
Indianapolis 23, Cleveland 17 (Dec. 10, 1989, at Ind.)
Cleveland 23, Minnesota 17 (Dec. 17, 1989, at Cle.)
Cleveland 30, San Diego 24 (Oct. 20, 1991, at S.D.)
Cleveland 29, Cincinnati 26 (Oct. 29, 1995, at Cin.)
Chicago 27, Cleveland 21 (Nov. 4, 2001, at Chi.)
Pittsburgh 15, Cleveland 12 (Nov. 11, 2001, at Cle.)
Cleveland 31, Tennessee 28 (Sept. 22, 2002, at Tenn.)
Pittsburgh 16, Cleveland 13 (Sept. 29, 2002, at Pit.)
Denver 23, Cleveland 20 (Dec. 14, 2003, at Den.)
Philadelphia 34, Cleveland 31 (Oct. 24, 2004, at Cle.)
Cleveland 31, Kansas City 28 (Dec. 3, 2006, at Cle.)
Cleveland 33, Seattle 30 (Nov. 4, 2007, at Cle.)
Cleveland 33, Baltimore 30 (Nov. 18, 2007, at Bal.)
Cincinnati 23, Cleveland 20 (Oct. 4, 2009, at Cle.)
N.Y. Jets 26, Cleveland 20 (Nov. 14, 2010, at Cle.)
Arizona 20, Cleveland 17 (Dec. 18, 2001, at Ariz.)
Dallas 23, Cleveland 20 (Nov. 18, 2012, at Dal.)

Overall Regular Season – 16-17-1 (.543)
Home Regular Season – 10-6-1 (.708)
Away Regular Season – 6-11 (.364)
Postseason – 1-1 (.500)

P

PALMER, CHRIS

Chris Palmer was the Browns' head coach from 1999-2000. His all-time record as Browns head coach was 5-27, 2-14 at home and 3-13 on the road.

PARRISH, BERNIE

Bernie Parrish was a Browns defensive back from 1959-66. He was a ninth-round draft pick of the Browns in 1958 from the University of Florida with one year of eligibility left in school. He was the Browns' leader in interceptions in 1961 with seven. He tied for the team lead in picks in 1959 with five and in '64 with four. He ranks seventh in team history with 29 career interceptions. Parrish returned three picks for touchdowns—a 37-yarder on October 18, 1959, against the Chicago Cardinals, a 92-yarder on December 11, 1960, against the Chicago Bears, and a 54-yarder off a long Don Meredith pass on October 18, 1964, that gave the Browns the lead for good against the Dallas Cowboys. He was picked to play in the Pro Bowl in 1960 and '63.

PARSEGHIAN, ARA

Ara Parseghian was a Browns running back from 1948-49. He was a 25th-round draft choice of the Browns in 1948 from Miami University.

PASS COMPLETIONS LEADERS

Please see Individual Statistics on page 225.

PASSING YARDS LEADERS

Please see Individual Statistics on page 225.

PAUL, DON

Don Paul was a Browns defensive back from 1954-58. A Washington State University product, Paul was acquired by the Browns on August 30, 1954, in a trade with the Washington Redskins for rookies Dale Atkinson and Johnny Carson. He returned an interception 65 yards for a touchdown on December 26, 1955, against the Rams in the NFL title game in Los Angeles. He returned a fumble 89 yards for a TD for the Browns' final score in a 24-0 win over Pittsburgh on November 10, 1957. He was voted to the All-NFL defensive team in 1955 by UP and was picked for the Pro Bowl from 1956-58.

PAYTON, EDDIE

Eddie Payton was a Browns kickoff returner in 1977. A Jackson State University product, Payton was acquired by the Browns in 1977. He is the older brother of the late Hall of Famer Walter Payton.

PERFECT SEASON

The Browns had a perfect season in 1948, finishing with a 14-0 record—15-0 including their 49-7 demolition of Buffalo in the AAFC Championship Game on December 19 in Cleveland. It was the first time to that point (and now second overall) in the history of pro football that a team went an entire season (regular season and postseason) undefeated and untied on the way to a championship. The 1972 Miami Dolphins went 17-0 in winning the NFL Championship that culminated with a victory in Super Bowl VII. The 1937 Los Angeles Bulldogs went 8-0 in winning an earlier AFL Championship when there was no postseason.

PERRY, MICHAEL DEAN

Michael Dean Perry was a defensive end for Cleveland from 1988-94. He was a second-round draft choice of the Browns in 1988 from Clemson University. He was the Browns' leader with 11.5 sacks in 1990, which rank fourth in team history. His 51.5 career sacks rank second in team annals. He was voted AFC Defensive Most Valuable Player in 1989 by UPI. He was voted to All-AFC defensive teams in 1989 by AP, PFW, FWA, SN, and UPI; in 1990 by AP, NEA, PFW, FWA, SN, and UPI; in 1991 by PFW and SN; in 1992 and 1993 by SN; and in 1994 by UPI. Perry was picked for the Pro Bowl from 1989-91 and 1993-94.

PHILADELPHIA EAGLES

The Philadelphia Eagles were opponents of the Browns in the NFL from 1950-95 and have been since 1999. The most famous game between the two teams occurred in the NFL's season opener on Saturday evening, September 16, 1950, in Philadelphia's Municipal Stadium. As two-time defending NFL Champions, the Eagles were heavy favorites. The Browns, despite having won four straight AAFC Championships, were considered inferior because the AAFC was considered inferior to the NFL. The Browns blew away the Eagles 35-10 in front of 71,237 fans. Philadelphia's all-time record against Cleveland is 16-31-1, 9-14 at home and 7-17-1 on the road.

PHILCOX, TODD

Todd Philcox was a Browns quarterback from 1991-93. A Syracuse University product, he was obtained by the Browns on April 1, 1991, as a free agent. Philcox took over as the starter after Bernie Kosar was released on November 8, 1993, and played the position until Vinny Testaverde returned from a separated shoulder injury less than a month later.

PHIPPS, MIKE

Mike Phipps was a Browns quarterback from 1970-76. He was a first-round draft choice of the Browns in 1970 from Purdue University. To get Phipps, the Browns traded the great Paul Warfield to Miami on January 26, 1970, for the Dolphins' first-round selection that was the third overall pick in the next day's Draft. Phipps had led the Boilermakers to 24 victories in 30 games, including a pair of AP Top 10 finishes, the three previous autumns. He did not become the Browns' full-time starter until Week 2 of the 1972 season. Veteran Bill Nelsen directed the Browns for the most part from 1970-71.

Phipps's best season with the Browns was 1972 when he completed 144 of 305 pass attempts for 1,994 yards, 13 touchdowns, and 16 interceptions. The Browns finished 10-4 that year, and despite Phipps's five interceptions, took the undefeated Dolphins down to the wire in an AFC Divisional Playoff Game in the Orange Bowl (a 20-14 Dolphins win). Things went downhill from there. Phipps's touchdown passes/interceptions ratio was quite unimpressive for the next three seasons: 9/20, 9/17, and 4/19. He held off a challenge from Brian Sipe in the 1976 training camp and started the opening game against the New York Jets at home. He passed for three second-quarter touchdowns en route to a 21-10 halftime lead, only to suffer a separated shoulder early in the third

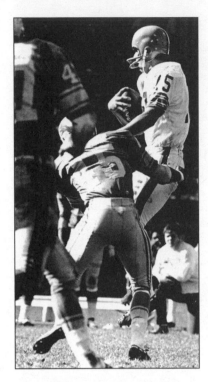

Mike Phipps is corralled by the Lions' Bobby Williams en route to a 40-24 Detroit victory on October 18, 1970. Photo courtesy of the Cleveland Press Collection.

quarter. Sipe came in and put the finishing touches on a 38-17 victory. Sipe went on to pass for 17 touchdowns and had just 14 interceptions as the Browns improved to 9-5 after a 3-11 finish the year before, and the starting job was his.

Phipps passed for 7,700 yards overall, ranking eighth in Browns history, while his 633 career completions rank seventh. He totaled 40 touchdown passes and 81 interceptions in his Browns career. He was traded to the Chicago Bears on May 3, 1977.

PITTS, FRANK

Frank Pitts was a Browns wide receiver from 1971-73. A Southern University product, he was acquired by the Browns on September 8, 1971, in a trade with the Kansas City Chiefs for a fourth-round draft pick in 1972 and a third-round pick in '73. Pitts led the Browns in touchdown receptions in 1971 with four and was the team leader in receptions (36), receiving yards (620), and touchdown catches (eight) in 1972. One of the '72 TD receptions was a game-winning 38-yarder from Mike Phipps with less then a minute to play on a Monday night in San Diego. Pitts was the team leader with 31 receptions and four touchdown catches in 1973.

PITTSBURGH STEELERS

The Pittsburgh Steelers were Browns opponents in the NFL from 1950-95 and have been since 1999. The Pittsburgh-Cleveland rivalry is one of the most heralded in the NFL. The series was dominated by the Browns early on, as Cleveland won 32 of the first 41 meetings. Things turned around in the 1970s as the Steelers won 20 of the next 26 meetings. The tables then turned once again as the Browns won 10 of the next 12 encounters. The teams were even for the most part in the early 1990s before the Steelers won the last five games prior to the Browns' relocation to Baltimore following the 1995 season.

Pittsburgh spoiled the "new era" Browns' return in 1999 by destroying them 43-0 on September 12 in brand new Cleveland Browns Stadium. The revenge-minded Browns won in Pittsburgh two months later 16-15 on a 39-yard field goal by Phil Dawson with 0:00 on the clock.

Pittsburgh and Cleveland have met twice in postseason play, a 29-9 Steelers victory in an AFC Divisional Playoff on January 7, 1995, in Pittsburgh, and a 36-33 Steelers win an AFC Wild Card Playoff on January 5, 2003, again in Pittsburgh. The Steelers' all-time record against the Browns is 65-57, 40-21 at home and 25-36 on the road. Their all-time postseason record against the Browns is 2-0 (home games).

PLAYER OF THE YEAR

1957   Jim Brown (NFL by AP)
1965   Jim Brown (NFL by AP)
1976   Jerry Sherk (NFL Defensive by NEA)
1980   Brian Sipe (NFL by AP; NFL Offensive by PFW)

PLAYERS FROM OHIO SCHOOLS REPRESENTED IN REGULAR DRAFTS, MOST TO LEAST

1.	Ohio State University	38
2.	Miami University	10
3.	Bowling Green State University	9
4.	University of Toledo	8
5.	Xavier University	6
6.	John Carroll University	5
	Kent State University	5
8.	Case Western Reserve University	3
	University of Akron	3
	University of Cincinnati	3
	University of Dayton	3
12.	Heidelberg College	2
	Ohio University	2
14.	Baldwin-Wallace College	1
	Wittenberg University	1
	Youngstown State University	1

PLAYERS' STRIKES

Contractual disputes between NFL players and owners resulted in players' strikes during the 1982 and '87 seasons. Both walkouts began two weeks into the season. The 1982 season was shortened to nine games, with one make-up game played on the weekend on which the wild card games were originally scheduled. In the Browns' case, the make-up game was at Pittsburgh, originally scheduled for October 24.

All postseason games other than the Super Bowl were pushed back a week, and there was only one week, rather than the usual two, in between the conference championship games and the Super Bowl. In addition, the postseason field was increased to 16 teams. The Browns finished 4-5 but still qualified for the playoffs as the eighth and final seed in the AFC. They lost 27-10 to the Los Angeles Raiders in the Los Angeles Memorial Coliseum in the first round.

The 1987 season was shortened to 15 games, but three weeks were played largely with "replacement players." In the Browns' "replacement games," they won at New England 20-10, lost at home to Houston 15-10, and won at Cincinnati 34-0. The one Browns game that was cancelled altogether was the Monday night matchup at home against Denver that was scheduled for September 28.

There was also a players' strike in 1974, but it only affected training camp as it ended in August.

PLAYOFF BOWL

The Playoff Bowl was an exhibition game played between the Eastern Conference and Western Conference runners-up in the Orange Bowl in Miami after the regular season from 1960-69. The Browns played in three Playoff Bowls, losing them all—to the Detroit Lions 17-16 on January 7, 1961, to the Packers 40-23 on January 5, 1964, and to the Rams 30-6 on January 7, 1968.

PLEASANT, ANTHONY

Anthony Pleasant was a Browns defensive end from 1990-95. He was a third-round draft choice of the Browns in 1990 from Tennessee State University. He was the Browns' leader with 11 sacks in 1993, which ties him for fifth in Browns history. His 33.5 career sacks rank sixth in team history.

PLUM, MILT

Milt Plum was a Browns quarterback from 1957-61. He was a second-round draft choice of the Browns in 1957 from Penn State University. He led the NFL in passing in 1960 and '61. With a 110.4 rating in 1960, he completed 110 of 250 attempts for 2,297 yards, 21 touchdowns, and just five interceptions. On October 23 of that year, he connected with Leon Clarke for an 86-yard pass play that went for a touchdown against the Eagles. In 1961 he completed 177 of 302 passes for 2,416 yards, 18 touchdowns and 10 interceptions, and had a 90.3 rating. Plum's 8,914 passing yards rank seventh all-time for the Browns. His 627 completions rank eighth all-time in team history. He was selected to play in the Pro Bowl in 1960 and '61.

PONTBRIAND, RYAN

Ryan Pontbriand was a Browns long snapper from 2003-11. He was a fifth-round draft choice of the Browns in 2003 out of Rice University.

POOL, BRODNEY

Brodney Pool was a Browns defensive back from 2005-09. He was a second-round draft choice of the Browns in 2005 out of the University of Oklahoma. He returned a Kyle Boller pass 100 yards for a touchdown to give the Browns a 27-14, third-quarter lead en route to a thrilling 33-30 victory over the Ravens in Baltimore. His four interceptions in 2009 tied for the team lead.

POSTSEASON

For a complete listing of all postseason games, please see Team Statistics on page 248.

POSTSEASON GAMES THE BROWNS LOST AND WHO THEY WOULD HAVE PLAYED HAD THEY WON

Please see Team Statistics on page 248.

POWELL, RONNIE

Ronnie Powell was a Cleveland kickoff returner in 1999. He was a Northwestern State University product obtained by the Browns as a free agent on April 23, 1999. He was the team leader that season both with 44 kickoff returns and 986 kickoff return yards.

PRESEASON

The Browns' all-time record in the preseason (not including four games against the college all-stars) is 148-149-4, 51-44-1 at home, 66-86-3 on the road, and 31-19 at neutral sites.

PRESEASON GAMES IN FOREIGN CITIES

N.Y. Jets 11, Cleveland 7 (Aug. 18, 1988, at Montreal)
Philadelphia 17, Cleveland 13 (Aug. 6, 1989, at London)
Cleveland 12, New England 9 (Aug. 14, 1993, at Toronto)

Overall – 1-2 (.333)

PRESEASON GAMES AT NEUTRAL SITES IN THE UNITED STATES

The following are neutral cities in the United States in which the Browns have played preseason games: Toledo, Ohio; Syracuse, New York; Portland, Oregon; Birmingham, Alabama; Canton, Ohio; Memphis, Tennessee; South Bend, Indiana; Ann Arbor, Michigan; Columbus, Ohio; Knoxville, Tennessee; Lincoln, Nebraska; and Stillwater, Oklahoma.

PRESEASON GAMES VS. THE BENGALS

The Browns have played the Bengals four times in the preseason, each team winning two. The first game was played on August 29, 1970, in Riverfront Stadium in Cincinnati, with the Bengals winning 31-14. The last three games were played in Ohio Stadium on the campus of Ohio State University in Columbus. The Bengals won the first one 27-21 on September 3, 1972. The Browns won the last two 24-6 on August 19, 1973, and 21-17 on September 1, 1974. Interest in the game in Columbus was rabid at first but waned dramatically. Attendance at the first game in the capital city was 84,816. The mark dropped to 73,421 in the second game. Only 36,326 showed up for the last game.

PRO BOWLERS

1950   Tony Adamle, Otto Graham, Lou Groza, Weldon Humble, Marion Motley, Mac Speedie, Bill Willis

1951   Tony Adamle, Ken Carpenter, Len Ford, Lou Groza, Otto Graham, Dub Jones, Dante Lavelli, Bill Willis

1952   Len Ford, Abe Gibron, Horace Gillom, Otto Graham, Lou Groza, Bill Willis

1953   Len Ford, Abe Gibron, Otto Graham, Lou Groza, Harry Jagade, Tommy James, Dante Lavelli, Ray Renfro

1954   Don Colo, Len Ford, Frank Gatski, Abe Gibron, Otto Graham, Lou Groza, Dante Lavelli

1955   Darrell Brewster, Don Colo, Abe Gibron, Lou Groza, Ken Konz, Fred Morrison

1956   Darrell Brewster, Mike McCormack, Walt Michaels, Don Paul

1957   Jim Brown, Bob Gain, Lou Groza, Mike McCormack, Walt Michaels, Don Paul, Ray Renfro

1958   Jim Brown, Don Colo, Bob Gain, Lou Groza, Walt Michaels, Don Paul, Jim Ray Smith

1959   Jim Brown, Bob Gain, Lou Groza, Art Hunter, Walt Michaels, Jim Ray Smith

1960   Jim Brown, Mike McCormack, Bobby Mitchell, Bernie Parrish, Milt Plum , Ray Renfro, Jim Ray Smith

1961   Jim Brown, Bob Gain, Mike McCormack, John Morrow, Milt Plum, Jim Ray Smith

1962   Jim Brown, Galen Fiss, Bob Gain, Bill Glass, Mike McCormack, Jim Ray Smith

1963   Jim Brown, Galen Fiss, Bill Glass, John Morrow, Bernie Parrish, Dick Schafrath

1964   Jim Brown, Bill Glass, Jim Houston, Dick Modzelewski, Frank Ryan, Dick Schafrath, Paul Warfield

1965   Jim Brown, Gary Collins, Gene Hickerson, Jim Houston, Frank Ryan, Dick Schafrath, Paul Wiggin, John Wooten

1966   Johnny Brewer, Gary Collins, Ernie Green, Gene Hickerson, Leroy Kelly, Frank Ryan, Dick Schafrath, John Wooten

1967   Bill Glass, Ernie Green, Gene Hickerson, Walter Johnson, Leroy Kelly, Milt Morin, Dick Schafrath, Paul Wiggin

1968   Erich Barnes, Gene Hickerson, Walter Johnson, Ernie Kellermann, Leroy Kelly, Milt Morin, Dick Schafrath, Paul Warfield

1969   Jack Gregory, Gene Hickerson, Fred Hoaglin, Jim Houston, Walter Johnson, Leroy Kelly, Bill Nelsen, Paul Warfield

1970   Gene Hickerson, Jim Houston, Leroy Kelly

1971   Leroy Kelly, Milt Morin

1973   Greg Pruitt, Clarence Scott, Jerry Sherk
1974   Greg Pruitt, Jerry Sherk
1975   Jerry Sherk
1976   Greg Pruitt, Jerry Sherk
1977   Greg Pruitt
1978   Thom Darden
1979   Tom DeLeone, Mike Pruitt
1980   Joe DeLamielleure, Tom DeLeone, Doug Dieken, Mike Pruitt,
       Brian Sipe
1981   Ozzie Newsome
1982   Chip Banks
1983   Chip Banks
1984   Ozzie Newsome
1985   Chip Banks, Bob Golic, Kevin Mack, Clay Matthews, Ozzie
       Newsome
1986   Chip Banks, Hanford Dixon, Bob Golic, Frank Minnifield, Cody
       Risien
1987   Hanford Dixon, Bob Golic, Bernie Kosar, Kevin Mack, Clay
       Matthews, Gerald McNeil, Frank Minnifield, Cody Risien
1988   Hanford Dixon, Clay Matthews, Frank Minnifield
1989   Mike Johnson, Clay Matthews, Frank Minnifield, Michael Dean
       Perry, Webster Slaughter
1990   Mike Johnson, Michael Dean Perry
1991   Michael Dean Perry
1993   Eric Metcalf, Michael Dean Perry
1994   Rob Burnett, Leroy Hoard, Pepper Johnson, Eric Metcalf, Michael
       Dean Perry, Eric Turner
2001   Jamir Miller
2007   Derek Anderson, Josh Cribbs, Braylon Edwards, Ryan Pontbriand,
       Joe Thomas, Kellen Winslow
2008   Ryan Pontbriand, Shaun Rogers, Joe Thomas
2009   Josh Cribbs, Joe Thomas
2010   Alex Mack, Joe Thomas
2011   Joe Thomas
2012   Josh Cribbs, Phil Dawson, Joe Thomas
2013   Jordan Cameron, Josh Gordon, Joe Haden, Alex Mack, Joe Thomas,
       T.J. Ward
2014   Tashaun Gipson, Joe Haden, Joe Thomas

PRUITT, GREG

Greg Pruitt was a Browns running back from 1973-81. He was a second-round draft choice of the Browns in 1973 from the University of Oklahoma. He led the Browns in rushing yards every season from 1974-78. In 1975 he gained 1,067 yards and a team-leading eight touchdowns. In 1976 he gained exactly 1,000 yards and tied Cleo Miller for the team lead with four touchdowns on the ground. In 1977 he gained 1,086 yards, and in 1978 he gained 960. He ranks fourth in Browns all-time rushing yards with 5,496.

Pruitt's 214 yards rushing on December 14, 1975, at home against the Chiefs are the eighth-most in team history. His 191 rushing yards on October 17, 1976, in Atlanta rank ninth. His longest run from scrimmage as a Brown was a 78-yard gain for a touchdown in a 44-7 romp over Kansas City on October 30, 1977. His 323 career receptions rank fifth in Browns annals.

Pruitt also returned punts and kickoffs. His 659 career punt return yards rank eighth for the Browns. He led the Browns in punt returns and punt return yards each season from 1973-75, kickoff returns in 1973 and '75, and kickoff return yards in 1973 and '74. On October 27, 1974, he returned a punt 72 yards late in the game that led to the winning touchdown in a dramatic home win over the Denver Broncos. Two weeks later on November 10 in New England he returned a kickoff 88 yards for a touchdown.

Pruitt's 1,798 combined net yards in 1975 rank ninth in team history. His 10,700 career combined net yards rank fourth in team history (######). He was selected for the Pro Bowl in 1973, '74, '76, and '77.

PRUITT, MIKE

Mike Pruitt was a running back for the Browns from 1976-84. He was a first-round draft choice of the Browns in 1976 from Purdue University. He was second on the Browns in rushing yards in 1978 with 560 but first in rushing touchdowns with five. He was the team leader in rushing yards every season from 1979-83: 1,294 in 1979, 1,034 in '80, 1,103 in '81, 516 in '82, and 1,184 in '83. His 1979 total was second in the AFC to Houston's Earl Campbell's 1,697 and ranks eighth in Cleveland history.

Pruitt led the Browns in rushing touchdowns with nine in 1979, six in '80, seven in '81, and 10 in '83. He tied Charles White in 1982 with three. His two longest runs as a Brown were a 79-yarder for a touchdown on December 9, 1979, at Oakland and a 71-yarder against the visiting Bills on October 29,

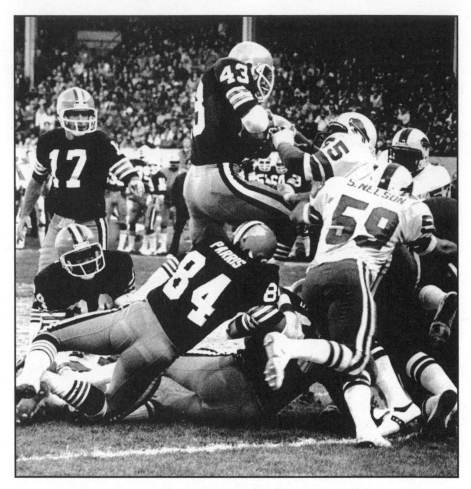

Mike Pruitt scores from a yard out at home against the Bills on October 29, 1978. Photo courtesy of the Cleveland Press Collection.

1978. His 6,540 rushing yards rank third all-time for the Browns. He totaled 8,538 combined net yards that rank sixth in team history (######). Pruitt was voted to All-AFC offensive teams in 1979 by PFW, SN, and UPI. He was picked for the Pro Bowl in 1979 and '80.

PUNT RETURN YARDS LEADERS

Please see Individual Statistics on page 225.

PUNT RETURNERS

Notable Cleveland punt returners include Cliff Lewis, Don Phelps, Ken Carpenter, Ray Renfro, Billy Reynolds, Chet Hanulak, Don Paul, Bobby Mitchell, Jim Shofner, Walter Roberts, Leroy Kelly, Ben Davis, Reece Morrison, Greg Pruitt, Keith Wright, Dino Hall, Gerald McNeil, Eric Metcalf, Dennis Northcutt, Josh Cribbs, and Travis Benjamin.

PUNT RETURNS LEADERS

Please see Individual Statistics on page 225.

PUNTERS

Notable Browns punters include Tom Colella, Horace Gillom, Gary Collins, Don Cockroft, Johnny Evans, Steve Cox, Jeff Gossett, Bryan Wagner, Brian Hansen, Tom Tupa, Chis Gardocki, Dave Zastudil, Reggie Hodges, and Spencer Lanning.

PUNTING YARDS LEADERS

Please see Individual Statistics on page 225.

PYNE, JIM

Jim Pyne was a Browns guard from 1999-2000. A Virginia Tech University product, Pyne was the Browns' first choice in the 1999 expansion draft.

QUARTERBACKS

Notable Browns quarterbacks include Otto Graham, George Ratterman, Tommy O'Connell, Milt Plum, Jim Ninowski, Frank Ryan, Bill Nelsen, Mike Phipps, Brian Sipe, Paul McDonald, Gary Danielson, Bernie Kosar, Vinny Testaverde, Tim Couch, Kelly Holcomb, Jeff Garcia, Trent Dilfer, Charlie Frye, Derek Anderson, Brady Quinn, Colt McCoy, Brandon Weeden, and Brian Hoyer.

QUINN, BRADY

Brady Quinn was a Browns quarterback from 2007-09. He was a first-round draft pick of the Browns in 2007 from the University of Notre Dame. He played very little his first two seasons and then split the quarterback duties with Derek Anderson in 2009, completing 136 of 256 passes for 1,339 yards, eight touchdowns, and seven interceptions.

R

RAINER, WALI

Wali Rainer was a Browns linebacker from 1999-2001. He was a fourth-round draft choice of Cleveland's in 1999 out of the University of Virginia.

RATTERMAN, GEORGE

George Ratterman was a Cleveland quarterback from 1952-56. He was a University of Notre Dame product acquired by Cleveland on April 18, 1952, in a trade with the New York Yanks for Stan Williams and Bill Forester. He backed up Otto Graham from 1952-55 and then rotated with Tommy O'Connell and Vito Parilli in 1956.

RECEIVING YARDS LEADERS

Please see Individual Statistics on page 225.

RECEPTIONS LEADERS

Please see Individual Statistics on page 225.

RED RIGHT 88

Red Right 88 was a play in which Browns quarterback Brian Sipe was intercepted by Oakland's Mike Davis in the Raiders' end zone on a pass intended for Ozzie Newsome with the less than a minute to go in an AFC Divisional Playoff on January 4, 1981, in frozen Cleveland Stadium. The Browns trailed 14-12 at the time. The Browns eschewed a field-goal try by Don Cockroft because the veteran kicker had been having a rough day, having missed two field goals and an extra point. The play originated from the Raiders' 13-yard-line.

REGULAR-SEASON GAMES IN JANUARY

Pittsburgh 37, Cleveland 21 (Jan. 2, 1983, at Pit.)
Pittsburgh 16, Cleveland 9 (Jan. 2, 1994, at Pit.)
Cleveland 22, Houston 14 (Jan. 2, 2005, at Hou.)
Cleveland 20, Baltimore 16 (Jan. 1, 2006, at Cle.)
Cleveland 23, Jacksonville 17 (Jan. 3, 2010, at Cle.)
Pittsburgh 41, Cleveland 9 (Jan. 2, 2011, at Cle.)
Pittsburgh 13, Cleveland 9 (Jan. 1, 2012, at Cle.)

Overall – 3-4 (.429)
Home – 2-2 (500)
Away – 1-2 (.333)

RELOCATION TO BALTIMORE

Majority owner Art Modell moved the Browns to Baltimore in 1996 and renamed them the Ravens.

RENFRO, RAY

Ray Renfro was a Browns wide receiver from 1952-63. He was a fourth-round draft choice of the Browns in 1952 out of North Texas State College. Renfro led the Browns in rushing yards in 1953. He led the team in touchdown receptions in 1955 (eight), '56 (four), and '57 (six) and in receiving yards and touchdown catches in 1958 (573 and six) and '59 (528 and six). He had highs of 48 receptions, 834 receiving yards, and six touchdown catches in 1961. He ranks fourth in Browns history with 5,508 career receiving yards. His 6,569 career combined net yards (######) and 330 all-time points each rank 10th in team history. He is tied for fourth in Browns annals for most points in a postseason game with 12, which occurred in Cleveland's NFL title-game rout of Detroit on December 26, 1954, in Cleveland. He was selected for the Pro Bowl in 1953 and '57.

RETIRED UNIFORM NUMBERS

14   Otto Graham
32   Jim Brown
45   Ernie Davis
46   Don Fleming
76   Lou Groza

REYNOLDS, BILLY

Billy Reynolds was a mainly a Browns punt and kickoff returner from 1953-54 and in 1957. He was a second-round draft pick by the Browns in 1953 out of the University of Pittsburgh. He was in the military from 1955-56. He led the Browns in punt returns in 1953 and '57, punt return yardage all three years he played, and kickoff returns and kickoff return yards in 1954. His kickoff returns of 42 and 46 yards helped set up touchdowns in the Browns' 56-10 rout of the Detroit Lions in the 1954 NFL title game.

RICHARDSON, TRENT

Trent Richardson was a Cleveland running back from 2012-13. He was a first-round draft pick—the third overall selection—of the Browns in 2012 out of the University of Alabama. Although he rushed for both a team-leading 950 yards and 11 touchdowns, and had 51 receptions for 367 yards and a touchdown in his rookie year of 2012, Richardson turned out to be a big disappointment. He averaged only 3.6 yards per carry in '12. Two games into the 2013 season, he was traded to the Indianapolis Colts.

RICOCHET, THE

There have been countless Browns games throughout the years that have provided crazy plays and wacky ways. But what occurred at the end of regulation in a game against the Baltimore Ravens on November 18, 2007, in M&T Bank Stadium might just take the cake. The Browns, just off a heartbreaking defeat in Pittsburgh and a thrilling triumph over the Seahawks prior to that, were in the midst of their third straight game that would go down to the wire. At 5-4, they were desperate for a win to keep playoff hopes from becoming little more than a pipe dream.

The Browns, suddenly an offensive juggernaut since Derek Anderson replaced the departed Charlie Frye following an embarrassing home loss to the Steelers in the season opener, seemed to have the game well in hand. They carried a 27-14 lead into the fourth quarter. The 4-5 Ravens, their playoff hopes in even bigger jeopardy than their visitors, refused to die. Three Matt Stover field goals and a 27-yard scoring strike from Kyle Boller to Devard Darling had Baltimore in the lead 30-27 with just 31 seconds to go.

A 39-yard kickoff return by Josh Cribbs gave the Browns the ball on their own 43-yard line. Completions from Anderson to Joe Jurevicius and Braylon Edwards put the ball on the Ravens' 34 with but three seconds remaining. Phil

Dawson, who had come up just short on a 52-yard field-goal try that would have forced overtime against the Steelers the week before, came on to attempt a 51-yarder. Dawson's boot had more than enough distance this time. However, the ball deflected off of the left upright and, incredibly, onto the top of the support beam beyond the crossbar, then ricocheted back in front of the bar before falling to the ground. It was an extraordinary sequence no observer had ever seen before. The initial ruling was that Dawson's kick was no good. The two officials beneath the goalpost saw only that the ball sprung backwards and tumbled down short of the crossbar.

Players from both sides were undressing in their respective locker rooms, thinking the game was over and that the teams were now tied for second place in the AFC North with 5-5 records when shocking news arrived—the game was not over. Although field goals, by rule, are not reviewable via instant replay, officials had huddled and reversed their original call—the correct decision—making Dawson's three-pointer good, thus knotting the score at 30 and forcing overtime.

Dawson's 33-yard—and somewhat anticlimactic—field goal 5:47 into the extra period gave the Browns an exhilarating 33-30 triumph, sending 71,055 fans home shocked, shaking their heads in disbelief.

RISIEN, CODY

Cody Risien was a Cleveland offensive tackle from 1979-83 and '85-89. He was a seventh-round draft pick of the Browns in 1979 out of Texas A&M University. He missed the entire 1984 season due to a knee injury suffered in the final preseason game in Philadelphia. He was voted to All-AFC offensive teams in 1983 by UPI and in 1986 by PFW and was voted to the Pro Bowl from 1986-87.

ROAD WON-LOST-TIED RECORDS

Please see Team Statistics on page 248.

ROBERTS, WALTER

Walter Roberts was a Browns wide receiver from 1964-66. He was a San Jose State University product acquired by the Browns as a free agent in 1964. He started in place of the injured Paul Warfield for part of the 1965 season. He had an 80-yard touchdown reception from Frank Ryan that year in a

Cody Risien and assistant coach Rod Humenuik drill in offensive line techniques in 1979. Photo courtesy of the Cleveland Press Collection.

season-opening win over Washington. He also saw time as a kickoff returner and punt returner. He was the Browns' leader in kickoff return yards (661) and co-leader in kickoff returns (24) in 1964. He was the team leader in kickoff returns (20) and kickoff return yards (454) in 1966. Roberts returned a kickoff 88 yards on November 7, 1965, at home against the Eagles. He led the Browns in punt returns from 1964-65. His 1,608 all-time punt return yards rank ninth in Browns history.

ROBERTSON, CRAIG

Craig Robertson has been a Browns linebacker since 2011. A product of the University of North Texas, he was signed by the Browns in 2011 as an undrafted free agent. Robertson tied for second on the team in interceptions in 2012.

ROBISKIE, BRIAN

Brian Robiskie was a Cleveland wide receiver from 2009-11. He was a second-round draft choice by the Browns in 2009 out of Ohio State University.

His best year came in 2010 when he caught 29 balls for 310 yards and three touchdowns, the latter which tied for the team lead.

ROGERS, DON

Don Rogers was a Browns safety from 1984-85. He was a first-round draft choice of the Browns in 1984 out of UCLA. He returned an interception of a Dan Marino pass 45 yards in an AFC Divisional Playoff loss at Miami on January 4, 1986. Rogers died tragically from a drug overdose some three-and-a-half weeks prior to the start of the 1986 training camp.

ROGERS, SHAUN

Shaun Rogers was a Browns defensive lineman from 2008-10. A product of the University of Texas, he was traded to the Browns from the Lions on March 1, 2008. He led the Browns in 2008 with 4.5 sacks.

ROGERS, TYRONE

Tyrone Rogers was a Browns defensive lineman from 1999-2004. He was a product of Alabama State University. He was second on the Browns with six sacks in 2001.

ROOKIE OF THE YEAR

1957   Jim Brown (NFL by AP, UP)
1982   Chip Banks (NFL Defensive by AP, PFW)
1985   Kevin Mack (AFC by UPI)

ROTH, MATT

Matt Roth was a Browns linebacker from 2009-10. A product of the University of Iowa, he was claimed off waivers by Cleveland on November 25, 2009. He had four sacks in only six games in 2009 and 3.5 sacks in 2010, the latter which were tied for second on the team.

ROYE, ORPHEUS

Orpheus Roye was a Browns defensive lineman from 2000-07. He attended Florida State University.

RUBBER BOWL

The Rubber Bowl in Akron, Ohio, was the venue where the Browns played their first preseason game on August 30, 1946, a 35-20 victory over the Brooklyn Dodgers.

RUBIN, AHTYBA

Ahtyba Rubin was a Browns nose tackle from 2008-14. Rubin was a sixth-round draft pick of the Browns in 2008 out of Iowa State University. He was second on the Browns in 2011 with five sacks.

RUCKER, FROSTEE

Frostee Rucker was a Cleveland defensive end in 2012. A product of the University of Southern California, he signed with the Browns on March 14, 2012. He had four sacks that season.

RUCKER, REGGIE

Reggie Rucker was a Browns wide receiver from 1975-81. A Boston University product, Rucker was acquired by the Browns on January 28, 1975, in a trade with New England for a fourth round draft choice that year. He was the

Reggie Rucker, 1978. Photo courtesy of the Cleveland Press Collection.

team leader in receptions from 1975-76 and in '78, receiving yards from 1975-78, and touchdown receptions in 1976 and '78. His 177 receiving yards in the Browns' 30-24 sudden-death victory over the Miami Dolphins on November 18, 1979, in Cleveland are tied for 10th in team history (#######). In that game, he caught a game-winning 39-yard touchdown pass from Brian Sipe 1:59 into overtime. He caught a 42-yard touchdown pass from Sipe for Cleveland's first score in its 27-24 AFC Central Division-clinching win in Cincinnati on December 21, 1980. Rucker caught 310 passes for 4,953 yards as a Brown, which rank eighth and seventh, respectively, in team history.

RUDD, DWAYNE

Dwayne Rudd was a Cleveland linebacker from 2001-02. He was a University of Alabama product acquired by the Browns on March 4, 2001, as a free agent. Unfortunately, Rudd is best known for his helmet-toss gaffe on September 8, 2002, against the Chiefs that cost the Browns a victory (*please see Helmet Toss, The*).

RUNNING BACKS

Notable Browns running backs have included Edgar Jones, Marion Motley, Bill Boedeker, Rex Bumgardner, Ken Carpenter, Harry Jagade, Billy Reynolds, Maurice Bassett, Fred Morrison, Ed Modzelewski, Preston Carpenter, Jim Brown, Bobby Mitchell, Ernie Green, Leroy Kelly, Bo Scott, Greg Pruitt, Cleo Miller, Mike Pruitt, Calvin Hill, Earnest Byner, Kevin Mack, Eric Metcalf, Leroy Hoard, William Green, Reuben Droughns, Jamal Lewis, Jerome Harrison, Peyton Hillis, Trent Richardson, Terrance West, and Isaiah Crowell.

RUSHING YARDS LEADERS

Please see Individual Statistics on page 225.

RUSSELL, BRIAN

Brian Russell was a Browns free safety from 2005-06. A product of San Diego State University, Russell was signed by the Browns as a free agent in 2005. He tied for the team lead in interceptions with three in 2005.

RUTIGLIANO, SAM

Sam Rutigliano was the Browns' head coach from 1978-84. Rutigliano led the Browns to some exciting times in the late 1970s and early '80s. His Kardiac Kids won several games in thrilling fashion during that period. Rutigliano's first of two playoff games as the Browns' head man ended with his team on the losing end of a thriller—a 14-12 AFC Divisional Playoff loss to the Oakland Raiders on January 4, 1981, in frigid Cleveland Stadium. Quarterback Brian Sipe was picked off in the end zone with less than a minute play. He was fired midway through the 1984 season the day after Cleveland's 12-9 last-second loss to the lowly Bengals in Cincinnati dropped the Browns' record to 1-7.

Rutigliano was voted AFC Coach of the Year from 1979-80 by UPI. His all-time record as the Browns' head coach was 47-50, 28-20 at home and 19-30 on the road. His all-time postseason record as Browns head coach was 0-2, 0-1 at home and 0-1 on the road.

RYAN, FRANK

Frank Ryan was a Browns quarterback from 1962-68. He was a Rice University product acquired by the Browns on July 12, 1962, as part of a five-player trade with the Los Angeles Rams. After sharing the signal-calling duties with Jim Ninowski in 1962, he completed 135 of 256 passes for 25 touchdowns and 13 interceptions in 1963 while directing the Browns to a 10-4 record and second-place finish in the Eastern Conference. In the season opener at home that year against the Redskins on September 15, Ryan connected with Jim Brown on an 83-yard pass play that went for a touchdown on the way to a 37-14 win. In 1964 he completed 174 of 334 passes for 2,404 yards, 25 touchdowns, and 19 interceptions as the Browns won the Eastern Conference with a 10-3-1 record. Three second-half TD passes to Gary Collins for 18, 42, and 51 yards led Cleveland to a 27-0 upset of Baltimore in the NFL Championship Game that year.

Ryan helped the Browns get off to a fine start the next year by completing an 80-yard touchdown pass to Walter Roberts in the season opener at Washington on September 19. He was instrumental in the team returning to the title game, but the Browns fell in the snow and sleet of Green Bay 23-12. He passed for team records (at the time) of 2,974 yards and 29 touchdowns in 1966 and had just 14 interceptions. He totaled 367 yards through the air on December 17 that year in a 38-10 rout of the St. Louis Cardinals. Ryan's 2,026 yards passing and 20 touchdown passes helped Cleveland to a 9-5 record and the Century Division Championship in 1967. The Browns were crushed, though, 52-14 in Dallas for the Eastern Conference title.

After arm problems surfaced, Ryan was replaced as the starter in favor of Bill Nelsen four games into the 1968 season. He ranks fifth all-time for the Browns in completions (907) and fourth in yards passing (13,361). His 35 completions and 534 passing yards in postseason play each rank fourth in team history. He was a Pro Bowl selection from 1964-66.

RYMKUS, LOU

Lou Rymkus was a Browns offensive tackle from 1946-51. He was a University of Notre Dame product acquired by Cleveland as a free agent. He was named to All-AAFC teams in 1946 by SP; in 1947 by C&O, NYN, OFF, and SP; in 1948 by AP, OFF, and UP; and in 1949 by UP. He was voted to the All-AAFC offensive team in 1949 by INS.

S

SABAN, LOU

Lou Saban was a Browns linebacker from 1946-49. An Indiana University product, Saban was acquired by the Browns as a free agent. His 39-yard interception return in the fourth quarter of the 1948 AAFC Championship Game against the Buffalo Bills was Cleveland's final touchdown in a 49-7 rout. He was voted to All-AAFC teams in 1948 by NYN and UP and in 1949 by AP, NYN, OFF, and UP. He was voted to the All-AAFC defensive team in 1949 by INS. He was a Browns television broadcaster in 1952.

SACKS LEADERS

Please see Individual Statistics on page 225.

SAN DIEGO CHARGERS

The San Diego Chargers were Browns opponents in the NFL from 1970-95 and have been since 1999. The Browns have some memorable win over the Chargers. Three came in San Diego—a 21-17 triumph on Monday night, November 13, 1972, on a 38-yard pass from Mike Phipps to Frank Pitts late in the game, a 30-24 overtime victory on September 25, 1983, when Brian Sipe hit Harry Holt on a 48-yard pass-and-run play, and 30-24 in overtime on October 20, 1991, on a 30-yard interception return by David Brandon. San Diego's all-time record Cleveland is 14-8-1, 6-4 at home and 8-4-1 on the road.

SAN FRANCISCO 49ERS

The San Francisco 49ers were opponents of the Browns in the AAFC from 1946-49 and the NFL from 1950-95 and have been since 1999. One memorable game between the Browns and 49ers was when the Browns upset eventual Super Bowl Champion San Francisco 15-12 on November 15, 1981, in Candlestick Park. Another memorable game was when the Browns upset the Niners again 23-13 on *Monday Night Football* on September 13, 1993, in Cleveland Stadium. Yet another eventful game between the two teams was on September 21, 2003, in 3Com Park when the Browns came back from a 12-0 deficit to win 13-12 on a touchdown pass from Kelly Holcomb to Andre Davis with just 29 seconds remaining.

The two teams have met once in the postseason—a 21-7 Browns victory in the 1949 AAFC Championship Game in Cleveland. San Francisco's all-time record against Cleveland is 9-17, 6-8 at home and 3-9 on the road. The 49ers' all-time record against Cleveland in the postseason is 0-1 (away game).

SANDUSKY, JOHN

John Sandusky was a Browns offensive tackle from 1950-55. He was a Browns second-round draft choice in 1950 from Villanova University.

SATURDAY AFTERNOON GAMES (REGULAR SEASON)

(Local starting times of earlier than 5 p.m.)
Cleveland 14, N.Y Giants 13 (Oct. 27, 1951, at Cle.)
Cleveland 13, San Francisco 10 (Dec. 15, 1962, at S.F.)
Cleveland 52, New York 20 (Dec. 12, 1964, at N.Y.)
Cleveland 38, St. Louis 10 (Dec. 17, 1966, at St.L.)
St. Louis 27, Cleveland 16 (Dec. 14, 1968, at St.L.)
Dallas 6, Cleveland 2 (Dec. 12, 1970, at Cle.)
Cleveland 27, Cincinnati 24 (Dec. 9, 1972, at Cin.)
Dallas 41, Cleveland 17 (Dec. 7, 1974, at Dal.)
N.Y. Jets 14, Cleveland 13 (Dec. 12, 1981, at Cle.)
Cleveland 19, Pittsburgh 13 (Dec. 26, 1987, at Pit.)
Cleveland 19, Dallas 14 (Dec. 10, 1994, at Dal.)
Cleveland 35, Seattle 9 (Dec. 24, 1994, at Cle.)
Minnesota 27, Cleveland 11 (Dec. 9, 1995, at Minn.)
Pittsburgh 41, Cleveland 0 (Dec. 24, 2005, at Cle.)
Baltimore 20, Cleveland 14 (Dec. 24, 2011, at Bal.)

Overall – 8-7 (.533)
Home – 2-3 (.400)
Away – 6-4 (.600)

SATURDAY NIGHT GAMES

(Local starting times of 5 p.m. or later)
Cleveland 7, New York 0 (Oct. 12, 1946, at N.Y.)
Cleveland 35, Philadelphia 10 (Sept. 16, 1950, at Phi.)
Cleveland 30, Pittsburgh 17 (Oct. 7, 1950, at Pit.)
Cleveland 21, Pittsburgh 20 (Oct. 4, 1952, at Pit.)
Cleveland 37, Philadelphia 13 (Oct. 10, 1953, at Cle.)
Cleveland 23, Pittsburgh 12 (Oct. 6, 1956, at Pit.)
Cleveland 23, Pittsburgh 12 (Oct. 5, 1957, at Pit.)
Pittsburgh 17, Cleveland 7 (Sept. 26, 1959, at Pit.)
Cleveland 35, Pittsburgh 23 (Oct. 5, 1963, at Cle.)
Pittsburgh 23, Cleveland 7 (Oct. 10, 1964, at Cle.)
Cleveland 24, Pittsburgh 19 (Oct. 9, 1965, at Cle.)
Cleveland 41, Pittsburgh 10 (Oct. 8, 1966, at Cle.)
Cleveland 21, Pittsburgh 10 (Oct. 7, 1967, at Cle.)
Cleveland 31, Pittsburgh 24 (Oct. 5, 1968, at Cle.)
Cleveland 42, Pittsburgh 31 (Oct. 18, 1969, at Cle.)
Cleveland 15, Pittsburgh 7 (Oct. 3, 1970, at Cle.)
Cleveland 24, Houston 20 (Dec. 23, 1989, at Hou.)

Overall – 15-2 (.882)
Home – 8-1 (.889)
Away – 7-1 (.875)

SATURDAY NIGHT GAMES VS.
THE PITTSBURGH STEELERS

(Local starting times of 5 p.m. or later)
Cleveland 30, Pittsburgh 17 (Oct. 7, 1950, at Pit.)
Cleveland 21, Pittsburgh 20 (Oct. 4, 1952, at Pit.)
Cleveland 23, Pittsburgh 12 (Oct. 6, 1956, at Pit.)
Cleveland 23, Pittsburgh 12 (Oct. 5, 1957, at Pit.)
Pittsburgh 17, Cleveland 7 (Sept. 26, 1959, at Pit.)
Cleveland 35, Pittsburgh 23 (Oct. 5, 1963, at Cle.)
Pittsburgh 23, Cleveland 7 (Oct. 10, 1964, at Cle.)
Cleveland 24, Pittsburgh 19 (Oct. 9, 1965, at Cle.)
Cleveland 41, Pittsburgh 10 (Oct. 8, 1966, at Cle.)
Cleveland 21, Pittsburgh 10 (Oct. 7, 1967, at Cle.)

Cleveland 31, Pittsburgh 24 (Oct. 5, 1968, at Cle.)
Cleveland 42, Pittsburgh 31 (Oct. 18, 1969, at Cle.)
Cleveland 15, Pittsburgh 7 (Oct. 3, 1970, at Cle.)

Overall – 11-2 (.846)
Home – 7-1 (.875)
Away – 4-1 (.800)

SCARRY, MIKE

Mike Scarry was a center for Cleveland from 1946-47. He was a Waynesburg College product acquired by the Browns as a free agent. He was named to All-AAFC teams in 1946 by NYN and in 1947 by C&O.

SCHAFRATH, DICK

Dick Schafrath was a Browns guard and offensive tackle from 1959-71. He was a second-round draft choice of Cleveland's in 1959 from Ohio State University. He was voted to All-NFL offensive teams in 1963 by AP and from 1964-65 by AP, NYN, and UPI. He was voted to the Pro Bowl from 1963-68.

SCHOTTENHEIMER, MARTY

Marty Schottenheimer was the Browns' head coach from 1984-88. He was promoted from his defensive coordinator duties for the team to head coach when the Browns were 1-7 in '84, replacing the fired Sam Rutigliano. He led the Browns to a 4-4 finish that year for a 5-11 final record. He led the team to AFC Central Division titles from 1985-87 and a wild card berth in 1988. The Browns lost heartbreaking AFC title games to Denver in 1986 and '87. Philosophical differences with Browns majority owner Art Modell led to Schottenheimer's resignation following the 1988 season.

Schottenheimer was named AFC Coach of the Year in 1986 by FWA and UPI. His all-time record as Browns head coach was 44-27, 23-12 at home and 21-15 on the road. His all-time postseason record as Browns head coach was 2-4, 2-2 at home and 0-2 on the road. He was a Browns assistant coach from 1980-84.

SCHWARTZ, MITCHELL

Mitchell Schwartz has been a Cleveland offensive tackle since 2012. He was a second-round draft pick of the Browns out of the University of California, Berkeley, in 2012.

SCORING LEADERS (POINTS)

Please see Individual Statistics on page 225.

SCOTT, BO

Bo Scott was a Browns running back from 1969-74. He was a Browns third-round draft choice in 1965 from Ohio State University despite having just one season—his sophomore year —under his belt. He played in the CFL from 1965-68. He was second on the Browns to Leroy Kelly every year from 1970-72 in rushing attempts and rushing yards. He was the team leader with seven rushing touchdowns in 1970 and second with nine in 1971 to Kelly's 10. Scott led the team in receptions with 40 in 1970 and tied Gary Collins for the team lead in TD catches that year with four. He was a kickoff returner in his rookie year of 1969 and led the Browns with 25 returns and 722 return yards. His 12 points in Cleveland's victory at Dallas in the Eastern Conference title game on December 28, 1969, are tied for fourth in Browns history.

SCOTT, CLARENCE

Clarence Scott was a Cleveland defensive back from 1971-83. A first-round draft choice by the Browns in 1971 from Kansas State University, Scott led the team with five interceptions in 1973 and four in 1981. He tied Charlie Hall for the team lead in picks in 1975. His 39 career interceptions rank third in team annals. He was named to the All-AFC defensive team by UPI and was a Pro Bowl selection in 1973.

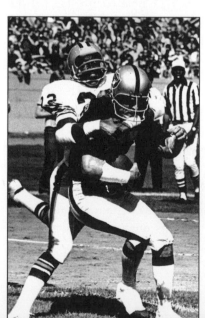

Clarence Scott grabs Oakland's Fred Biletnikoff as the Raiders' wide receiver scores on an 11-yard touchdown pass from Ken Stabler. The Browns lost 40-24 on October 6, 1974. Photo courtesy of the Cleveland Press Collection.

SEASON POINTS DIFFERENTIALS

FIVE BEST
1. +286 (423-137) (1946)
2. +225 (410-185) (1947)
3. +199 (389-190) (1948)
4. +186 (348-162) (1953)
5. +179 (331-152) (1951)

FIVE WORST
1. -258 (161-419) (2000)
2. -234 (228-462) (1990)
3. -220 (217-437) (1999)
4. -154 (218-372) (1975)
5. -130 (245-375) (2009)

SEATTLE SEAHAWKS

The Seattle Seahawks were Browns opponents in the NFL from 1976-95 and have been since 1999. The most memorable game between the Seahawks and Browns came on November 4, 2007, in Cleveland Browns Stadium when the Browns recovered from a 21-6 second-quarter deficit to win an overtime thriller 33-30. Seattle's all-time record against the Browns is 11-6, 7-3 at home and 4-3 on the road.

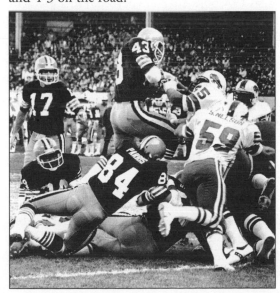

Mike Pruitt scores from a yard out in a 29-24 loss to Seattle in Cleveland Stadium on November 11, 1979.

SEPTEMBER

-6, 1946

The Browns defeated the Miami Seahawks 44-0 in Cleveland in the Browns' first game ever.

-16, 1950

Cleveland defeated Philadelphia 35-10 in Philadelphia in the NFL's Saturday-night season opener. The Browns were four-time defending AAFC Champions, and the NFL matched them up with the two-time defending NFL Champion Eagles right off the bat.

-21, 1970

The Browns defeated the New York Jets 31-21 in Cleveland in the first ABC *Monday Night Football* game. Cleveland's Homer Jones returned the second-half kickoff 94 yards for a touchdown. Browns linebacker Billy Andrews put the game away when he made a diving interception of a Joe Namath pass, got up and returned it 25 yards for a touchdown with 35 seconds left.

-24, 1979

The Browns shocked the Dallas Cowboys 26-7 in Cleveland in a battle of unbeatens on ABC *Monday Night Football.* The Browns scored 20 points in the first half of the first *quarter* before the Cowboys recorded a first down.

-3, 1984

The Browns were embarrassed by the Seattle Seahawks 33-0 in Seattle in the season opener played on a Monday afternoon due to a scheduling conflict the day before with Major League Baseball's Seattle Mariners, who were co-tenants of the Kingdome with the Seahawks.

-7, 1986

The NFL utilized its new instant replay method of officiating questionable referees' calls for the first time during the Browns-Bears game in Soldier Field in Chicago. On the third play of the game, Browns safety Al Gross appeared to recover an errant Chicago snap in the Bears' end zone. The debate was whether or not Gross gained possession of the ball before sliding across the end line. After a review, referees ruled that Gross did indeed gain possession of the ball in time for a touchdown. Gross's score gave Cleveland a 7-0 lead, but the defending Super Bowl Champion Bears went on to win a wild one 41-31.

-28, 1987

The Browns were to play the Denver Broncos at home on ABC *Monday Night Football*, but the game was cancelled due to the NFL players' strike. The game would have been a rematch of the Browns' AFC Championship-Game defeat to Denver some nine months earlier.

-10, 1989

The Browns bombed the Pittsburgh Steelers 51-0 in Pittsburgh in the season opener, while yielding just 53 total net yards, the fewest ever given up in one game by the Browns. Cleveland forced eight Steelers turnovers and had seven sacks. This was the Browns' fourth straight win in Three Rivers Stadium after 16 consecutive losses there from 1970-85.

-4, 1994

It didn't take long for the NFL's first two-point conversion to be scored in the first year of its use. Tom Tupa earned the honors against the Bengals in Cincinnati. As the holder on Matt Stover's apparent extra-point attempt following Leroy Hoard's 11-yard touchdown catch from Vinny Testaverde, Tupa ran over the left side to give the Browns an 11-0 first-quarter lead en route to a season-opening 28-20 triumph.

-8, 1998

The NFL awarded the city of Cleveland an expansion team called the "Browns" that, beginning with its first season in 1999, would continue the history—the uniform colors and statistics—of the original Browns, who relocated to Baltimore in 1996 and became the Ravens.

-12, 1999

The Browns experienced their worst home loss ever in a 43-0 defeat at the hands of the Pittsburgh Steelers. The game, the first in Cleveland Browns

Stadium, was the Browns' first game of the "new era" after three seasons of football-less autumns in Cleveland. Unfortunately for the Browns, the game was broadcast on national television.

-16, 2001

Because of terrorist activities against the United States five days before, the Browns game with the Steelers in Pittsburgh, along with the other NFL games that week, was cancelled and rescheduled for some four months later as the season finale. Originally, the Browns-Steelers game was scheduled as a nationally-televised Sunday night game on ESPN. But the game was switched to an early-afternoon game and was replaced on ESPN that night by the Eagles vs. Buccaneers contest. It was the first time in NFL history that games were canceled for reasons other than a players' strike.

-22, 2002

Tim Couch led the Browns back from 28-14 down in the fourth quarter to a 31-28 sudden-death win over the Titans at Tennessee. An eight-yard touchdown pass from Couch to Dennis Northcutt with 12 seconds left tied the game at 28. Phil Dawson's 33-yard field goal 4:13 into overtime won it.

-14, 2003

Jamal Lewis rushed for 295 yards and two touchdowns to lead the Ravens to a 33-13 triumph over the Browns in Baltimore. Three-and-a-half months later, Lewis rushed for 205 yards and two more TDs in a 35-0 Ravens rout of the Browns in Cleveland. In two games against the Browns in 2003, Lewis rushed for 500 yards and four touchdowns.

-16, 2007

The Browns defeated the Bengals 51-45 in Cleveland as the two teams totaled a staggering 1,085 total yards. The Browns' Derek Anderson was 20-for-33 for 328 yards with five touchdown passes and one interception. The Bengals' Carson Palmer was 33-of-50 for 401 yards with six touchdown passes and two interceptions. Jamal Lewis rushed for 216 yards, including a 66-yard TD run. The Bengals' Rudi Johnson rushed for 118 yards and scored the first touchdown of the game in the first quarter when he caught a 13-yard pass from Palmer.

-22, 2013

Brian Hoyer completed a seven-yard touchdown pass to Jordan Cameron with 51 seconds to go to give the Browns a 31-27 win over the Vikings in Minnesota.

SHAFFER, KEVIN

Kevin Shaffer was a Browns offensive tackle from 2006-08. A product of the University of Tulsa, he signed with the Browns as an unrestricted free agent on March 11, 2006.

SHANLEY, GIB

Gib Shanley was a Browns radio broadcaster from 1961-84.

SHEA, AARON

Aaron Shea was a Browns tight end from 2000-05. He was a fourth-round draft pick of the Browns in 2000 out of the University of Michigan. He tied for the team lead in touchdown receptions in his rookie year of 2000, and his four TD catches in 2004 tied for second.

SHEARD, JABAAL

Jabaal Sheard was a Cleveland defensive lineman and linebacker from 2011-14. He was a second-round draft pick of the Browns in 2011 out of the University of Pittsburgh. Sheard led the Browns in sacks in his rookie year of 2011 (8.5), 2012 (7), and 2013 (5.5). His 23 career sacks rank ninth in team history.

SHERK, JERRY

Jerry Sherk was a Browns defensive tackle from 1970-81. A second-round draft choice of the Browns in 1970 from Oklahoma State University, Sherk was voted NFL Defensive Player of the Year in 1976 by NEA. He was named to All-AFC defensive teams in 1975 by SN and in 1976 by AP, NEA, PFW, FWA, SN, and UPI. He was selected to play in the Pro Bowl from 1973-76.

SHOFNER, JIM

Jim Shofner was a Browns defensive back from 1958-63. He was a Browns first-round draft choice in 1958 from Texas Christian University. His eight interceptions in 1960 not only tied Bobby Franklin for the team lead but are also tied for eighth in team history.

As a coach in the Browns organization, Shofner was promoted from his offensive coordinator duties to head coach for the last seven games of the 1990 season after Bud Carson was fired. His all-time record as head coach of the Browns was 1-6, 1-3 at home and 0-3 on the road. He was a Browns assistant coach from 1978-80 and in 1990.

SHULA, DON

Don Shula was a Browns defensive back from 1951-52. He was a ninth-round draft choice of the Browns in 1951 from John Carroll University. He ranked third on the team in 1951 with four interceptions.

SHUTOUTS

For a list of Cleveland games in which either the Browns or the other team did not score, please see Team Statistics on page 248.

SIPE, BRIAN

Brian Sipe was a Browns quarterback from 1974-83. A 13th-round draft choice of the Browns in 1972 from San Diego State University, Sipe spent two seasons on the practice squad before making the regular roster in 1974. He filled in for the interception-prone Mike Phipps on occasion that season and was instrumental in three wins. One was a stirring comeback at home against Denver in which he scored twice—the second with 1:56 left—after relieving Phipps in the fourth quarter.

Sipe replaced Phipps once and for all when the Browns' 1970 first-round draft choice went down with a separated shoulder while the Browns were leading the New York Jets 21-10 early in the second half of the 1976 season opener. Sipe directed the Browns to a victory in that game and went on to complete 178 of 312 passes that year for 2,113 yards, 17 touchdowns and 14 interceptions, becoming the first Cleveland quarterback in seven years to throw for more TDs than picks. The Browns improved to 9-5 after 4-10 and 3-11 finishes the two previous seasons, respectively.

Sipe had the starting job all to himself when the 1977 season opened with Phipps's transfer to Chicago by way of an offseason trade. With the Browns in first place in the AFC Central Division at 5-3, Sipe suffered a separated left

Brian Sipe (left) and Sam Rutigliano during training camp in July 1981. Photo courtesy of the Cleveland Press Collection.

shoulder in a loss to the Steelers that caused him to miss the rest of the season. He had completed 112 of 195 passes for 1,233 yards and nine touchdowns but had thrown 14 interceptions that year. The last-place Browns finished 6-8.

In 1978 the arrival of new head coach Sam Rutigliano meant a more pass-oriented offense. Sipe passed for 2,906 yards on 222 completions out of 399 attempts, with 21 touchdown passes and 15 interceptions as the Browns improved to 8-8 in the tough AFC Central. He really started coming into his own in 1979 when he completed 286 of 535 attempts for 3,793 yards, 28 touchdown passes (tied with New England's Steve Grogan for the NFL high that year), and 26 interceptions. His feats helped lead the Browns to numerous down-to-the-wire victories and a 9-7 record as the Browns became known as the Kardiac Kids. A late-season letdown, though, left the Browns out of the playoffs for the seventh straight year.

Sipe passed for a team record 4,132 yards on 337 completions, another team record, in 554 attempts in 1980, becoming just the second quarterback in NFL annals to pass for 4,000 yards in one season. He had 30 touchdown passes (tied with San Diego's Dan Fouts for most in the AFC) and just 14 interceptions. He was the NFL's passing leader with a 91.4 rating. On October 19 of that year he passed for 391 yards in a 26-21 home win over Green Bay, a game in which he hit Dave Logan for a 46-yard touchdown pass with 16 seconds to go. Both Sipe and the Browns' magical season, another Kardiac Kids year, came to a crushing end when number 17 was intercepted in Oakland's end zone with less than a minute to play in a 14-12 divisional playoff loss to the Raiders in Cleveland Stadium.

Sipe completed 313 of 567 pass attempts for 3,876 yards in 1981. However, he threw for only 17 touchdowns and was picked off 25 times as the Browns fell to 5-11 and last place. He did have his moments, though, that year. He had 375 passing yards in a season-opening Monday-night loss to San Diego, and he had a team-record 444 yards through the air in a 42-28 home win over Baltimore on October 25. Rutigliano benched Sipe after six games in 1982 in favor of third-year lefty Paul McDonald, who finished out the strike-shortened season that ended with a losing record and first-round playoff elimination by the Raiders in Los Angeles. Sipe regained his starting job during the 1983 training camp and had a fine season, starting in all but two games. He completed 291 of 496 pass attempts for 3,566 yards, an AFC-high 26 touchdowns but also 23 interceptions as the Browns wound up 9-7 and barely missed the playoffs.

Sipe's 23,713 career passing yards and 1,944 career completions both are tops in Browns history. In 1980 Sipe was voted NFL Most Valuable Player by FWA and SN; NFL Player of the Year by AP; NFL Offensive Player of the Year by PFW; and AFC Most Valuable Player by UPI. He was voted to All-AFC offensive teams that year by AP, NEA, PFW, FWA, SN, and UPI, and was also voted to the Pro Bowl.

SIX TOUCHDOWNS IN ONE GAME

Wide receiver Dub Jones scored six touchdowns in one game on November 25, 1951, in the Browns' 42-21 victory over the Chicago Bears in Cleveland Municipal Stadium. He broke the team record of four, set by Dante Lavelli on October 14, 1949, when each of his scores came on receptions in a 61-14 rout of the Los Angeles Dons. Jones matched the NFL record set by Ernie Nevers, who totaled six touchdown catches and led the Chicago Cardinals to a 40-6 thumping of the crosstown Bears on Thanksgiving Day 1929. While Lavelli and Nevers scored their touchdowns on receptions alone, Jones tallied his in the air and on the ground, scoring four on runs and two on catches. Even more remarkable was that all six of his touchdowns came in the final three quarters. On top of all that, Jones scored the last six times he touched the ball.

SKORICH, NICK

Nick Skorich was the Browns' head coach from 1971-74. He led the Browns to 9-5 and 10-4 finishes in 1971 and '72, respectively. The '71 team won the AFC Central Division, and the '72 team qualified for the playoffs as the AFC's wild card entrant. Both years, the Browns were ousted in the divisional playoffs. Until Eric Mangini in 2009, Skorich was the only Browns head coach ever who had prior NFL head-coaching experience (with the Philadelphia Eagles from 1961-63). His all-time record as the Browns' head coach was 30-24-2, 16-11-1 at home and 14-13-1 on the road. His all-time postseason record as Cleveland's head coach was 0-2, 0-1 at home and 0-1 on the road. He was a Browns assistant coach from 1964-70.

SKRINE, BUSTER

Buster Skrine has been a Browns defensive back since 2011. He was a fifth-round draft choice of the Browns in 2011 out of the University of Tennessee at Chattanooga. Skrine was second on the Browns with four interceptions in 2014.

SLAUGHTER, WEBSTER

Webster Slaughter was a Browns wide receiver from 1986-91. He was a second-round draft choice of the Browns in 1986 from San Diego State University. He had 47 receptions for a Browns-leading 806 yards in 1987. He also led the team with seven touchdown catches that year. He had a career year in 1989, with a team-leading 65 receptions, 1,236 receiving yards (third in team history), and a team-leading six touchdown catches. He totaled 186 and 184 receiving yards in consecutive weeks that year—on October 23 against the Bears and on October 29 against the Oilers, both in Cleveland. His 186-yard performance ranks sixth in Browns history, and his 184-yard performance ranks seventh (#######). In the '89 Bears game, which was on *Monday Night Football,* Slaughter was on the receiving end of a 97-yard pass play from Bernie Kosar that went for a touchdown, the second-longest pass play in team history. His 59 receptions, 847 receiving yards, and four touchdown catches led the Browns in 1990. His 64 receptions and 906 receiving yards led the Browns in 1991.

Slaughter's 305 receptions rank ninth in team history and his 4,834 receiving yards rank eighth. His 30 career points in the postseason are tied for fifth in team annals. He totaled 381 postseason receiving yards with the Browns, which rank third all-time in Browns history (##). He is tied for fourth for most points scored in a postseason game with 12, and he did it twice—against Houston in the 1988 AFC Wild Card Game and Buffalo in a 1989 AFC Divisional Playoff affair. He was voted to the All-AFC offensive team by UPI in 1989 and was also picked to play in the Pro Bowl that year.

SMITH, AKILI

Akili Smith was a Cincinnati Bengals quarterback from 1999-2002. He was nearly selected by the Browns with the number one overall pick in the 1999 NFL Draft from the University of Oregon. Instead, the Browns chose University of Kentucky quarterback Tim Couch. The rivalry between Smith and Couch—Smith believed he should have been the Browns' selection—was the only thing needed to re-energize the rivalry between the Browns and Bengals upon Cleveland's return to the NFL in 1999. Intense feelings came to a boil on October 10 of that year in Cleveland Browns Stadium. Smith's two-yard touchdown pass to Carl Pickens with five seconds to go lifted Cincinnati to an 18-17 victory. After the game, Smith visibly taunted Browns fans that he claimed had been overly uncouth verbally to him all afternoon. He finished the day with 25 completions in 41 pass attempts for 221 yards and two touchdowns. Couch, meanwhile, was 15 of 27 for 164 yards and an interception. Smith led the Bengals to a 44-28 victory over the Browns in Cincinnati in the rematch on December 12 that year.

Smith was outplayed by Couch in a 24-7 loss to the Browns on September 10, 2000, in Cincinnati, completing just 15 of 43 passes for a touchdown and pair of interceptions. He quarterbacked the Bengals to a 12-3 win in Cleveland on October 29 that year. Smith was benched in favor of Jon Kitna before the 2001 season began and barely played against the Browns that year, attempting just two passes in the second meeting that year between the teams in Cleveland on November 25.

SMITH, JIM RAY

Jim Ray Smith was a Browns guard from 1956-62. He was a sixth-round draft choice of Cleveland's in 1954 from Baylor University with one year of eligibility left in school. He spent the 1955 season and the first half of the 1956 campaign in the military. He was voted to All-NFL offensive teams in 1959 and '60 by AP, NYN, NEA, and UPI; in 1961 by AP, NYN, NEA, PFI, and UPI; and in 1962 by NEA. He was voted to the Pro Bowl from 1958-62.

SMITH, ROBAIRE

Robaire Smith was a Browns defensive end from 2007-10. A product of Michigan State University, he signed with Cleveland as a free agent on March 16, 2007. Smith tied for the team lead with four sacks in 2007.

SMITH, SHAUN

Shaun Smith was a Cleveland defensive lineman from 2007-08. A product of the University of South Carolina, he signed with the Browns as a restricted free agent on March 16, 2007.

SMITH, TERRELLE

Terrelle Smith was a Browns fullback from 2004-06. A product of Arizona State University, he signed with Cleveland as an unrestricted free agent on March 11, 2004, and was mainly a blocking back.

SONGS

Two of the more popular songs written about the Browns are "Dawg Fever" sung by Greg Barnhill and "Somebody Let the Dawgs Out" sung by Kim Carnes.

SORENSEN, NICK

Nick Sorensen was a Browns defensive back from 2007-10. A product of Virginia Tech University, he signed with the Browns on October 24, 2007.

SPEEDIE, MAC

Mac Speedie was a Browns wide receiver from 1946-52. He was a University of Utah product acquired by the Browns as a free agent. He led Cleveland in receptions in 1947 (67), '48 (58), '49 (62), '50 (42), and '52 (62). His total receptions in 1947 rank fifth all-time for the Browns. He was the team leader in receiving yards in 1947 (1,146), '48 (816), '49 (1,028), '51 (589), and '52 (911). His 1947 and '49 totals rank fourth and eighth in team history. His 5,602 receiving yards and 349 receptions each rank third in Browns annals.

Speedie was on the receiving end of several long touchdown strikes from Otto Graham, including a 78-yarder on November 3, 1946, against the Los Angeles Dons; a 70-yarder on September 26, 1947, against the Chicago Rockets; and a 99-yarder that is tied for the longest pass play in Browns history on November 2, 1947, against the Buffalo Bills. He also caught an 82-yard strike from Graham on November 23, 1947, against the New York Yankees. Speedie's 228 receiving yards at Brooklyn-New York on November 20, 1949, are the most ever in one game by a Browns player (#######). His 27 postseason receptions are tied for second in Browns history (###). He is tied for second in team history for most receptions in a postseason game, as he totaled seven against Buffalo on December 4, 1949, and against Los Angeles on December 23, 1951 (#####).

Speedie was voted to All-AAFC teams in 1946 by NYN and UP; in 1947 by AP, C&O, NYN, OFF, and SP; in 1948 by AP, NYN, OFF, SN, and UP; and in 1949 by AP, NYN, OFF, and UP. He was named to the All-AAFC offensive team by INS in 1949. He was voted to All-NFL teams in 1950 by NYN and UP and in 1952 by UP. He was voted to the Pro Bowl in 1950.

SPORTS ILLUSTRATED COVERS

Fourteen *Sports Illustrated* covers have featured the Browns. The following are the dates and names of those who appeared:

Oct. 8, 1956   Paul Brown, George Ratterman
Sept. 26, 1960 Jim Brown
Jan. 4, 1965   Frank Ryan
Sept. 27, 1965 Frank Ryan
Nov. 21, 1966 Ross Fichtner
Aug. 30, 1982 Tom Cousineau
Aug. 26, 1985 Bernie Kosar
Jan. 12, 1987   Ozzie Newsome
Aug. 29, 1988 Bernie Kosar
Dec. 4, 1995   Art Modell
April 19, 1999 Big Dawg, Tim Couch, Akili Smith (never played for the Browns)
Sept. 1, 1999   Jim Brown, Tim Couch (a special commemorative issue honoring the return of the Browns to the NFL after three seasons without NFL football in Cleveland)
Aug. 6, 2007   Jamal Lewis
May 19, 2014   Johnny Manziel

ST. LOUIS RAMS

The St. Louis Rams were opponents of the Browns in the NFL from 1950-95 and have been since 1999. The Rams were located in Los Angeles through 1994. One memorable Browns victory against the Rams came on October 26, 1987, when the host Browns—led by Felix Wright's two interceptions, one for a pick-six—defeated the Rams 30-17 in the first *Monday Night Football* game since a players' strike came to an end.

The Browns and Rams have met three times in postseason play—all NFL Championship Games. The Browns won 30-28 on December 24, 1950, in Cleveland on Lou Groza's 16-yard field goal with 28 seconds left. The Rams won 24-17 on December 23, 1951, in Los Angeles on a 73-yard pass play from Norm Van Brocklin to Tom Fears that broke a 17-17 fourth-quarter tie. The Browns won the rubber match 38-14 on December 26, 1955, in Los Angeles as Otto Graham passed for two touchdowns and ran for two more in his final game.

The Rams' all-time record against the Browns is 10-9, 5-4 at home and 5-5 on the road. Their all-time postseason record against Cleveland is 1-2, 1-1 at home and 0-1 on the road.

STANDING-ROOM-ONLY

Standing-room-only tickets for Browns home games were tickets that were sold for home games that allowed patrons to stand to watch games when no tickets were left. Standing-room-only tickets for Browns home games were sold from 1946 through the November 3, 1980, Monday night game against the Chicago Bears. Sales of them ceased due to safety concerns.

STEINBACH, ERIC

Eric Steinbach was a Browns guard from 2007-11. A product of the University of Iowa, he signed with Cleveland as a free agent on March 2, 2007.

STOKES, BARRY

Barry Stokes was a Browns offensive lineman from 2002-03. A product of Eastern Michigan University, he played both guard and tackle.

STOVER, MATT

Matt Stover was a Browns kicker from 1991-95. He was a Louisiana State University product acquired by the Browns on March 15, 1991, as a free agent. He ranks seventh in all-time Browns scoring with 480 points. His 113 points in 1995 and 110 in 1994 rank sixth and seventh, respectively, in team history. He failed on just two of 158 extra-point attempts as a Brown. Stover kicked four field goals of 50 yards or more—a 55-yarder in Houston on November 17, 1991, a 53-yarder in Houston on December 12, 1993, a 51-yarder at home against Pittsburgh on October 11, 1992, and a 50-yarder at home against Philadelphia on November 10, 1991.

STREAKS

The longest winning streak in Browns history occurred in 1948 when the team finished 14-0 for a perfect season. The longest losing streak occurred in 1975 when the club lost its first nine games of the season. *For more streaks, please see Team Statistics on page 248.*

STROCK, DON

Don Strock was a Browns quarterback in 1988. He was a Virginia Tech University product acquired by the Browns on September 11, 1988, due to injuries to Bernie Kosar and Gary Danielson. He engineered a memorable, season-ending 28-23 comeback victory over Houston in the snow after the Browns trailed 23-7. The win earned the team the AFC Wild Card Playoff berth. Strock became the fourth Browns' quarterback to go down in 1988 when he injured his right hand early in the second quarter while trying to recover his own fumble in a wild card loss to the Oilers that was a rematch from the week before.

SUGGS, LEE

Lee Suggs was a Browns running back from 2003-05. He was a fourth-round draft pick of the Browns in 2003 out of Virginia Tech University. He was second on the Browns in rushing touchdowns in his rookie year of 2003. He was the team leader in 2004 with 744 rushing yards and tied for the team lead in rushing touchdowns. That year he also had 20 receptions for 178 yards and a touchdown.

SUMNER, WALT

Walt Sumner was a Cleveland defensive back from 1969-74. He was a Browns seventh-round draft choice in 1969 from Florida State University. He ranked second on the Browns with four interceptions in both 1969 and '70. He was the team leader in picks in 1971 with five. He finished his Browns career with 15 interceptions. Sumner's most memorable pick was his 88-yard return of a Craig Morton pass for a touchdown in the fourth quarter of the 1969 Eastern Conference Championship Game against the Dallas Cowboys in the Cotton Bowl. Sumner's return set up a touchdown on the next play, which increased the Browns' lead to 38-7 en route to a 38-14 triumph.

SUNDAY NIGHT GAMES

(Local starting times of 5 p.m. or later)

Denver 24, Cleveland 14 (Sept. 16, 1984, at Cle.)
San Francisco 38, Cleveland 24 (Nov. 29, 1987, at S.F.)
Houston 28, Cleveland 24 (Nov. 17, 1991, at Hou.)
Pittsburgh 43, Cleveland 0 (Sept. 12, 1999, at Cle.)
Baltimore 26, Cleveland 21 (Oct. 6, 2002, at Cle.)
Cleveland 33, Pittsburgh 13 (Oct. 5, 2003, at Pit.)
Baltimore 27, Cleveland 13 (Nov. 7, 2004, at Bal.)
Miami 10, Cleveland 7 (Dec. 26, 2004, at Mia.)
Pittsburgh 34, Cleveland 21 (Nov. 13, 2005, at Pit.)
Pittsburgh 10, Cleveland 6 (Sept. 14, 2008, at Cle.)

Overall – 1-9 (.100)
Home – 0-4 (.000)
Away – 1-5 (.000)

T

TAMPA BAY BUCCANEERS

The Tampa Bay Buccaneers were Browns opponents in the NFL from 1976-95 and have been since 1999. Their all-time record against Cleveland is 3-6, 2-3 at home and 1-3 on the road.

TANNEHILL, RAY

Ray Tannehill was a Browns radio broadcaster in 1962.

TAYLOR, BEN

Ben Taylor was a Browns linebacker from 2002-05. He was a fourth-round draft pick of Cleveland's in 2002 from Virginia Tech University.

TAYLOR, PHIL

Phil Taylor has been a Cleveland offensive lineman since 2011. He was a first-round draft choice by the Browns in 2011 out of Baylor University. He had four sacks in his rookie year of 2011.

TEAM TOP FIVES

For team top five statistics, please see Team Statistics on page 248.

TENNESSEE TITANS

The Tennessee Titans were Browns opponents in the NFL from 1970-95 and have been since 1999. They relocated from Houston, where they were known as the Oilers, in 1997. They were re-named "Titans" in 1999. The series was dominated by the Browns early on as Cleveland won the first nine meetings. The Titans took 10 of the next 15 games before dropping 12 of the next 15. Then they won 13 of the next 18 encounters.

One of the more memorable games between the two teams was on November 30, 1980, when the Browns upset the Oilers 17-14 in Houston in a battle for the AFC Central Division lead. Another memorable game between the two clubs was when the Browns defeated the Oilers, again in Houston, 24-20 in a season-ending battle for the AFC Central title. The teams have met once in postseason play with the Browns falling 24-23 in the AFC Wild Card Game on Christmas Eve 1988 in Cleveland.

Tennessee's all-time record against the Browns is 28-34, 13-19 at home and 15-15 on the road. The Titans' all-time postseason mark against Cleveland is 1-0 (away game).

TESTAVERDE, VINNY

Vinny Testaverde was a Browns quarterback from 1993-95. A University of Miami product who won the 1987 Heisman Trophy, Testaverde was obtained by the Browns on March 31, 1993, as a free agent. He was in the middle of a month-long quarterback controversy with Browns icon Bernie Kosar early in the 1993 season when he came off the bench to replace his ex-college teammate and lead the Browns' remarkable, last-second comeback victory over the Raiders in Los Angeles on September 19 to give Cleveland its first 3-0 start in fourteen years. His first start as a Brown was three weeks later against the Bengals in Cincinnati when he passed for three touchdowns in a 28-17 victory. He suffered a separated shoulder late in a home game against Pittsburgh a week later that sidelined him until December 5. That is when, with Kosar having been released and Todd Philcox not cutting the mustard, Testaverde returned in the second quarter of a home game against New Orleans. He helped the Browns to a 17-13 win that snapped a four-game losing streak and preserved Cleveland's postseason hopes, at least for another week or two.

In the second-to-last week of the '93 season, Testaverde completed 21 of 23 passes for a 91.3 percent completions rate in the Browns' 42-14 rout of the Los Angeles Rams in L.A. His performance set an NFL record at the time for the highest completion percentage by a quarterback with at least 20 attempts in one game. Incredibly, both of his incompletions were intentional! Although the Browns failed to qualify for the playoffs, he enjoyed a fine season despite a tumultuous first half. He wound up with 130 completions in 230 attempts for 1,797 yards, 14 touchdowns, and nine interceptions. Testaverde led the Browns to their first playoff berth in five years the next season, completing 207 of 376 passes for 2,575 yards and 16 touchdowns, but also 18 interceptions. Mark Rypien relieved him for a few games due to a recurring concussion. On

September 18 of that year, Testaverde hooked up with Derrick Alexander for an 81-yard pass play that went for a touchdown in a 32-0 rout of the Arizona Cardinals in Cleveland Stadium. He completed 20 of 30 passes for 268 yards and a touchdown in the Browns' 20-13 triumph over New England in an AFC Wild Card Game on New Year's Day 1995.

Testaverde completed 241 of 392 passes for 2,883 yards, 17 touchdowns, and 10 interceptions in 1995. He was replaced by rookie Eric Zeier as the starter for the Browns' October 29 game in Cincinnati even though he was leading the AFC in passing. Head coach Bill Belichick thought the change would give the team, which had lost three straight, a spark. Zeier led the Browns to an exciting overtime win with a strong performance, but he tailed off after that and gave way to Testaverde three weeks later during a loss to the Green Bay Packers.

Testaverde ranks ninth in Browns career passing yards (7,255) and 10th in career completions (578). His 33 career postseason completions rank fifth in team annals.

THANKSGIVING DAY GAMES

Cleveland 27, Los Angeles 17 (Nov. 27, 1947, at L.A.)
Cleveland 31, Los Angeles 14 (Nov. 25, 1948, at L.A.)
Cleveland 14, Chicago 6 (Nov. 24, 1949, at Chi.)
Dallas 26, Cleveland 14 (Nov. 24, 1966, at Dal.)
Dallas 31, Cleveland 14 (Nov. 25, 1982, at Dal.)
Detroit 13, Cleveland 10 (Nov. 23, 1989, at Det.)

Overall – 3-3 (.600) (Away games)

THOMAS, JOE

Joe Thomas has been a Browns offensive tackle since 2007. He was a first-round draft pick—the third pick overall—of Cleveland's in 2007 out of the University of Wisconsin. Thomas has been First-Team All-Pro five times, from 2009-11 and '13-14. He has been a Pro Bowler in each of his eight seasons.

THOMPSON, CHAUN

Chaun Thompson was a Browns linebacker from 2003-07. He was a second-round draft pick of the team in 2003 out of West Texas A&M University. Thompson tied for the team lead with five sacks in 2005.

THOMPSON, TOMMY

Tommy Thompson was a Browns linebacker from 1949-53. He was a seventh-round draft choice of the Browns in 1948 from the College of William & Mary with one year of school eligibility remaining. He was voted to All-NFL defensive teams in 1953 by AP and UP.

THREE RIVERS JINX

The Three Rivers Jinx was the nickname attributed to Cleveland's 16-game losing streak in Pittsburgh's Three Rivers Stadium from 1970-85. The heart of the streak occurred from 1977-81 when the games hinged on thrilling finishes, suspect officiating calls and, as usual, hard hits. The Steelers won those five games by an average of only 4.4 points per contest (35-31, 15-9 [OT], 33-30 [OT], 16-13, 13-7, respectively).

The Browns resorted to extreme measures in trying to halt the Jinx. They traveled by plane, by bus, and by car. They even changed hotels several times. Nothing worked until October 5, 1986, when Gerald McNeil's 100-yard kickoff return for a touchdown sparked the Browns' 27-24 triumph. It was the start of four straight wins for Cleveland in what had been their own personal house of horrors. The following are the 16 games that comprised the Three Rivers Jinx:

Pittsburgh 28, Cleveland 9 (Nov. 29, 1970)
Pittsburgh 26, Cleveland 9 (Nov. 7, 1971)
Pittsburgh 30, Cleveland 0 (Dec. 3, 1972)
Pittsburgh 33, Cleveland 6 (Sept. 23, 1973)
Pittsburgh 20, Cleveland 16 (Oct. 20, 1974)
Pittsburgh 31, Cleveland 17 (Dec. 7, 1975)
Pittsburgh 31, Cleveland 14 (Sept. 19, 1976)
Pittsburgh 35, Cleveland 31 (Nov. 13, 1977)
Pittsburgh 15, Cleveland 9 (OT) (Sept. 24, 1978)
Pittsburgh 33, Cleveland 30 (OT) (Nov. 25, 1979)
Pittsburgh 16, Cleveland 13 (Nov. 16, 1980)
Pittsburgh 13, Cleveland 7 (Oct. 11, 1981)
Pittsburgh 37, Cleveland 21 (Jan. 2, 1983)
Pittsburgh 44, Cleveland 17 (Oct. 16, 1983)
Pittsburgh 23, Cleveland 20 (Dec. 9, 1984)
Pittsburgh 10, Cleveland 9 (Nov. 3, 1985)

THREE-THOUSAND-YARD PASSERS

For team top five statistics, please see Individual Statistics on page 225.

THURSDAY NIGHT GAMES

(Not including Thanksgiving Day games)
(Local starting times of 5 p.m. or later)

Houston 17, Cleveland 13 (Dec. 3, 1981, at Hou.)
Cleveland 17, Cincinnati 7 (Sept. 15, 1983, at Cle.)
Cincinnati 30, Cleveland 13 (Sept. 18, 1986, at Cle.)
Cleveland 11, Houston 8 (Oct. 13, 1994, at Hou.)
Pittsburgh 27, Cleveland 7 (Dec. 7, 2006, at Pit.)
Denver 34, Cleveland 30 (Nov. 6, 2008, at Cle.)
Cleveland 13, Pittsburgh 6 (Dec. 10, 2009, at Cle.)
Pittsburgh 14, Cleveland 3 (Dec. 12, 2011, at Pit.)
Baltimore 23, Cleveland 16 (Sept. 27, 2012, at Bal.)
Cleveland 37, Buffalo 24 (Oct. 3, 2013, at Cle.)
Cleveland 24, Cincinnati 3 (Nov. 6, 2014, at Cin.)

Overall – 5-6 (.400)
Home – 3-2 (.600)
Away – 2-4 (.333)

TIES

New York 28, Cleveland 28 (Nov. 23, 1947, at N.Y.)
Buffalo 28, Cleveland 28 (Sept. 5, 1949, at Buf.)
Cleveland 7, Buffalo 7 (Nov. 13, 1949, at Cle.)
New York 35, Cleveland 35 (Nov. 27, 1955, at N.Y.)
Washington 30, Cleveland 30 (Nov. 17, 1957, at Was.)
St. Louis 17, Cleveland 17 (Nov. 27, 1960, at St.L.)
New York 7, Cleveland 7 (Dec. 17, 1961, at N.Y.)
Cleveland 14, Philadelphia 14 (Nov. 4, 1962, at Cle.)
Cleveland 33, St. Louis 33 (Sept. 20, 1964, at Cle.)
Cleveland 21, St. Louis 21 (Oct. 26, 1969, at Cle.)
Cleveland 16, San Diego 16 (Oct. 28, 1973, at Cle.)
Kansas City 20, Cleveland 20 (Dec. 2, 1973, at K.C.)
Cleveland 10, Kansas City 10 (OT) (Nov. 19, 1989, at Cle.)

TIGHT ENDS

Notable Browns tight ends include Johnny Brewer, Milt Morin, Gary Parris, Oscar Roan, Ozzie Newsome, Steve Heiden, Kellen Winslow, Ben Watson, Even Moore, and Jordan Cameron.

TRADES

The following are seven notable Browns trades:

April 29, 1952

The Browns traded three players to the Green Bay Packers for linebacker Walt Michaels, who originally was a seventh-round draft choice of the Browns in 1951 but was traded to the Packers on August 20 of that year.

January 26, 1970

The Browns traded wide receiver Paul Warfield to the Miami Dolphins for a first-round draft pick in the next day's draft in order to select Purdue University quarterback Mike Phipps.

September 1, 1980

Cleveland traded a second-round draft choice in 1981 and a third-round pick in '82 to the Buffalo Bills for guard Joe DeLamielleure.

April 28, 1982

The Browns traded defensive end Lyle Alzado to the Los Angeles Raiders for a draft choice that year.

April 28, 1982

The Browns traded running back Greg Pruitt to the Los Angeles Raiders for a draft choice in 1983.

September 11, 2007

Cleveland traded quarterback Charlie Frye to the Seattle Seahawks for a 2008 sixth-round draft choice two days after Frye had been the Browns' starting quarterback in the season opener.

September 19, 2013

The Browns traded running back Trent Richardson to the Indianapolis Colts for a first-round draft pick in 2014. The deal sent shockwaves throughout Northeast Ohio, considering the Browns had traded up in 2012 to select Richardson with the third overall pick that year.

TRAINING CAMP

Browns training camps have been held at the following venues in Ohio:

Bowling Green State University	1946-51
Hiram College	1952-74
Kent State University	1975-81
Lakeland Community College	1982-91
Cleveland Browns Training and Administrative Complex (Berea)	1992-95, since 1999

TUCKER, RYAN

Ryan Tucker was a Browns offensive lineman from 2002-08. A product of Texas Christian University, he was acquired by Cleveland as an unrestricted free agent on March 7, 2002.

TUESDAY NIGHT GAMES

Cleveland 34, Miami 0 (Dec. 3, 1946, at Mia.)
Cleveland 14, Baltimore 10 (Oct. 5, 1948, at Bal.)
Overall – 2-0 (1.000) (away games)

TUPA, TOM

Tom Tupa was a Browns punter from 1993-95. He was an Ohio State University product obtained by Cleveland off waivers on November 10, 1993. He was waived on November 24, 1993, and then re-signed on March 24, 1994. Tupa has the distinction of scoring the NFL's first-ever two-point conversion in the Browns' season-opening 28-20 win over the Bengals on September 4, 1994, in Cincinnati.

TURNER, ERIC

Eric Turner was a Browns safety from 1991-95. A first-round draft choice of Cleveland's in 1991 from UCLA, Turner had a 42-yard interception return off Jim McMahon for a touchdown on November 10, 1991, at home against Philadelphia. His five interceptions in 1993 led the Browns. His nine picks in 1994 not only topped the team and are tied for fourth in Browns annals, they also tied for the league lead that year. One was a 93-yard return for a touchdown in a 32-0 rout of the Cardinals at home on September 18. Turner intercepted 17 passes all-time for Cleveland. He was voted to All-AFC defensive teams by AP, PFW, and UPI and was named to the Pro Bowl in 1994.

TWELVE DAYS OF A CLEVELAND BROWNS CHRISTMAS, THE

"The Twelve Days of a Cleveland Browns Christmas" was a popular song on Cleveland-area radio airwaves in late December 1980 and early January 1981. It honored the Browns' first AFC Central Division title in nine years and first playoff berth in eight years.

TWO ONE-THOUSAND-YARD RUSHERS IN ONE SEASON

The 1985 Browns became the third team in NFL history to have two players gain at least 1,000 yards rushing in one season when Kevin Mack and Earnest Byner did it. Mack totaled 1,104 yards, Byner 1,002. The two previous teams to accomplish the feat were the 1972 Miami Dolphins (Larry Csonka, Mercury Morris) and the 1976 Pittsburgh Steelers (Franco Harris, Rocky Bleier).

U

ULINSKI, ED

Ed Ulinski was a Browns guard from 1946-49. He was a Marshall University product obtained by the Browns as a free agent. Ulinski was a Browns assistant coach from 1954-70.

UPSHAW, MARVIN

Marvin Upshaw was a Browns defensive lineman from 1968-69. Upshaw was a first-round draft pick of the Browns in 1968 out of Trinity University.

UNITED STATES FOOTBALL LEAGUE

The United States Football League existed from 1983-86. Only three seasons were played, however (1983-85). The seasons were held mainly during the spring and summer. The USFL competed with the NFL for college players and lured several, including three consecutive Heisman Trophy winners from 1983-85 and future Browns stars Kevin Mack, Gerald McNeil, and Frank Minnifield.

Prior to the 1985 season, the USFL, experiencing severe financial problems, sued the NFL and commissioner Pete Rozelle for violation of the Sherman Antitrust Act, seeking actual damages of $567 million that, when trebled, would amount to more than $1.7 billion. The league also announced that it would switch to a fall season in 1986 to compete head-to-head with the NFL. At the end of the 48-day trial on July 29, 1986, a United States District Court jury found the NFL liable on one of nine antitrust charges, assessing just $1 in actual damages, though, $3 when trebled. The USFL's own mismanagement was cause of its financial problems, according to the jury. More than $160 million in debt, the USFL folded on August 4, 1986.

V

VERBA, ROSS

Ross Verba was a Browns offensive lineman from 2001-02 and in '04. He is a product of the University of Iowa.

VICKERS, LAWRENCE

Lawrence Vickers was a Browns fullback from 2006-10. He was a sixth-round draft pick by the Browns in 2006 out of the University of Colorado. He was mainly a blocking back.

VS. DOMED-STADIUM TEAMS AT HOME

Please see Team Statistics on page 248.

VS. NFL CHAMPIONS (1950-69) AND SUPER BOWL CHAMPIONS (1970-95, SINCE 1999) OF SEASON AT HAND

Please see Team Statistics on page 248.

VS. PACIFIC TIME ZONE TEAMS AT HOME

Please see Team Statistics on page 248.

W

WAGNER, BRYAN

Bryan Wagner was a Browns punter from 1989-90. He was a California State University, Northridge product acquired by Cleveland as a free agent on March 30, 1989. His 3,817 punting yards in 1989 rank fifth in Browns history. He is fifth in Browns career postseason punting yards with 451. His 338 yards in the 1989 AFC Championship loss to Denver rank second for Cleveland all-time.

WAITERS, VAN

Van Waiters was a Browns linebacker from 1988-91. He was a third-round draft choice of Cleveland's in 1988 from Indiana University. His most memorable moment as a Brown actually came on special teams when he caught a game-winning 14-yard touchdown pass from Mike Pagel on a fake field goal that beat the visiting Vikings 23-17 in overtime in a crucial contest on December 17, 1989.

WALKER, NATE

Nate Walker is the Browns fan to whom the Browns' 1983 NFL Films highlights video is dedicated.

WARD, CARL

Carl Ward was a Browns defensive back from 1967-68. He was a Browns fourth-round draft pick in 1967 from the University of Michigan. He also returned punts and kickoffs, including a 104-yard kickoff return for a touchdown against the Redskins on November 26, 1967.

WARD, T.J.

T.J. Ward was a Browns strong safety from 2010-13. He was a second-round draft pick of the Browns in 2010 out of the University of Oregon.

He scored two touchdowns in 2013. The first was a memorable 44-yard interception return off Jeff Tuel for a touchdown that put the icing on the cake in a nationally-televised 37-24 victory over the Buffalo Bills on October 3 in a rocking FirstEnergy Stadium. The second was a 51-yard fumble return for a touchdown against the visiting Chicago Bears on December 15.

WARFIELD, PAUL

Paul Warfield was a wide receiver for the Browns from 1964-69 and '76-77. He was a first-round draft choice of the Browns in 1964 from Ohio State University. He was traded to the Miami Dolphins on January 26, 1970, for the Dolphins' first-round pick in the next day's draft. The Browns made the trade in order to draft Purdue University quarterback Mike Phipps. Warfield was reacquired in 1976 after five playoff seasons—including two Super Bowl Championships—with the Dolphins and one season in the WFL (that folded before the season was finished).

Warfield led the Browns in receptions (52), receiving yards (920), and touchdown receptions (nine) his rookie year. He was injured for most of the 1965 season. He had 36 catches for 741 yards and five touchdowns in 1966 and caught 32 balls for a team-leading 702 yards and eight touchdowns in 1967. He was the team leader in receptions (50), receiving yards (1,067), and touchdown catches (12) in 1968. His receiving yardage total that year ranks seventh in team history. He became the first Browns player since 1949 to accumulate 1,000 yards receiving in one season. Warfield caught 42 passes for a team-leading 886 yards and 10 touchdowns in 1969. Against the St. Louis Cardinals on December 14 that year, he was on the receiving end of an 82-yard pass play from Bill Nelsen that went for a touchdown. He averaged an incredible 20.7 yards per catch from 1964-69, a period in which the Browns appeared in four NFL title games. He caught 56 balls for 864 yards and eight touchdowns in 1976 and '77 combined.

Warfield's 5,210 career receiving yards rank sixth in Browns history. His 404 career postseason receiving yards rank second in team annals (##), and his 24 postseason receptions rank fifth (###). He had eight receptions in Dallas in the Eastern Conference Championship Game on December 28, 1969, the most in Browns history (#####). He won All-NFL offensive acclaim in 1964 by NEA, in 1968 by NEA, PFW, and UPI, and in 1969 by NEA, OFF, PFW, and SI. He was picked for the Pro Bowl in 1964 and from '68-69 and was enshrined into the Pro Football Hall of Fame in 1983.

WARREN, GERARD

Gerard Warren was a Browns defensive tackle from 2001-04. He was a first-round draft choice of the Browns in 2001 from the University of Florida. He had 16.5 career sacks.

WASHINGTON REDSKINS

The Washington Redskins were Browns opponents in the NFL from 1950-95 and have been since 1999. Their all-time record against Cleveland is 11-33-1, 4-16-1 at home and 7-17 on the road.

WATSON, BEN

Ben Watson was a Browns tight end from 2010-12. A product of the University of Georgia, Watson signed with Cleveland on March 12, 2010. His best year with the Browns was 2011 when he led the team with both 68 receptions and 763 receiving yards and tied for the team lead with three touchdown receptions.

WATTRICK, DON

Don Wattrick was a Browns television broadcaster in 1952.

WDOK-FM 102.1

WDOK-FM 102.1 was a Browns' co-flagship radio station from 1986-89 and '94-95.

WEEDEN, BRANDON

Brandon Weeden was a Browns quarterback from 2012-13. He was a first-round draft pick of the Browns in 2012 out of Oklahoma State University. In his rookie year of 2012 Weeden completed 297 of 517 passes for 3,385 yards, 14 touchdown passes, and 17 interceptions. In 2013 he shared the quarterbacking duties mainly with Jason Campbell and was 141-for-267 with nine TD passes and nine interceptions.

WERE-AM 1300

WERE-AM 1300 was the flagship radio station of the Browns from 1950-51 and '62-67.

WEST, TERRANCE

Terrance West has been a Browns running back since 2014. He was a third-round draft pick of the Browns in 2014 out of Towson University. West led the Browns with 673 rushing yards, and tied for second with four rushing touchdowns, in '14. He also had 11 receptions for 64 yards and a touchdown.

WEST COAST, ON THE

Please see Team Statistics on page 248.

WESTERN DIVISION

The Western Division was the home of the Browns from 1946-49. Cleveland won the division all four years with records of 12-2, 12-1-1, 14-0 and 9-1-2, respectively.

WGAR-AM 1220

WGAR-AM 1220 was the flagship radio station of the Browns from 1946-49, in '54, and from '56-61.

WHITE, CHARLES

Charles White was a Browns running back from 1980-82 and in 1984. He was a first-round draft choice by the Browns in 1980 from the University of Southern California where he won the 1979 Heisman Trophy. White missed the 1983 season due to a broken ankle suffered in the second preseason game at Buffalo. He was second behind Mike Pruitt in rushing yards in his first three seasons. He ranked second behind Pruitt with five rushing touchdowns in 1980 and tied him for the team lead in 1982 with three.

WHITE, JAMEL

Jamel White was a Cleveland running back from 2000-03. He was a product of the University of South Dakota acquired by the Browns via waivers on August 29, 2000. White was the team's leader with five rushing touchdowns in 2001 and was second with 443 rushing yards. He was also second on the club with 44 receptions that year. He posted a career-best 216 yards from scrimmage on 131 yards rushing—including a 51-yarder—and 85 yards receiving against Green Bay in Lambeau Field on December 23, 2001.

The 131 rushing yards were the most by a Brown in 14 years. He also led the Browns in kickoff returns (43) and kickoff return yards (935) in 2000.

WHITNER, DONTE

Donte Whitner has been a Cleveland strong safety since 2014. An Ohio State University product, he signed with the Browns on March 11, 2014. Whitner was a Pro Bowler in '14.

WHK - AM 1420

WHK-AM 1420 was the Browns' flagship radio station from 1968-85 and co-flagship radio station from 1990-93.

WIDE RECEIVERS

Notable wide receivers throughout Browns history include Dante Lavelli, Mac Speedie, Horace Gillom, Dub Jones, Darrell Brewster, Ray Renfro, Gary Collins, Paul Warfield, Fair Hooker, Frank Pitts, Reggie Rucker, Ricky Feacher, Dave Logan, Brian Brennan, Reggie Langhorne, Webster Slaughter, Michael Jackson, Mark Carrier, Derrick Alexander, Kevin Johnson, Quincy Morgan, Andre Davis, Dennis Northcutt, Antonio Bryant, Braylon Edwards, Joe Jurevicius, Mohamed Massaquoi, Josh Cribbs, Greg Little, Jordan Norwood, Travis Benjamin, Josh Gordon, Taylor Gabriel, Andrew Hawkins, and Miles Austin.

WIGGIN, PAUL

Paul Wiggin was a Browns defensive end from 1957-67. He was a sixth-round draft choice of the Browns in 1956 from Stanford University with one year of eligibility in school remaining. He was voted to the Pro Bowl in 1965 and '67.

WILD CARD GAMES

Houston 24, Cleveland 23 (AFC, Dec. 24, 1988, at Cle.)
Cleveland 20, New England 13 (AFC, Jan. 1, 1995, at Cle.)
Pittsburgh 36, Cleveland 33 (AFC, Jan. 5, 2003, at Pit.)

Overall – 1-2 (.333)
Home – 1-1 (.500)
Away – 0-1 (.000)

WILLIS, BILL

Bill Willis was a Cleveland guard and linebacker from 1946-53. A product of Ohio State University, he was acquired by the Browns as a free agent. He saved the day in the Browns' 8-3 victory over the New York Giants in an American Conference Playoff on December 17, 1950, in Cleveland when he tackled fullback Eugene Roberts from behind at the Browns' four-yard line late in the game. Willis was named to All-AAFC teams in 1946 by OFF and SP, in 1947 by OFF, and in 1948 by AP, NYN, OFF, and UP. He was voted to the All-NFL offensive team in 1950 by UP. He was voted to All-NFL defensive teams in 1950 by NYN, in 1951 by AP, NYN, and UP, in 1952 by AP and NYN, and in 1953 by AP. He was selected to play in the Pro Bowl from 1950-52 and was inducted into the Pro Football Hall of Fame in 1977.

WIMBLEY, KAMERION

Kamerion Wimbley was a Cleveland linebacker from 2006-09. He was a Browns 2006 first-round draft choice out of Florida State University. He led the team in sacks in 2006 (11), '07 (5), and '09 (6.5). He was second on the team in 2008 with four sacks. His '06 sacks total is tied for fifth in Browns history, and his 26.5 career sacks rank eighth.

WINN, BILLY

Billy Winn has been a Cleveland defensive lineman since 2012. He was a sixth round draft pick by the Browns in 2012 from Boise State University. He has intercepted two passes—one against Pittsburgh on November 25, 2012, and one against Carolina on December 21, 2014.

WINSLOW, KELLEN

Kellen Winslow was a Browns tight end in 2004 and from 2006-08. A first-round draft pick of the Browns in 2004 out of the University of Miami, Winslow missed most of his rookie season of 2004 due to a Week 2 leg injury. He missed the entire 2005 season due to another leg injury from an offseason motorcycle accident. He recovered nicely, though, for in 2006 he had a team-leading 89 receptions for 875 yards and three touchdowns. In 2007 Winslow caught a team-leading 82 balls for 1,106 yards and five TDs. His '06 receptions total is tied for first in Browns history, and his '07 total is sixth. His receiving yards total in 2006 ranks fifth in team annals. He tied for the team lead in touchdown receptions in 2008.

WJW-CHANNEL 8

WJW-Channel 8 was the television station that broadcast Browns road games from 1954-67.

WKNR-AM 850

WKNR-AM 850 has been a co-flagship radio station of the Browns since 2013.

WKNR-AM 1220

WKNR-AM 1220 was a co-flagship radio station of the Browns from 1994-95.

WKRK-FM 92.3

WKRK-FM 92.3 has been a co-flagship radio station of the browns since 2013.

WMJI-FM 105.7

WMJI-FM 105.7 was a Browns co-flagship radio station from 1999-2012.

WMMS-FM 100.7

WMMS-FM 100.7 was a co-flagship radio station of the Browns from 1990-93.

WNCX-FM 98.5

WNCX-FM 98.5 has been a co-flagship radio station of the Browns since 2013.

WOHLABAUGH, DAVE

Dave Wohlabaugh was a Browns center from 1999-2002. A product of Syracuse University, Wohlabaugh was obtained by the Browns on February 16, 1999, as a free agent.

WON-LOST-TIED RECORDS, POSTSEASON

Please see Team Statistics on page 248.

WOOTEN, JOHN

John Wooten was a Browns guard from 1959-67. He was a fifth-round draft choice of the Browns in 1959 from the University of Colorado. He was voted to the All-NFL offensive team in 1966 by NYN and was picked for the Pro Bowl from 1965-66.

WORD, MARK

Mark Word was a Browns defensive lineman from 2002-03. A product of Jacksonville State University, Word signed with Cleveland on July 20, 2001. He led the Browns with eight sacks in 2002. He had four sacks in 2003.

WRIGHT, ERIC

Eric Wright was a Browns cornerback from 2007-10. He was a second-round draft pick of Cleveland's in 2007 out of the University of Nevada, Las Vegas. He tied for the team lead with four interceptions in 2009.

WRIGHT, FELIX

Felix Wright was a safety for the Browns from 1985-90. A product of Drake University, Wright was acquired by Cleveland as a free agent on April 13, 1985. He tied Frank Minnifield for the team lead in interceptions in 1987 with four, including a pair returned for 68 and 40 yards, respectively, in the first half against the Los Angeles Rams on *Monday Night Football* on October 26, the second of which went for a touchdown. He led the Browns in picks in 1988 with five, '89 with nine, and '90 with three. His 1989 total led the NFL and is tied for fourth in Browns annals. His 26 career interceptions are tied for 10th in Browns history.

WRIGHT, JASON

Jason Wright was a Browns running back from 2005-08. A product of Northwestern University, he was signed by the Browns off waivers on September 13, 2005.

WRIGHT, KEITH

Keith Wright was a Cleveland punt and kickoff returner from 1978-80. Wright was a Browns fifth-round draft choice in 1978 from Memphis State

University. He led the team in kickoff return yards in 1978 and returned the opening kickoff 86 yards against the Chiefs in Kansas City on October 22 that year. His 1,767 career kickoff return yards rank eighth in team history. He led the team in punt returns and punt return yards in 1978 and '80. He also was a wide receiver on occasion and caught three passes—all for touchdowns—in 1980. He was voted to the All-AFC offensive team in 1978 by PFW.

WTAM-AM 1100

WTAM-AM 1100 was the Browns' flagship radio station from 1952-53 and in 1955 and co-flagship radio station from 1999-2012.

WWWE-AM 1100

WWWE-AM 1100 was a Browns co-flagship radio station from 1986-89.

WXEL-CHANNEL 9

WXEL-Channel 9 was the television station that broadcast Browns road games from 1952-53.

WYCHE, SAM

Sam Wyche was the Cincinnati Bengals' head coach from 1984-91 and the Tampa Bay Buccaneers' head coach from 1992-95. Many Browns fans disliked Wyche, especially during his tenure with the Bengals. One memorable incident that added to the animosity occurred during a Bengals-Seahawks game in Cincinnati on December 10, 1989. That is when, while boisterous fans hurled snowballs at Seattle players, the Bengals' coach grabbed the public address microphone and shouted, "You don't live in Cleveland, you live in Cincinnati!"

X

X-RAYS IN '88

Browns quarterbacks needed several x-rays in 1988 due to a seemingly never-ending series of injuries. It all started when Bernie Kosar was blindsided by Chiefs safety Lloyd Burruss early in the second quarter of Cleveland's 6-3 opening-day win in Kansas City. Kosar suffered strained ligaments in his right elbow and missed the next six games. Gary Danielson replaced Kosar, but the next week against the New York Jets at home he went down with a broken left ankle in the third quarter.

Danielson was replaced by Mike Pagel, who started the next four games before suffering a second-quarter shoulder separation on October 9 at home against Seattle while trying to make a tackle on a blocked field goal. Don Strock, who had signed with the Browns on September 11, took over and made his first start in five years the following week at home against Philadelphia, tossing a pair of touchdown passes en route to a 19-3 victory.

Kosar made his return the next week and completed 25 of 43 passes for 314 yards and three touchdowns in a 29-21 victory over the Phoenix Cardinals in the desert. Kosar started the next seven games before suffering strained ligaments in his left knee during a 38-31 loss in Miami on Monday night, December 12, leaving the game in the fourth quarter. Strock took over and performed brilliantly against his former team, completing seven of 10 passes for 70 yards, including two touchdown passes that tied the score at 31 with just 59 seconds left.

Strock started the next week in the season finale at home against Houston. In a do-or-die situation regarding the playoffs, the veteran rallied his troops from a 16-point third-quarter deficit to a dramatic 28-23 triumph, throwing two touchdown passes in a driving snowstorm. During the AFC Wild Card Game the next week in a rematch with the Oilers on Christmas Eve in Cleveland, Strock injured his right hand early in the second quarter while failing to recover his own fumble deep in Cleveland territory with the Browns trailing 7-3. The Oilers scored on the very next play, upping their lead to 14-3. Pagel came in and completed 17 of 25 passes for 179 yards and two touchdowns to rally the Browns, but they fell short 24-23.

Y

YONAKOR, JOHN

John Yonakor was a Browns defensive end from 1946-49. He was a product of the University of Notre Dame acquired by Cleveland as a free agent.

YOUNG, GEORGE

George Young was a Cleveland defensive end from 1946-53. He was a product of the University of Georgia acquired by the Browns as a free agent. He returned a fumble 47 yards for a touchdown in the Browns' 45-0 triumph over the Washington Redskins on October 14, 1951, in Cleveland Municipal Stadium.

YOUNG, GLEN

Glen Young was a Browns kickoff returner from 1984-85 and '87-88. He was a product of the University of Mississippi obtained by Cleveland as a free agent on November 14, 1984. He was waived in 1986 and was out of football that year. He was re-acquired as a free agent on March 9, 1987. Young was the Browns' leader in kickoff returns and kickoff return yards in 1985 and from '87-88. He led the AFC in 1985 when he averaged 25.7 yards per return on 35 attempts for 898 yards. His 2,079 career kickoff return yards rank fourth in team annals.

YOUNG, USAMA

Usama Young was a Cleveland safety from 2011-12. A product of Kent State University, he signed as a free agent with the Browns on July 28, 2011. Young tied for the team lead with three interceptions in 2012.

Z

ZASTUDIL, DAVE

Dave Zastudil was a Browns punter from 2006-09. A homegrown product of Bay Village High School, and Ohio University, he signed with Cleveland on March 12, 2006. His 3,563 punting yards in 2006 rank 10th in Browns history. His 11,207 career punting yards rank fifth in team annals.

ZEIER, ERIC

Eric Zeier was a Browns quarterback in 1995. He was a third-round draft choice of the Browns in 1995 from the University of Georgia. He saw limited playing time behind starter Vinny Testaverde but did start four games, including his first—and most impressive—performance on October 29 in Cincinnati when he completed 26 of 46 passes for 310 yards and led the Browns to a dramatic 29-26 overtime win.

ZUKAUSKAS, PAUL

Paul Zukauskas was a Browns offensive lineman from 2001-04. He was a Browns seventh-round draft pick in 2001 out of Boston College.

BROWNS
TRIVIA

FAST FACTS

Otto Graham was not the Browns' starting quarterback in their first game.

The Browns were shut out by the New York Giants 6-0 on October 1, 1950, but were not bageled again until a 27-0 loss to the Denver Broncos on October 24, 1971.

When Dub Jones broke a Browns record, and tied an NFL mark, by scoring six touchdowns on November 25, 1951, against the Bears, he crossed the goal line the last five times he touched the ball.

Harry Jagade rushed for 104 yards on 15 carries and scored the Browns' only touchdown on a short run in the third quarter in a loss to the Lions in the 1952 NFL title game. Remarkably, Jagade rushed for 104 yards on 15 carries and scored the Browns' only touchdown on a short run in the third quarter in a loss to the Lions in the 1953 NFL title game.

The Browns' majority owner in the eight seasons prior to Art Modell's reign was a gentleman by the name of Dave Jones.

Marion Motley once played for the Pittsburgh Steelers.

Jim Brown missed only one half of one game in his nine-year career.

The Browns tallied 30 or more points in seven consecutive weeks during the 1968 season.

The only season the attendance figure for every Browns home game was at least 80,000 was 1969.

The first ABC *Monday Night Football* game on September 21, 1970, between the Browns and New York Jets drew 85,703 fans, the largest regular season or postseason crowd—home or away—in Browns history.

Mike Phipps threw more than two interceptions for every touchdown in his days with the Browns.

Despite the popular belief that the 1970s were a disastrous decade, the Browns actually won at a .507 clip.

The point total was in the 20s in each of the Browns' 10 victories in 1972.

The Browns sent no players to the Pro Bowl in 1972 despite posting a 10-4 record and earning the AFC's wild card berth.

In between Leroy Kelly's 1966-72 reign and Greg Pruitt's 1974-78 reign as the Browns' season leader in rushing yards, a player by the name of Ken Brown was the leading ground gainer in 1973.

The only two Browns tie games since 1970—in 1973 and '89—were against the Chiefs, and both times the Browns entered play with seven wins and three defeats (though the 1973 team had a previous tie).

Forrest Gregg began his tenure as Browns head coach in 1975 0-9, and ended his tenure in 1977 1-5, but went 17-9 in between.

The Browns wore orange pants from 1975-83.

In an upset of the visiting Bengals on November 23, 1975, the Browns entered the game with an 0-9 record, while the Bengals came to town with an 8-1 mark.

Paul Warfield closed out his stellar career with a second stint with the Browns in 1976 and 1977.

The Browns began the 1976 season 1-0, the 1977 season 2-0, the 1978 season 3-0, and the 1979 season 4-0 yet failed to make the playoffs each year. However, when they began the 1980 season 0-2 they made the playoffs.

Even though they finished in last place in 1977, the Browns had the best road record in the AFC Central Division.

The average margin of defeat in the Browns' five losses in Three Rivers Stadium from 1977-81 was just 4.4 points.

The Browns once had three head coaches in a fifteen-day span—Forrest Gregg, Dick Modzelewski, and Sam Rutigliano from December 13-28, 1977.

In retrospect, the Browns would have qualified for the playoffs in 1979 had they beaten the Bengals on the final Sunday by at least 33 points (due to the complicated NFL tiebreaking formula).

When Brian Sipe passed for 4,132 yards in 1980, he became just the second quarterback in NFL history to throw for 4,000 yards in one season.

Brian Sipe won Player-of-the-Year and Most Valuable Player honors in 1980, was benched during the 1982 season, then came back to lead the AFC in touchdown passes in 1983.

The attendance figure of 83,224 at the Browns' Monday night triumph over the Bears on November 3, 1980, was the time the team drew at least 80,000 fans at a home game. This was the last Browns home game in which standing-room-only tickets were sold, due to safety concerns.

The Browns beat both Super Bowl teams—the Bengals and 49ers—in 1981, and on the road!

The Browns qualified for the playoffs in 1982 despite posting a losing record, becoming just the second team in NFL history to do so (the other team, the Lions, did so the same year finishing 4-5).

The Browns' experiment of using orange numbers on brown jerseys in a preseason home game with the Pittsburgh Steelers in 1984 was a bust, as it was extremely difficult for media personnel and fans to identify players due to the excessive blending of orange and brown.

The Browns' 1984 opener in Seattle was played on a Monday afternoon.

In retrospect, had the Browns hung on to upset the Dolphins in an AFC Divisional Playoff on January 4, 1986, in the Orange Bowl, they would have hosted the AFC Championship game the following week despite posting just an 8-8 record during the regular season.

The one Browns game in the strike-shortened 1987 season that was canceled was the one the entire city of Cleveland had hungered for since the schedule was published five months earlier—the home game against the Denver Broncos September 28 (the Broncos had beaten the Browns in the AFC Championship game ["The Drive" game] the previous January in the same venue).

In their 51-0 destruction of the Pittsburgh Steelers in the 1989 season opener, the Browns incredibly scored all of their points from 5:42 remaining in the first quarter to 11:34 left in the game.

In Cleveland's 37-21 defeat in Denver in the 1989 AFC title game, the Browns trailed by just three points entering the fourth quarter.

Travis Prentice is the only player to score all of Cleveland's rushing touchdowns in one season when he had seven in 2000.

Because of the September 11, 2001, terrorist attacks on the United States, the Browns' September 16 nationally-televised Sunday night game in Pittsburgh—and the christening of Heinz Field—was rescheduled for January

6, 2002, on the weekend the wild card games were supposed to have been played.

The Browns blew a 14-point lead with 28 seconds to go on November 4, 2001, in Chicago against the Bears. A 21-7 lead turned into a 27-21 defeat in overtime.

On September 22, 2002, Tim Couch brought the Browns back from a 28-14 fourth-quarter deficit to beat the Titans 31-28 at Tennessee. It was the second time in less than nine months that Couch led the Browns back from a 14-point, fourth-quarter deficit to beat the Titans on the road, for on December 30, 2001, he had brought the Browns back from 38-24 down to a 41-38 triumph.

The Browns were gashed for the appalling total of 500 yards on the ground by Baltimore's Jamal Lewis in the Ravens' two wins over the Browns in 2003. Lewis rushed for 295 yards in the Ravens' 33-13 victory on September 14 in Baltimore and ran for 205 in the Ravens' 35-0 rout on December 21 in Cleveland.

The 106 points scored in the Browns' 58-48 loss to the Bengals on November 28, 2004, are the second-most points ever scored in an NFL game.

The Browns scored just 31 points—and not one single offensive touchdown—in their final six games of the 2008 season.

Josh Cribbs returned two kickoffs for touchdowns in the Browns 41-34 victory over the Chiefs in Kansas City on December 27, 2009.

Jerome Harrison rushed for 561 (65 percent) of his team-leading 862 yards in the Browns' final three games of the 2009 season.

When the Browns upset the New Orleans Saints on October 24, 2010, it marked the third straight season that the Browns beat the defending Super Bowl champ. They beat the Pittsburgh Steelers in 2009 and the New York Giants in 2008.

Josh Gordon set an NFL record in 2013 for most receiving yards in a four-game stretch with 774 from November 17 to December 8. The Browns, though, lost all four games.

THE LAST TIME . . .

* Does not include 2014 season

The last time a Browns player rushed for 100 yards in a game was on October 5, 2014, when Ben Tate totaled 124 yards in a 29-28 win over the Titans in Tennessee.

. . . an opposing player of the Browns rushed for 100 yards in a game was on December 28, 2014, when the Ravens' Justin Forsett gained 119 yards in a 20-10 win over the Browns in Baltimore.

. . . a Browns player passed for 400 yards in a game was on November 28, 2004, when Kelly Holcomb totaled 413 yards in a 58-48 defeat to the Bengals in Cincinnati.

. . . an opposing player of the Browns passed for 400 yards in a game was on December 8, 2013, when the Patriots' Tom Brady totaled 418 yards in a 27-26 win over the Browns in New England.

. . . a Browns player was unsuccessful on an extra point attempt was on November 1, 2009, when Phil Dawson had one blocked in a 30-6 defeat to the Bears in Chicago.

. . . an opposing player of the Browns was unsuccessful on an extra point attempt was on September 27, 2012, when the Ravens' Justin Tucker's kick was aborted in a 23-16 victory over the Browns in Baltimore.

* . . . a Browns player blocked a field goal was on December 5, 2010, when Shaun Rogers blocked a 41-yard attempt by Dan Carpenter in a 13-10 victory over the Dolphins in Miami.

* . . . an opposing player of the Browns blocked a field goal was on September 29, 2013, when Cincinnati's Carlos Dunlap blocked Billy Cundiff's attempt in a 17-6 defeat to the Browns in Cleveland.

. . . a Cleveland player returned an interception for a touchdown was on December 7, 2014, when Justin Gilbert returned an Andrew Luck pass 23 yards in a 25-24 loss to the Colts in Cleveland.

. . . an opposing player of Cleveland's returned an interception for a touchdown was on December 15, 2013, when Chicago's Zack Bowman returned a Jason Campbell pass 43 yards in a 38-31 win over the Browns in Cleveland.

. . . a Browns player returned a fumble for a touchdown was on December 7, 2014, when Craig Robertson recovered an Andrew Luck fumble in the end zone in the Browns' 25-24 loss to the Colts in Cleveland.

. . . an opposing defensive player of the Browns returned a fumble for a touchdown was on November 30, 2014, when the Bills' Jerry Hughes returned a Terrance West fumble 18 yards in a 26-10 victory over the Browns in Buffalo.

* . . . a Browns player blocked a punt was on November 30, 2003, when the team blocked one by Tom Rouen in the Browns' 34-7 defeat to the Seahawks in Seattle.

* . . . an opposing player of the Browns blocked a punt was on November 17, 2013, when the Bengals' Jayson DiManche blocked one by Spencer Lanning in a 41-20 victory over the Browns in Cincinnati.

. . . a Browns player returned a punt for a touchdown was on October 3, 2013, when Travis Benjamin returned one by Shawn Powell 79 yards in a 37-24 victory over the Bills in Cleveland.

. . . an opposing player of the Browns returned a punt for a touchdown was on September 16, 2012, when the Bengals' Adam Jones returned one by Reggie Hodges 81 yards in a 34-27 victory over the Browns in Cincinnati.

. . . a Browns player returned a kickoff for a touchdown was on December 20, 2009, when Josh Cribbs returned one 103 yards in a 41-34 win over the Chiefs in Kansas City.

. . . an opposing player of the Browns returned a kickoff for a touchdown was on October 16, 2011, when the Raiders' Jacoby Ford returned one 101 yards in a 24-17 victory over the Browns in Oakland.

. . . a Browns player scored a safety was on November 22, 2009, when Tank Carder blocked a Brett Kerns punt out of the end zone in the Browns' 29-28 win over the Titans in Tennessee.

. . . an opposing player of the Browns scored a safety was on December 1, 2013, when Brandon Weeden was called for a penalty in the end zone in Jacksonville's 32-28 win over the Browns in Cleveland.

. . . the Browns gained 500 total net yards in one game was on September 16, 2007, when they totaled 554 in a 51-45 win over the Bengals in Cleveland.

. . . a Browns opponent gained 500 total net yards in one game was on September 7, 2014, when the Steelers totaled 503 in a 30-27 victory over the Browns in Pittsburgh.

. . . the Browns posted a shutout was on December 16, 2007, when they beat Buffalo 8-0 in Cleveland.

. . . a Browns opponent posted a shutout was on December 14, 2014, when Cincinnati defeated the Browns 30-0 in Cleveland.

THE LAST TIME THE BROWNS BEAT (CURRENT TEAMS)...
* Denotes only victory

TEAM	AT HOME	AWAY
Arizona	Nov. 16, 2003	Oct. 23, 1988
Atlanta	Dec. 29, 2002	Nov. 23, 2014
Baltimore	Nov. 3, 2013	Nov. 18, 2007
Buffalo	Oct. 3, 2013	Oct. 11, 2009
Carolina	*Nov. 28, 2010	Never
Chicago	Oct. 9, 2005	Nov. 30, 1969
Cincinnati	Sept. 29, 2013	Nov. 6, 2014
Dallas	Dec. 4, 1988	Dec. 10, 1994
Denver	Oct. 1, 1989	Oct. 8, 1990
Detroit	Sept. 23, 2001	*Sept. 11, 1983
Green Bay	Oct. 18, 1992	Sept. 18, 2005
Indianapolis	Sept. 19, 1988	Sept. 18, 2011
Jacksonville	Nov. 20, 2011	Oct. 26, 2008
Kansas City	Dec. 9, 2012	Dec. 20, 2009
Miami	Sept. 25, 2011	Dec. 5, 2010
Minnesota	Dec. 17, 1989	Sept. 22, 2013
New England	Nov. 7, 2010	Oct. 25, 1992
New Orleans	Sept. 14, 2014	Oct. 24, 2010
New York Giants	Oct. 13, 2008	Dec. 1, 1985
New York Jets	Oct. 29, 2006	Dec. 9, 2007
Oakland	Oct. 26, 2014	Dec. 2, 2012
Philadelphia	Oct. 16, 1988	Nov. 13, 1994
Pittsburgh	Oct. 12, 2014	Oct. 5, 2003
St. Louis	Oct. 26, 1987	Oct. 28, 2007
San Diego	Oct. 28, 2012	Oct. 20, 1991
San Francisco	Dec. 30, 2007	Sept. 21, 2003
Seattle	Oct. 23, 2011	Nov. 12, 1989
Tampa Bay	Nov. 2, 2014	Nov. 5, 1989
Tennessee	Nov. 6, 2005	Oct. 5, 2014
Washington	Oct. 3, 2004	Nov. 27, 1988

Coaches And Assistant Coaches

Head Coaches

Paul Brown (1946-62)
Blanton Collier (1963-70)
Nick Skorich (1971-74)
Forrest Gregg (1975-77)
Dick Modzelewski (1977)
Sam Rutigliano (1978-84)
Marty Schottenheimer (1984-88)
Bud Carson (1989-90)
Jim Shofner (1990)
Bill Belichick (1991-95)
Chris Palmer (1999)
Butch Davis (2001-04)
Terry Robiskie (2004)
Romeo Crennel (2005-08)
Eric Mangini (2009-10)
Pat Shurmur (2011-12)
Rob Chudzinski (2013)
Mike Pettine (2014-)

Assistant Coaches

John Brickels (1946-48)
Blanton Collier (1946-53, '62, '75-76)
William "Red" Conkright (1946)
Fritz Heisler (1946-70)
Bob Voigts (1946)
Bill Edwards (1947-48)
Dick Gallagher (1947-49, '55-59)
Weeb Ewbank (1949-53)
Timmy Temerario (1950-51)
Howard Brinker (1952-73)
Paul Bixler (1954-62)
Ed Ulinski (1954-70)
Dick Evans (1960-63)
Dub Jones (1963-67)
Nick Skorich (1964-70)
Bob Nussbaumer (1966-71)
Dick Modzelewski (1968-77)
Howard Keys (1970-71)
Richie McCabe (1971-75)
Ray Prochaska (1971-72)
Jerry Williams (1971)
John David Crow (1972-73)
Fran Polsfoot (1972-74)
Al Tabor (1972-77)
Jerry Smith (1973)
Forrest Gregg (1974)
Dale Lindsey (1974)
Dick Wood (1974)
Walt Corey (1975-77)
Doug Gerhart (1975)
Rod Humenuik (1975-82)
George Sefcik (1975-77, '89-90)
Raymond Berry (1976-77)
Billy Kinard (1976-77)
Buck Buchanan (1978)
Jim Garrett (1978-84)
Rich Kotite (1978-82)
Dick MacPherson (1978-80)

John Petercuskie (1978-84)
Jim Shofner (1978-80, '90)
Chuck Weber (1978-79)
Dave Adolph (1979-84, '86-88)
Len Fontes (1980-82)
Marty Schottenheimer (1980-84)
Paul Hackett (1981-82)
Tom Pratt (1981-88)
Dave Redding (1982-88)
Joe Scannella (1982-84)
Joe Daniels (1983-84)
Howard Mudd (1983-88)
Darvin Wallis (1983-88)
Larrye Weaver (1983)
Keith Rowen (1984)
Tom Bettis (1985)
Bill Cowher (1985-88)
Steve Crosby (1985, '91-95)
Greg Landry (1985)
Richard Mann (1985-93)
Tom Olivadotti (1985-86)
Joe Pendry (1985-88)
Charlie Davis (1986-87)
Lindy Infante (1986-87)
Kurt Schottenheimer (1987-88)
Ray Braun (1988)
Marc Trestman (1988-89)
Jed Hughes (1989)
Hal Hunter (1989-92)
Stan Jones (1989-90)
Paul Lanham (1989-90)
Joe Popp (1989-90)
Dan Radakovich (1989-90)
Lionel Taylor (1989-90)
John Teerlinck (1989-90)
Gary Wroblewski (1989-90)
Zeke Bratkowski (1990)
Mike Faulkiner (1990)
Jim Vechiarella (1990)

Ernie Adams (1991-95)
Jim Bates (1991-93, 1995)
Don Blackmon (1991)
John Mitchell (1991-93)
Scott O'Brien (1991-95)
Nick Saban (1991-94)
Phil Savage (1991-93)
Jerry Simmons (1991-95)
Kevin Spencer (1991-94)
Gary Tranquill (1991-93)
Al Groh (1992)
Kirk Ferentz (1993-95)
Pat Hill (1993-95)
Mike Sheppard (1993-95)
Woody Widenhofer (1993-94)
Chuck Bresnahan (1994-95)
Jacob Burney (1994-95)
Rod Dowhower (1994)
Rick Venturi (1994-95)
Eric Mangini (1995)
John Settle (1995, 2013)
Tom Spann (1995)
Clarence Brooks (1999)
Jerry Butler (1999-2000)
Keith Butler (1999-2002)
Bill Davis (1999, 2011-12)
Jerry Holmes (1999-2000)
John Hufnagel (1999-2000)
Tim Jorgensen (1999-2001)
Mark Michaels (1999-2000)
Bob Palcic (1999)
Ray Perkins (1999-2000)
Dick Portee (1999)
Bob Slowik (1999)
Aril Smith (1999)
Tony Sparano (1999-2000)
Ken Whisenhunt (1999)
Pete Carmichael (2000)
Pete Carmichael, Jr. (2000)

Romeo Crennel (2000)
John Fabris (2000)
Joe Kim (2000)
Mike Pitts (2000)
Bruce Arians (2001-03)
Phil Banko (2001-04)
Todd Bowles (2001-04)
Foge Fazio (2001-02)
Pete Garcia (2001)
Steve Hagen (2001-04, '09-12)
Ray Hamilton (2001-02)
Todd McNair (2001-03)
Chuck Pagano (2001-04)
Rob Phillips (2001-04)
Terry Robiskie (2001-06)
Jerry Rosburg (2001-06)
Carl Smith (2001-03, '09-10)
Larry Zierlein (2001-04)
Buddy Morris (2002-04)
Mike Sullivan (2002-04, '07-08, '13)
Dave Campo (2003-04)
Andre Patterson (2003-04)
Clancy Pendergast (2003)
Rob Chudzinski (2004, '07-08)
George Edwards (2004)
Fred Graves (2004)
Taver Johnson (2004)
Tom Myslinski (2004, '07-09)
Kennedy Pola (2004)
Dave Atkins (2005-08)
Maurice Carthon (2005-06)
Ben Coates (2005-06)
Carl Crennel II (2005-06)
Jeff Davidson (2005-06)
Todd Grantham (2005-07)
Mike Haluchak (2005-08)
John Lott (2005-06)
Marwan Maalouf (2005-06)
Randy Melvin (2005-08)

Rip Scherer (2005-08)
Bob Trott (2005-08)
Mel Tucker (2005-08)
Jeff Uhlenhake (2005-06)
Cory Undlin (2005-08)
Wes Chandler (2007-08)
Ted Daisher (2007-08)
Alan DeGennaro (2007-09)
Umberto Leone (2007-08)
Anthony Lynn (2007-08)
Steve Marshall (2007-08)
Alfredo Roberts (2007-08)
Frank Verducci (2007-08)
Chris Caminiti (2008)
Richard McNutt (2008)
Gary Brown (2009-12)
Bryan Cox (2009-10)
Brian Daboll (2009-10)
Andy Dickerson (2009-10)
Matt Eberflus (2009-10)
Jerome Henderson (2009-11)
Rick Lyle (2009-12)
George McDonald (2009-10)
Rob Ryan (2009-10)
Brad Seely (2009-10)
George Warhop (2009-13)
Kent Johnston (2010-12)
Chris Beake (2011-12)
Dwaine Board (2011-12)
Chuck Bullough (2011-12)
Keith Gilbertson (2011)
Dick Jauron (2011-12)
Shawn Mennenga (2011-14)
Ray Rhodes (2011-12)
Luke Steckel (2011-12)
Chris Tabor (2011-14)
Mark Whipple (2011-12)
Mike Wilson (2011-12)
Brad Childress (2012)

Nolan Cromwell (2012)
Tim Hauck (2012)
Bobby Babich (2013-14)
Brian Baker (2013)
Louie Cioffi (2013)
Joe Cullen (2013)
Chris DiSanto (2013)
Jon Embree (2013)
Ken Flajole (2013)
Steve Gera (2013)
Ray Horton (2013)
Derik Keyes (2013-14)
Daron Roberts (2013)
Brad Roll (2013)
Shane Steichen (2013)
Norv Turner (2013)
Scott Turner (2013)

Brian Angelichio (2014)
George DeLeone (2014)
Chuck Driesbach (2014)
Brian Fleury (2014)
Aaron Glenn (2014)
Jeff Hafley (2014)
Richard Hightower (2014)
Dowell Loggains (2014)
Mike McDaniel (2014)
Andy Moeller (2014)
Wilbert Montgomery (2014)
Jim O'Neil (2014)
Paul Ricci (2014)
Kyle Shanahan (2014)
Tony Tuioti (2014)
Anthony Weaver (2014)
Mike Wolf (2014)

ATTENDANCE
STATISTICS

(The Browns' home attendance figures were based on the number of tickets purchased from 1946-72 and the number of tickets used from 1973-95 and since 1999. Standing-room-only [SRO] tickets for home games were included in attendance figures from 1946 to November 3, 1980, and not included from November 23, 1980, to 1995 and since 1999.)

REGULAR SEASON

TEN HIGHEST HOME FIGURES, 1946-NOVEMBER 3, 1980

1. 85,703   Cleveland 31, N.Y. Jets 21 (Sept. 21, 1970)
2. 84,850   Cleveland 42, Dallas 10 (Nov. 2, 1969)
3. 84,721   Cleveland 30, Dallas 21 (Oct. 23, 1966)
4. 84,684   Cleveland 35, Pittsburgh 23 (Oct. 5, 1963)
5. 84,349   Cleveland 15, Pittsburgh 7 (Oct. 3, 1970)
6. 84,285   Oakland 34, Cleveland 20 (Oct. 4, 1971)
7. 84,213   New York 33, Cleveland 6 (Oct. 27, 1963)
8. 84,078   Cleveland 42, Pittsburgh 31 (Oct. 18, 1969)
9. 83,943   Green Bay 21, Cleveland 20 (Sept. 18, 1966)
10.83,819   Kansas City 31, Cleveland 7 (Oct. 8, 1972)

TEN HIGHEST HOME FIGURES, NOVEMBER 23, 1980-95

1. 79,700   Cleveland 17, Cincinnati 7 (Sept. 15, 1983)
2. 79,543   Cleveland 34, Pittsburgh 10 (Sept. 20, 1987)
3. 79,483   Houston 9, Cleveland 3 (Sept. 13, 1981)
4. 79,253   Cleveland 31, Cincinnati 7 (Nov. 23, 1980)
5. 79,147   Cleveland 23, Cincinnati 16 (Oct. 30, 1988)
6. 79,042   Cleveland 17, Pittsburgh 7 (Sept. 16, 1985)
7. 78,986   Cleveland 42, Baltimore 28 (Oct. 25, 1981)
8. 78,904   San Diego 44, Cleveland 14 (Sept. 7, 1981)
9. 78,860   Dallas 26, Cleveland 14 (Sept. 1, 1991)
10. 78,840   Pittsburgh 17, Cleveland 7 (Oct. 15, 1989)

TEN HIGHEST HOME FIGURES SINCE 1999

1. 73,718   Pittsburgh 23, Cleveland 20 (Nov. 3, 2002)
2. 73,688   Baltimore 26, Cleveland 21 (Oct. 6, 2002)
3. 73,658   Pittsburgh 13, Cleveland 6 (Nov. 23, 2003)
4. 73,528   Cleveland 24, Atlanta 16 (Dec. 29, 2002)
5. 73,428   Cincinnati 21, Cleveland 14 (Sept. 28, 2003)
6. 73,358   Cleveland 20, Cincinnati 7 (Sept. 15, 2002)
             Indianapolis 9, Cleveland 6 (Sept. 7, 2003)
8. 73,318   Cleveland 13, Oakland 7 (Oct. 12, 2003)
9. 73, 248   Cleveland 34, Houston 17 (Oct. 20, 2002)
10. 73,238   San Diego 26, Cleveland 20 (Oct. 19, 2003)

TEN LOWEST HOME FIGURES

1. 16,506   Cleveland 35, Chicago 2 (Nov. 6, 1949)
2. 20,564   Cleveland 17, Philadelphia 14 (Dec. 2, 1956)
3. 20,621   Cleveland 21, Baltimore 0 (Sept. 11, 1949)
4. 21,908   Cleveland 20, Washington 14 (Nov. 19, 1950)
5. 22,511   Cleveland 7, Buffalo 7 (Nov. 13, 1949)
6. 22,878   Washington 20, Cleveland 17 (Nov. 25, 1956)
7. 24,101   Cleveland 31, Chi. Cardinals 7 (Oct. 10, 1954)
8. 24,499   Cleveland 27, Chi. Cardinals 16 (Nov. 29, 1953)
9. 24,559   Cleveland 7, San Francisco 0 (Dec. 1, 1974)
10. 25,158   Cleveland 62, Washington 3 (Nov. 7, 1954)

TEN HIGHEST ROAD FIGURES

1. 90,487   Washington 14, Cleveland 11 (Oct. 19, 2008)
2. 81,936   Dallas 23, Cleveland 20 (OT) (Nov. 18, 2012)
3. 79,911   N.Y. Giants 41, Cleveland 27 (Oct. 7, 2012)
4. 78,560   Kansas City 41, Cleveland 20 (Nov. 9, 2003)
5. 78,521   N.Y. Giants 27, Cleveland 10 (Sept. 26, 2004)
6. 78,502   Cleveland 24, N.Y. Jets 21 (Oct. 27, 2002)
7. 78,266   Buffalo 22, Cleveland 13 (Nov. 1, 1981)
8. 77,804   Green Bay 31, Cleveland 13 (Oct. 20, 2013)
9. 77,045   Cleveland 42, New Orleans 7 (Oct. 1, 1967)
10. 76,957   N.Y. Jets 24, Cleveland 13 (Dec. 22, 2013)

TEN LOWEST ROAD FIGURES

1. 5,031 Cleveland 14, Chicago 6 (Nov. 24, 1949)
2. 9,083 Cleveland 34, Miami 0 (Dec. 3, 1946)
3. 9,821 Cleveland 31, Brooklyn 21 (Dec. 5, 1948)
4. 14,600   Cleveland 66, Brooklyn 14 (Dec. 8, 1946)
5. 14,830   Cleveland 20, New England 10 (Oct. 4, 1987)
6. 15,201   Cleveland 31, Baltimore 0 (Sept. 24, 1950)
7. 16,263   Cleveland 24, Philadelphia 9 (Dec. 16, 1951)
8. 18,450   Cleveland 41, Chicago 21 (Sept. 26, 1947)
9. 18,876   Cleveland 55, Brooklyn 7 (Sept. 12, 1947)
10. 19,742   Cleveland 34, Chi. Cardinals 17 (Nov. 4, 1951)

HIGHEST, LOWEST HOME FIGURES VS. EACH TEAM
* Denotes only game played

TEAM	HIGHEST	LOWEST
Arizona Cardinals	81,186 (Oct. 26, 1969)	24,101 (Oct. 10, 1954)
Atlanta Falcons	78,283 (Sept. 27, 1981)	46,536 (Dec. 16, 1990)
Baltimore Colts (original)	44,257 (Sept. 21, 1947)	21,621 (Sept. 11, 1949)
Baltimore Ravens	73,688 (Oct. 6, 2002)	63,648 (Dec. 4, 2011)
Brooklyn Dodgers	43,713 (Oct. 6, 1946)	30,279 (Nov. 9, 1947)
Brooklyn-New York Yankees	*26,312 (Sept. 18, 1949)	*26,312 (Sept. 18, 1949)
Buffalo Bills (current)	78,409 (Nov. 15, 1987)	50,764 (Nov. 17, 1985)
Buffalo Bisons-Bills (original)	63,263 (Sept. 5, 1947)	22,511 (Nov. 13, 1949)
Carolina Panthers	72,818 (Nov. 21, 1999)	72,718 (Dec. 1, 2002)
Chicago Bears	83,224 (Nov. 3, 1980)	38,155 (Dec. 11, 1960)
Chicago Rockets	60,457 (Nov. 17, 1946)	16,506 (Nov. 6, 1949)
Cincinnati Bengals	83,520 (Oct. 11, 1970)	51,774 (Dec. 2, 1984)
Dallas Cowboys	84,850 (Nov. 2, 1969)	43,638 (Oct. 1, 1961)
Denver Broncos	81,065 (Oct. 5, 1980)	60,478 (Oct. 27, 1974)
Detroit Lions	83,577 (Oct. 18, 1970)	34,168 (Dec. 19, 1954)
Green Bay Packers	83,943 (Sept. 18, 1966)	51,482 (Oct. 23, 1955)
Indianapolis Colts	80,132 (Oct. 14, 1962)	42,404 (Nov. 11, 1956)
Jacksonville Jaguars	72,818 (Dec. 16, 2001)	63,498 (Nov. 20, 2011)
Kansas City Chiefs	83,819 (Oct. 8, 1972)	44,368 (Dec. 14, 1975)

Los Angeles Dons	71,134 (Oct. 20, 1946)	63,124 (Oct. 12, 1947)
Miami Dolphins	80,374 (Nov. 18, 1979)	66,651 (Sept. 25, 2011)
Miami Seahawks	*60,135 (Sept. 6, 1946)	*60,135 (Sept. 6, 1946)
Minnesota Vikings	83,505 (Oct. 31, 1965)	68,064 (Sept. 28, 1975)
New England Patriots	76,418 (Sept. 26, 1977)	48,618 (Dec. 19, 1993)
New Orleans Saints	76,059 (Oct. 18, 1981)	44,753 (Nov. 30, 1975)
New York Giants	84,213 (Oct. 27, 1963)	30,448 (Oct. 31, 1954)
New York Jets	85,703 (Sept. 21, 1970)	36,881 (Dec. 10, 1978)
New York Yankees	80,067 (Oct. 5, 1947)	46,912 (Oct. 24, 1948)
Oakland Raiders	84,285 (Oct. 4, 1971)	65,247 (Oct. 6, 1974)
Philadelphia Eagles	79,289 (Nov. 29, 1964)	20,645 (Dec. 2, 1956)
Pittsburgh Steelers	84,684 (Oct. 5, 1963)	28,064 (Dec. 12, 1954)
St. Louis Rams	82,514 (Sept. 29, 1968)	54,713 (Sept. 29, 1963)
San Diego Chargers	80,047 (Nov. 1, 1970)	54,064 (Dec. 5, 1982)
San Francisco 49ers	82,769 (Nov. 14, 1948)	24,559 (Dec. 1, 1974)
Seattle Seahawks	78,605 (Oct. 9, 1988)	54,180 (Dec. 24, 1994)
Tampa Bay Buccaneers	69,603 (Dec. 24, 2006)	56,091 (Nov. 13, 1983)
Tennessee Titans	80,243 (Sept. 15, 1980)	30,898 (Dec. 11, 1977)
Washington Redskins	82,581 (Sept. 28, 1969)	25,158 (Nov. 7, 1954)

HIGHEST, LOWEST ROAD FIGURES VS. EACH TEAM

(In cases where teams relocated cities, figures are based on those teams' stays in each city. The Browns never played a road game against the Boston Patriots.)

* Denotes only game played

TEAM	HIGHEST	LOWEST
Arizona-Phoenix Cardinals	64,791 (Dec. 2, 2007)	39,148 (Oct. 8, 2000)
Atlanta Falcons	70,793 (Nov. 12, 2006)	28,280 (Nov. 18, 1984)
Baltimore Colts (original)	36,837 (Sept. 25, 1949)	15,201 (Sept. 24, 1950)
Baltimore Colts (second)	60,238 (Oct. 20, 1968)	35,235 (Nov. 2, 1975)
Baltimore Ravens	71,119 (Sept. 26, 2010)	68,361 (Nov. 26, 2000)
Brooklyn Dodgers	18,876 (Sept. 12, 1947)	9,821 (Dec. 5, 1948)

Brooklyn-New York Yankees	*50,711 (Nov. 20, 1949)	*50,711 (Nov. 20, 1949)
Buffalo Bills (current)	78,266 (Nov. 1, 1981)	33,343 (Nov. 4, 1984)
Buffalo Bisons-Bills (original)	43,167 (Nov. 2, 1947)	30,302 (Sept. 22, 1946)
Chicago Bears	66,944 (Nov. 4, 2001)	38,717 (Dec. 10, 1961)
Chicago Cardinals	38,456 (Nov. 5, 1950)	19,742 (Nov. 4, 1951)
Chicago Rockets	51,962 (Sept. 13, 1946)	5,031 (Nov. 24, 1949)
Cincinnati Bengals	68,356 (Nov. 17, 2013)	40,179 (Oct. 18, 1987)
Dallas Cowboys	81,936 (Nov. 18, 2012)	23,500 (Dec. 3, 1961)
Denver Broncos	76,351 (Dec. 23, 2012)	51,001 (Dec. 20, 1970)
Detroit Lions	75,283 (Nov. 9, 1975)	43,170 (Nov. 22, 2009)
Green Bay Packers	77,804 (Oct. 20, 2013)	28,590 (Nov. 4, 1956)
Green Bay Packers (at Milwaukee)	54,089 (Nov. 6, 1983)	22,604 (Sept. 27, 1953)
Houston Oilers	58,852 (Dec. 23, 1989)	29,746 (Dec. 11, 1983)
Indianapolis Colts	65,035 (Sept. 18, 2011)	50,766 (Sept. 6, 1992)
Jacksonville Jaguars	66,007 (Dec. 24, 1995)	46,267 (Dec. 8, 2002)
Kansas City Chiefs	78,560 (Nov. 9, 2003)	34,340 (Dec. 12, 1976)
Los Angeles Dons	60,031 (Nov. 25, 1948)	24,800 (Nov. 3, 1946)
Los Angeles Raiders	65,461 (Nov. 16, 1986)	40,275 (Dec. 20, 1987)
Los Angeles Rams	73,948 (Dec. 16, 1973)	34,155 (Dec. 26, 1993)
Miami Dolphins	75,313 (Oct. 25, 1970)	58,444 (Oct. 8, 1989)
Miami Seahawks	*9,083 (Dec. 3, 1946)	*9,083 (Dec. 3, 1946)
Minnesota Vikings	63,814 (Nov. 27, 2005)	42,202 (Dec. 14, 1980)
New England Patriots	68,756 (Oct. 7, 2007, Dec. 8, 2013)	14,830 (Oct. 4, 1987)
New Orleans Saints	77,045 (Oct. 1, 1967)	48,817 (Oct. 31, 1999)
New York Giants	79,911 (Oct. 7, 2012)	27,707 (Dec. 9, 1956)
New York Jets	78,502 (Oct. 27, 2002)	48,472 (Sept. 2, 1979)
New York Yankees	70,060 (Nov. 23, 1947)	34,252 (Oct. 12, 1946)
Oakland Raiders	61,426 (Oct. 1, 2006)	41,862 (Dec. 18, 2005)
Philadelphia Eagles	71,237 (Sept. 16, 1950)	16,263 (Dec. 16, 1951)
Pittsburgh Steelers	65,168 (Oct. 17, 2010)	24,229 (Dec. 9, 1951)
St. Louis Cardinals	47,845 (Oct. 28, 1979)	23,256 (Oct. 21, 1962)
St. Louis Rams	65,866 (Oct. 24, 1999)	62,777 (Oct. 28, 2007)

San Diego Chargers	65,558 (Nov. 5, 2006)	35,683 (Nov. 3, 1974)
San Francisco 49ers	69,732 (Oct. 30, 2011)	31,359 (Nov. 3, 1968)
Seattle Seahawks	64,680 (Nov. 30, 2003)	51,435 (Dec. 20, 1981)
Tampa Bay Buccaneers	69,162 (Nov. 5, 1989)	36,390 (Nov. 21, 1976)
Tennessee Titans	69,143 (Dec. 7, 2008, Oct. 5, 2014)	65,904 (Sept. 19, 1999)
Washington Redskins	90,487 (Oct. 19, 2008)	21,761 (Dec. 5, 1954)

FIVE HIGHEST SEASON AVERAGE HOME FIGURES, 1946-80

(Although SRO tickets were not sold for the last two games of the 1980 season, that season is included since SRO tickets were sold for six of the eight home games that year.)

1. 82,623 (1969)
2. 81,054 (1970)
3. 79,612 (1965)
4. 78,476 (1964)
5. 77,830 (1967)

FIVE HIGHEST SEASON AVERAGE HOME FIGURES, 1981-95

1. 77,018 (1988)
2. 76,677 (1989)
3. 75,216 (1981)
4. 72,967 (1986)
5. 71,469 (1991)

FIVE HIGHEST SEASON AVERAGE HOME FIGURES SINCE 1999

1. 73,287 (2002)
2. 73,196 (2003)
3. 73,105 (2004)
4. 73,001 (2007)
5. 72,887 (2001)

FIVE LOWEST SEASON AVERAGE HOME FIGURES

1. 30,579 (1954)
2. 31,601 (1949)
3. 33,387 (1950)
4. 36,941 (1956)
5. 38,569 (1951)

POSTSEASON ATTENDANCE

(Browns home attendance figures were based on the number of tickets purchased from 1946-72 and the number of tickets used from 1973-95 and have been since 1999. Standing-room-only [SRO] tickets for home games were included in attendance figures from 1946 to November 3, 1980.)

HOME FIGURES, HIGHEST TO LOWEST, 1946-79

1. 81,497   Cleveland 31, Dallas 20 (Eastern Conference Championship, Dec. 21, 1968)
2. 80,628   Baltimore 34, Cleveland 0 (NFL Championship, Dec. 29, 1968)
3. 79,544   Cleveland 27, Baltimore 0 (NFL Championship, Dec. 27, 1964)
4. 74,082   Baltimore 20, Cleveland 3 (AFC Divisional Playoff, Dec. 26, 1971)
5. 50,934   Detroit 17, Cleveland 7 (NFL Championship, Dec. 28, 1952)
6. 43,827   Cleveland 56, Detroit 10 (NFL Championship, Dec. 26, 1954)
7. 40,489   Cleveland 14, New York 9 (AAFC Championship, Dec. 22, 1946)
8. 33,054   Cleveland 8, N.Y. Giants 3 (American Conference Playoff, Dec. 17, 1950)
9. 29,751   Cleveland 30, Los Angeles 28 (NFL Championship, Dec. 24, 1950)
10. 22,981   Cleveland 49, Buffalo 7 (AAFC Championship, Dec. 19, 1948)
11. 22,550   Cleveland 21, San Francisco 7 (AAFC Championship, Dec. 11, 1949)
12. 17,270   Cleveland 31, Buffalo 21 (AAFC Playoff, Dec. 4, 1949)

HOME FIGURES, HIGHEST TO LOWEST, 1980-95 AND SINCE 1999

1. 79,915   Denver 23, Cleveland 20 (OT) (AFC Championship, Jan. 11, 1987)

2. 78,586   Cleveland 38, Indianapolis 21 (AFC Divisional Playoff, Jan. 9, 1988)
3. 78,106   Cleveland 23, N.Y. Jets 20 (20T) (AFC Divisional Playoff, Jan. 3, 1987)
4. 77,706   Cleveland 34, Buffalo 30 (AFC Divisional Playoff, Jan. 6, 1990)
5. 77,655   Oakland 14, Cleveland 12 (AFC Divisional Playoff, Jan. 4, 1981)
6. 77,452   Cleveland 20, New England 13 (AFC Wild Card, Jan. 1, 1995)
7. 74,977   Houston 24, Cleveland 23 (AFC Wild Card, Dec. 24, 1988)

ROAD FIGURES, HIGHEST TO LOWEST

1. 87,695   Cleveland 38, Los Angeles 14 (NFL Championship, Dec. 26, 1955)
2. 80,010   Miami 20, Cleveland 14 (AFC Divisional Playoff, Dec. 24, 1972)
3. 76,046   Denver 37, Cleveland 21 (AFC Championship, Jan. 14, 1990)
4. 75,993   Denver 38, Cleveland 33 (AFC Championship, Jan. 17, 1988)
5. 75,128   Miami 24, Cleveland 21 (AFC Divisional Playoff, Jan 4, 1986)
6. 70,786   Dallas 52, Cleveland 14 (Eastern Conference Championship, Dec. 24, 1967)
7. 69,321   Cleveland 38, Dallas 14 (Eastern Conference Championship, Dec. 28, 1969)
8. 62,595   Pittsburgh 36, Cleveland 33 (AFC Wild Card, Jan. 5, 2003)
9. 61,879   Cleveland 14, New York 3 (AAFC Championship, Dec. 14, 1947)
10. 61,174   New York 10, Cleveland 0 (Eastern Conference Playoff, Dec. 21, 1958)
11. 58,185   Pittsburgh 29, Cleveland 9 (AFC Divisional Playoff, Jan. 7, 1995)
12. 57,540   Los Angeles 24, Cleveland 17 (NFL Championship, Dec. 23, 1951)
13. 56,555   L.A. Raiders 27, Cleveland 10 (AFC First-Round, Jan. 8, 1983)
14. 55,263   Detroit 59, Cleveland 14 (NFL Championship, Dec. 21, 1957)
15. 54,577   Detroit 17, Cleveland 16 (NFL Championship, Dec. 27, 1953)
16. 50,852   Green Bay 23, Cleveland 12 (NFL Championship, Jan. 2, 1966)
17. 47,900   Minnesota 27, Cleveland 7 (NFL Championship, Jan. 4, 1970)

INDIVIDUAL STATISTICS

COMBINED NET YARDS LEADERS
(Does not include fumble return yardage for various seasons)

1946 Edgar Jones	1,055		1973 Greg Pruitt	1,112
1947 Marion Motley	1,332		1974 Greg Pruitt	1,769
1948 Marion Motley	1,493		1975 Greg Pruitt	1,798
1949 Mac Speedie	1,028		1976 Greg Pruitt	1,368
1950 Marion Motley	961		1977 Greg Pruitt	1,557
1951 Dub Jones	1,062		1978 Greg Pruitt	1,283
1952 Dub Jones	921		1979 Mike Pruitt	1,666
1953 Dante Lavelli	783		1980 Mike Pruitt	1,505
1954 Maurice Bassett	813		1981 Mike Pruitt	1,545
1955 Fred Morrison	1,009		1982 Mike Pruitt	656
1956 Preston Carpenter	1,279		1983 Mike Pruitt	1,341
1957 Jim Brown	1,133		1984 Ozzie Newsome	1,001
1958 Jim Brown	1,749		1985 Earnest Byner	1,462
1959 Jim Brown	1,607		1986 Gerald McNeil	1,366
1960 Jim Brown	1,761		1987 Earnest Byner	986
1961 Jim Brown	1,917		1988 Earnest Byner	1,152
1962 Jim Brown	1,513		1989 Eric Metcalf	1,748
1963 Jim Brown	2,131		1990 Eric Metcalf	1,752
1964 Jim Brown	1,786		1991 Webster Slaughter	1,018
1965 Jim Brown	1,872		1992 Eric Metcalf	1,501
1966 Leroy Kelly	2,014		1993 Eric Metcalf	1,932
1967 Leroy Kelly	1,677		1994 Leroy Hoard	1,365
1968 Leroy Kelly	1,555		1995 Earnest Byner	1,024
1969 Leroy Kelly	1,138		1999 Terry Kirby	1,210
1970 Leroy Kelly	982		2000 Jamel White	1,180
1971 Leroy Kelly	1,420		2001 Kevin Johnson	1,214
1972 Leroy Kelly	1,055		2002 Andre Davis	1,528

2003 Andre Davis	1,414	2009 Josh Cribbs	2,510
2004 Dennis Northcutt	1,257	2010 Peyton Hillis	1,654
2005 Reuben Droughns	1,720	2011 Josh Cribbs	1,905
2006 Josh Cribbs	1,647	2012 Josh Cribbs	1,722
2007 Josh Cribbs	2,312	2013 Josh Gordon	1,734
2008 Josh Cribbs	1,523	2014 Andrew Hawkins	839

INDIVIDUAL TOP FIVES (CAREER) (POSTSEASON)

SCORING (POINTS)

1. Lou Groza	83
2. Matt Bahr	46
3. Otto Graham	36
Earnest Byner	36
5. Edgar Jones	30
Dante Lavelli	30
Marion Motley	30
Gary Collins	30
Webster Slaughter	30

RUSHING YARDS

(Does not include Browns games against the Buffalo Bills on December 4, 1949, and Los Angeles Rams on December 24, 1950, for Otto Graham and Marion Motley, and the Browns game against the New York Giants on December 17, 1950, for Motley)

1. Marion Motley	512
2. Earnest Byner	480
3. Leroy Kelly	427
4. Kevin Mack	424
5. Otto Graham	247

PASSING YARDS

1. Otto Graham	2,001
2. Bernie Kosar	1,860
3. Bill Nelsen	839
4. Frank Ryan	534
5. Kelly Holcomb	429

PASS COMPLETIONS

1. Otto Graham	159
2. Bernie Kosar	146
3. Bill Nelsen	68
4. Frank Ryan	35
5. Vinny Testaverde	33

RECEIVING YARDS

(Does not include Browns games against the New York Giants on December 17, 1950, and Los Angeles Rams on December 24, 1950, and a portion of the Browns game against the Buffalo Bills on December 4, 1949)

1. Dante Lavelli	526
2. Paul Warfield	404
3. Webster Slaughter	381
4. Ozzie Newsome	373
5. Reggie Langhorne	370

RECEPTIONS

(Does not include the Browns game against the New York Giants on December 17, 1950, and a portion of Browns games against the Buffalo Bills on December 4, 1949, and Los Angeles Rams on December 24, 1950)

1.	Dante Lavelli	30
2.	Mac Speedie	27
	Ozzie Newsome	27
4.	Reggie Langhorne	26
5.	Paul Warfield	24

PUNTING YARDS

1.	Horace Gillom	1,943
2.	Don Cockroft	965
3.	Jeff Gossett	792
4.	Gary Collins	595
5.	Bryan Wagner	451

INDIVIDUAL TOP FIVES (GAME) (POSTSEASON)
vs. – Denotes home

SCORING (POINTS)

1.	Marion Motley	18 (Dec. 19, 1948, vs. Buffalo)
	Otto Graham	18 (Dec. 26, 1954, vs. Detroit)
	Gary Collins	18 (Dec. 27, 1964, vs. Baltimore)
4.	Edgar Jones	12 (Dec. 19, 1948, vs. Buffalo)
	Dante Lavelli	12 (Dec. 24, 1950, vs. Los Angeles)
	Ray Renfro	12 (Dec. 26, 1954, vs. Detroit)
	Otto Graham	12 (Dec. 26, 1955, at Los Angeles)
	Leroy Kelly	12 (Dec. 21, 1968, vs. Dallas)
	Bo Scott	12 (Dec. 28, 1969, at Dallas)
	Earnest Byner	12 (Jan. 4, 1986, at Miami)
	Earnest Byner	12 (Jan. 9, 1988, vs. Indianapolis)
	Earnest Byner	12 (Jan. 17, 1988, at Denver)
	Webster Slaughter	12 (Dec. 24, 1988, vs. Houston)
	Webster Slaughter	12 (Jan. 6, 1990, vs. Buffalo)
	Brian Brennan	12 (Jan. 14, 1990, at Denver)
	Dennis Northcutt	12 (Jan. 5, 2003, at Pittsburgh)

RUSHING YARDS

1. Earnest Byner   161 (Jan. 4, 1986, at Miami)
2. Marion Motley   133 (Dec. 19, 1948, vs. Buffalo)
3. Earnest Byner   122 (Jan. 9, 1988, vs. Indianapolis)
4. Jim Brown   114 (Dec. 27, 1964, vs. Baltimore)
5. Marion Motley   109 (Dec. 14, 1947, at New York)

PASSING YARDS

1. Bernie Kosar   489 (Jan. 3, 1987, vs. New York Jets)
2. Kelly Holcomb   429 (Jan. 5, 2003, at Pittsburgh)
3. Bernie Kosar   356 (Jan. 17, 1988, at Denver)
4. Otro Graham   326 (Dec. 4, 1949, vs. Buffalo)
5. Otto Graham   298 (Dec. 24, 1950, vs. Los Angeles)

PASS COMPLETIONS

1. Bernie Kosar   33 (Jan. 3, 1987, vs. New York Jets)
2. Bernie Kosar   26 (Jan. 17, 1988, at Denver)
 Kelly Holcomb   26 (Jan. 5, 2003, at Pittsburgh)
4. Otto Graham   22 (Dec. 4, 1949, vs. Buffalo)
 Otto Graham   22 (Dec. 24, 1950, vs. Los Angeles)

RECEIVING YARDS
(Does not include a portion of Browns games against the Buffalo Bills on December 4, 1949, and Los Angeles Rams on December 24, 1950)

1. Kevin Johnson   140 (Jan. 5, 2003, at Pittsburgh)
2. Gary Collins   130 (Dec. 27, 1964, vs. Baltimore)
3. Ricky Feacher   124 (Jan. 8, 1983, at Los Angeles Raiders)
4. Michael Jackson   122 (Jan. 1, 1995, vs. New England)
5. Earnest Byner   120 (Jan. 17, 1988, at Denver)

RECEPTIONS
(Does not include the Browns game against the Los Angeles Rams on December 24, 1950, and a portion of the Browns game against the Buffalo Bills on December 4, 1949)

l. Paul Warfield   8 (Dec. 28, 1969, at Dallas)
2. Mac Speedie   7 (Dec. 4, 1949, vs. Buffalo)
   Mac Speedie   7 (Dec. 23, 1951, at Los Angeles)
   Herman Fontenot   7 (Jan. 11, 1987, vs. Denver)
   Earnest Byner   7 (Jan. 17, 1988, at Denver)
   Michael Jackson   7 (Jan. 1, 1995, vs. New England)

PUNTING YARDS

1. Horace Gillom   363 (Dec. 17, 1950, vs. New York)
2. Bryan Wagner   338 (Jan. 14, 1990, at Denver)
3. Jeff Gossett   310 (Jan. 3, 1987, vs. New York Jets)
4. Dick Deschaine   304 (Dec. 21, 1958, at New York)
5. Steve Cox   291 (Jan. 8, 1983, at Los Angeles Raiders)

INDIVIDUAL TOP TENS (CAREER)

SCORING (POINTS)		RUSHING YARDS	
1. Lou Groza	1,608	1. Jim Brown	12,312
2. Phil Dawson	1,271	2. Leroy Kelly	7,274
3. Don Cockroft	1,080	3. Mike Pruitt	6,540
4. Jim Brown	756	4. Greg Pruitt	5,496
5. Matt Bahr	677	5. Kevin Mack	5,123
6. Leroy Kelly	540	6. Marion Motley	4,712
7. Matt Stover	480	7. Earnest Byner	3,364
8. Gary Collins	420	8. Ernie Green	3,204
9. Dante Lavelli	372	9. Jamal Lewis	2,806
10. Ray Renfro	330	10. Bobby Mitchell	2,297

PASSING YARDS

1. Brian Sipe   23,713
2. Otto Graham   23,584
3. Bernie Kosar   21,904
4. Frank Ryan   13,361
5. Tim Couch   11,131
6. Bill Nelsen   9,725
7. Milt Plum   8,914
8. Mike Phipps   7,700
9. Vinny Testaverde   7,255
10. Derek Anderson   7,083

PASS COMPLETIONS

1. Brian Sipe   1,944
2. Bernie Kosar   1,853
3. Otto Graham   1,464
4. Tim Couch   1,025
5. Frank Ryan   907
6. Bill Nelsen   689
7. Mike Phipps   633
8. Milt Plum   627
9. Derek Anderson   587
10. Vinny Testaverde   578

RECEIVING YARDS

1. Ozzie Newsome   7,980
2. Dante Lavelli   6,488
3. Mac Speedie   5,602
4. Ray Renfro   5,508
5. Gary Collins   5,299
6. Paul Warfield   5,210
7. Reggie Rucker   4,953
8. Webster Slaughter   4,834
9. Dave Logan   4,247
10. Milt Morin   4,208

RECEPTIONS

1. Ozzie Newsome   662
2. Dante Lavelli   386
3. Mac Speedie   349
4. Gary Collins   331
5. Greg Pruitt   323
6. Brian Brennan   315
   Kevin Johnson   315
8. Reggie Rucker   310
9. Webster Slaughter   305
10. Eric Metcalf   297

INTERCEPTIONS

1. Thom Darden   45
2. Warren Lahr   44
3. Clarence Scott   39
4. Tommy James   34
5. Cliff Lewis   30
   Ken Konz   30
7. Bernie Parrish   29
8. Ross Fichtner   27
   Mike Howell   27
10. Hanford Dixon   26
    Felix Wright   26

SACKS

1. Clay Matthews   62
2. Michael Dean Perry   51.5
3. Rob Burnett   40.5
4. Carl Hairston   37.5
5. Reggie Camp   35
6. Anthony Pleasant   33.5
7. Chip Banks   27.5
8. Kamerion Wimbley   26.5
9. Jabaal Sheard   23
10. Jamir Miller   22.5
    Kenard Lang   22.5

PUNTING YARDS

1. Don Cockroft   26,262
2. Horace Gillom   21,206
3. Chris Gardocki   20,220
4. Gary Collins   13,764
5. Dave Zastudil   11,207
6. Jeff Gossett   10,307
7. Brian Hansen   10,112
8. Reggie Hodges   8,979
9. Johnny Evans   8,463
10. Steve Cox   7,974

PUNT RETURN YARDS

1. Josh Cribbs   2,154
2. Dennis Northcutt   2,149
3. Gerald McNeil   1,545
4. Eric Metcalf   1,341
5. Leroy Kelly   990
6. Dino Hall   901
7. Cliff Lewis   710
8. Greg Pruitt   659
9. Bobby Mitchell   607
10. Ken Konz   556

KICKOFF RETURN YARDS

1. Josh Cribbs   10,015
2. Dino Hall   3,185
3. Eric Metcalf   2,806
4. Glen Young   2,079
5. Randy Baldwin   1,872
6. Andre Davis   1,871
7. Leroy Kelly   1,784
8. Keith Wright   1,767
9. Walter Roberts   1,608
10. Bobby Mitchell   1,550

COMBINED NET YARDS
(Does not include fumble return yardage for part of Browns history)

1. Jim Brown   15,459
2. Josh Cribbs   14,065
3. Leroy Kelly   12,329
4. Greg Pruitt   10,700
5. Eric Metcalf   9,108
6. Mike Pruitt   8,538
7. Ozzie Newsome   8,144
8. Marion Motley   7,019
9. Kevin Mack   6,725
10. Ray Renfro 6,569

INDIVIDUAL TOP TENS (GAME)
vs. – Denotes home

RUSHING YARDS

1. Jerome Harrison   286 (Dec. 20, 2009, at Kansas City)
2. Jim Brown   237 (Nov. 24, 1957, vs. Los Angeles)
   Jim Brown   237 (Nov. 19, 1961, vs. Philadelphia)
4. Bobby Mitchell   232 (Nov. 15, 1959, at Washington)
   Jim Brown   232 (Sept. 22, 1963, at Dallas)

6. Jim Brown   223 (Nov. 3, 1963, at Philadelphia)
7. Jamal Lewis   216 (Sept. 16, 2007, vs. Cincinnati)
8. Greg Pruitt   214 (Dec. 14, 1975, vs. Kansas City)
9. Greg Pruitt   191 (Oct. 17, 1976, at Atlanta)
10. Marion Motley   188 (Oct. 29, 1950, vs. Pittsburgh)
    Jim Brown   188 (Oct. 18, 1964, at Dallas)
    Earnest Byner   188 (Dec. 16, 1984, at Houston)

PASSING YARDS

1. Brian Sipe   444 (Oct. 25, 1981, vs. Baltimore)
2. Bernie Kosar   414 (Nov. 23, 1986, vs. Pittsburgh)
3. Kelly Holcomb   413 (Nov. 28, 2004, at Cincinnati)
4. Otto Graham   401 (Oct. 4, 1952, at Pittsburgh)
   Bernie Kosar   401 (Nov. 10, 1986, vs. Miami)
6. Kelly Holcomb   392 (Nov. 16, 2003, vs. Arizona)
7. Brian Sipe   391 (Oct. 19, 1980, vs. Green Bay)
   Jason Campbell   391 (Dec. 8, 2013, at New England)
9. Otto Graham   382 (Nov. 20, 1949, at Brooklyn-New York)
10. Brian Sipe   375 (Sept. 7, 1981, vs. San Diego)

RECEIVING YARDS
(Does not include Browns games against the Brooklyn Dodgers on December 8, 1946, and Baltimore Colts on December 7, 1947)

1. Josh Gordon   261 (Dec. 1, 2013, vs. Jacksonville)
2. Josh Gordon   237 (Nov. 24, 2013, vs. Pittsburgh)
3. Mac Speedie   228 (Nov. 20, 1949, at Brooklyn-New York)
4. Dante Lavelli   209 (Oct. 14, 1949, at Los Angeles)
5. Ozzie Newsome   191 (Oct. 14, 1984, vs. New York Jets)
6. Webster Slaughter   186 (Oct. 23, 1989, vs. Chicago)
7. Webster Slaughter   184 (Oct. 29, 1989, vs. Houston)
8. Dante Lavelli   183 (Oct. 27, 1946, vs. San Francisco)
9. Pete Brewster   182 (Dec. 6, 1953, vs. New York)
10. Gern Nagler   177 (Nov. 20, 1960, at Pittsburgh)
    Reggie Rucker   177 (Nov. 18, 1979, vs. Miami)
    Eric Metcalf   177 (Sept. 20, 1992, at Los Angeles Raiders)

INDIVIDUAL TOP TENS (SEASON)

SCORING (POINTS)

1. Jim Brown	126	(1965)
2. Leroy Kelly	120	(1968)
Phil Dawson	120	(2007)
4. Phil Dawson	116	(2012)
5. Lou Groza	115	(1964)
6. Matt Stover	113	(1995)
7. Matt Stover	110	(1994)
8. Lou Groza	108	(1953)
Jim Brown	108	(1958)
Jim Brown	108	(1962)
Phil Dawson	108	(2008)

RUSHING YARDS

1. Jim Brown	1,863	(1963)
2. Jim Brown	1,544	(1965)
3. Jim Brown	1,527	(1958)
4. Jim Brown	1,446	(1964)
5. Jim Brown	1,408	(1961)
6. Jim Brown	1,329	(1959)
7. Jamal Lewis	1,304	(2007)
8. Mike Pruitt	1,294	(1979)
9. Jim Brown	1,257	(1960)
10. Leroy Kelly	1,239	(1968)

PASSING YARDS

1. Brian Sipe	4,132	(1980)
2. Brian Sipe	3,876	(1981)
3. Bernie Kosar	3,854	(1986)
4. Brian Sipe	3,793	(1979)
5. Derek Anderson	3,787	(2007)
6. Brian Sipe	3,566	(1983)
7. Bernie Kosar	3,533	(1989)
8. Bernie Kosar	3,487	(1991)
9. Paul McDonald	3,472	(1984)
10. Brandon Weeden	3,385	(2012)

PASS COMPLETIONS

1. Brian Sipe	337	(1980)
2. Brian Sipe	313	(1981)
3. Bernie Kosar	310	(1986)
4. Bernie Kosar	307	(1991)
5. Bernie Kosar	303	(1989)
6. Derek Anderson	298	(2007)
7. Brandon Weeden	297	(2012)
8. Brian Sipe	291	(1983)
9. Brian Sipe	286	(1979)
10. Tim Couch	273	(2002)

RECEIVING YARDS

1. Josh Gordon	1,646	(2013)
2. Braylon Edwards	1,289	(2007)
3. Webster Slaughter	1,236	(1989)
4. Mac Speedie	1,146	(1947)
5. Kellen Winslow	1,106	(2007)
6. Kevin Johnson	1,097	(2001)
7. Paul Warfield	1,067	(1968)
8. Mac Speedie	1,028	(1949)
9. Antonio Bryant	1,009	(2005)
10. Ozzie Newsome	1,002	(1981)

RECEPTIONS

1. Ozzie Newsome	89 (1983)
Ozzie Newsome	89 (1984)
Kellen Winslow	89 (2006)
4. Josh Gordon	87 (2013)
5. Kevin Johnson	84 (2001)
6. Kellen Winslow	82 (2007)
7. Braylon Edwards	80 (2007)
Jordan Cameron	80 (2013)
9. Ozzie Newsome	69 (1981)
Antonio Bryant	69 (2005)

INTERCEPTIONS

1. Tom Colella	10 (1946)
Thom Darden	10 (1978)
Anthony Henry	10 (2001)
4. Cliff Lewis	9 (1948)
Tommy James	9 (1950)
Felix Wright	9 (1989)
Eric Turner	9 (1994)
8. Warren Lahr	8 (1950)
Bobby Franklin	8 (1960)
Jim Shofner	8 (1960)
Ross Fichtner	8 (1966)
Mike Howell	8 (1966)
Ben Davis	8 (1968)
Thom Darden	8 (1974)

SACKS

1. Reggie Camp	14 (1984)
2. Jamir Miller	13 (2001)
3. Clay Matthews	12 (1984)
4. Michael Dean Perry	11.5 (1990)
5. Chip Banks	11 (1985)
Anthony Pleasant	11 (1993)

Kamerion Wimbley	11 (2006)
Paul Kruger	11 (2014)
9. Rob Burnett	10 (1994)
10. Rob Burnett	9 (1992)
Clay Matthews	9 (1992)
Rob Burnett	9 (1993)

PUNTING YARDS

1. Chris Gardocki	4,919 (2000)
2. Chris Gardocki	4,645 (1999)
3. Chris Gardocki	4,249 (2001)
4. Spencer Lanning	4,119 (2014)
5. Bryan Wagner	3,817 (1989)
6. Reggie Hodges	3,766 (2012)
7. Spencer Lanning	3,679 (2013)
8. Don Cockroft	3,643 (1974)
9. Brian Hansen	3,632 (1993)
10. Dave Zastudil	3,563 (2006)

PUNT RETURN YARDS

1. Gerald McNeil	496 (1989)
2. Eric Metcalf	464 (1993)
3. Josh Cribbs	457 (2012)
4. Josh Cribbs	452 (2009)
5. Dennis Northcutt	432 (2004)
6. Eric Metcalf	429 (1992)
7. Josh Cribbs	405 (2007)
8. Josh Cribbs	388 (2011)
9. Gerald McNeil	386 (1987)
10. Dennis Northcutt	368 (2005)

KICKOFF RETURN YARDS

1. Josh Cribbs   1,809 (2007)
2. Josh Cribbs   1,542 (2009)
3. Josh Cribbs   1,494 (2006)
4. Josh Cribbs   1,178 (2012)
5. Josh Cribbs   1,110 (2008)
6. Josh Cribbs   1,094 (2005)
7. Andre Davis   1,068 (2002)
8. Eric Metcalf   1,052 (1990)
9. Richard Alston   1,016 (2004)
10. Dino Hall   1,014 (1979)

COMBINED NET YARDS

1. Josh Cribbs   2,510 (2009)
2. Josh Cribbs   2,312 (2007)
3. Jim Brown   2,131 (1963)
4. Leroy Kelly   2,014 (1966)
5. Eric Metcalf   1,932 (1993)
6. Jim Brown   1,917 (1961)
7. Josh Cribbs   1,905 (2011)
8. Jim Brown   1,872 (1965)
9. Greg Pruitt   1,798 (1975)
10. Jim Brown   1,786 (1964)

INTERCEPTIONS LEADERS

1946 –	Tom Colella	10
1947 –	Tom Colella	6
1948 –	Cliff Lewis	9
1949 –	Cliff Lewis	6
1950 –	Tommy James	9
1951 –	Warren Lahr	5
	Cliff Lewis	5
1952 –	Bert Rechichar	6
1953 –	Tommy James	5
	Ken Konz	5
	Warren Lahr	5
1954 –	Ken Konz	7
1955 –	Ken Konz	5
	Warren Lahr	5
	Chuck Noll	5
1956 –	Don Paul	7
1957 –	Ken Konz	4
	Don Paul	4
1958 –	Ken Konz	4
	Don Paul	4
1959 –	Bernie Parrish	5
	Junior Wren	5
1960 –	Bobby Franklin	8
	Jim Shofner	8
1961 –	Bernie Parrish	7
1962 –	Ross Fichtner	7
1963 –	Larry Benz	7
	Vince Costello	7
1964 –	Walter Beach	4
	Larry Benz	4
	Bernie Parrish	4
1965 –	Larry Benz	5
1966 –	Ross Fichtner	8
	Mike Howell	8
1967 –	Erich Barnes	4
	Ross Fichtner	4
1968 –	Ben Davis	8
1969 –	Mike Howell	6
1970 –	Erich Barnes	5
1971 –	Walt Sumner	5
1972 –	Thom Darden	3
	Ben Davis	3
1973 –	Clarence Scott	5
1974 –	Thom Darden	8
1975 –	Charlie Hall	2
	Clarence Scott	2
1976 –	Thom Darden	7
1977 –	Thom Darden	6
1978 –	Thom Darden	10

1979 – Thom Darden	5
1980 – Ron Bolton	6
1981 – Clarence Scott	4
1982 – Hanford Dixon	4
Lawrence Johnson	4
1983 – Tom Cousineau	4
1984 – Hanford Dixon	5
Al Gross	5
1985 – Al Gross	5
1986 – Hanford Dixon	5
1987 – Frank Minnifield	4
Felix Wright	4
1988 – Felix Wright	5
1989 – Felix Wright	9
1990 – Felix Wright	3
1991 – Stephen Braggs	3
1992 – Vince Newsome	3
1993 – Eric Turner	5
1994 – Eric Turner	9
1995 – Stevon Moore	5
1999 – Marquez Pope	2
2000 – Corey Fuller	3
2001 – Anthony Henry	10
2002 – Earl Little	4
2003 – Earl Little	6
2004 – Anthony Henry	4
2005 – Leigh Bodden	3
Brian Russell	3
2006 – Daven Holly	5
Sean Jones	5
2007 – Leigh Bodden	6
2008 – Brandon McDonald	5
2009 – Brodney Pool	4
Eric Wright	4
2010 – Joe Haden	6
2011 – Mike Adams	3
2012 – Sheldon Brown	3
Joe Haden	3
Usama Young	3

2013 – Tashaun Gipson	5
2014 – Tashaun Gipson	6

KICKOFF RETURN YARDS LEADERS

1946 – Edgar Jones	307
1947 – Marion Motley	322
1948 – Marion Motley	337
1949 – Marion Motley	262
1950 – Don Phelps	325
1951 – Ken Carpenter	196
1952 – Ken Carpenter	234
1953 – Ken Carpenter	367
1954 – Billy Reynolds	413
1955 – Bob Smith	320
1956 – Preston Carpenter	381
1957 – Milt Campbell	263
1958 – Bobby Mitchell	454
1959 – Bobby Mitchell	236
1960 – Bobby Mitchell	432
1961 – Bobby Mitchell	428
1962 – Tom Wilson	307
1963 – Charley Scales	432
1964 – Walter Roberts	661
1965 – Leroy Kelly	621
1966 – Walter Roberts	454
1967 – Ben Davis	708
1968 – Charlie Leigh	322
1969 – Bo Scott	722
1970 – Homer Jones	739
1971 – Ken Brown	330
1972 – Ken Brown	473
1973 – Greg Pruitt	453
1974 – Greg Pruitt	606
1975 – Billy Lefear	412
1976 – Steve Holden	461
1977 – Brian Duncan	298

1978 – Keith Wright	789
1979 – Dino Hall	1,014
1980 – Dino Hall	691
1981 – Dino Hall	813
1982 – Dino Hall	430
1983 – Dwight Walker	627
1984 – Earnest Byner	415
1985 – Glen Young	898
1986 – Gerald McNeil	997
1987 – Glen Young	412
1988 – Glen Young	635
1989 – Eric Metcalf	718
1990 – Eric Metcalf	1,052
1991 – Eric Metcalf	351
1992 – Randy Baldwin	675
1993 – Randy Baldwin	444
1994 – Randy Baldwin	753
1995 – Earnest Hunter	518
1999 – Ronnie Powell	986
2000 – Jamel White	935
2001 – Ben Gay	513
2002 – Andre Davis	1,068
2003 – Andre Davis	803
2004 – Richard Alston	1,016
2005 – Josh Cribbs	1,094
2006 – Josh Cribbs	1,494
2007 – Josh Cribbs	1,809
2008 – Josh Cribbs	1,110
2009 – Josh Cribbs	1,542
2010 – Josh Cribbs	814
2011 – Josh Cribbs	974
2012 – Josh Cribbs	1,178
2013 – Fozzy Whittaker	482
2014 – Marlon Moore	322

KICKOFF RETURNS LEADERS

1946 – Edgar Jones	12
1947 – Marion Motley	13
1948 – Marion Motley	14
1949 – Marion Motley	12
1950 – Don Phelps	12
1951 – Ken Carpenter	9
1952 – Ken Carpenter	11
1953 – Ken Carpenter	16
1954 – Billy Reynolds	14
1955 – Bob Smith	13
1956 – Preston Carpenter	15
1957 – Milt Campbell	11
1958 – Bobby Mitchell	18
1959 – Bobby Mitchell	11
1960 – Bobby Mitchell	17
1961 – Bobby Mitchell	16
Preston Powell	16
1962 – Ernie Green	13
1963 – Ernie Green	18
1964 – Leroy Kelly	24
Walter Roberts	24
1965 – Leroy Kelly	24
1966 – Walter Roberts	20
1967 – Ben Davis	27
1968 – Charlie Leigh	14
1969 – Bo Scott	25
1970 – Homer Jones	29
1971 – Ken Brown	15
1972 – Ken Brown	20
1973 – Greg Pruitt	16
1974 – Billy Lefear	26
1975 – Greg Pruitt	14
1976 – Steve Holden	19
1977 – Brian Duncan	15
1978 – Larry Collins	32
1979 – Dino Hall	50

1980 – Dino Hall	32
1981 – Dino Hall	36
1982 – Dino Hall	22
1983 – Dwight Walker	29
1984 – Earnest Byner	22
1985 – Glen Young	35
1986 – Gerald McNeil	47
1987 – Glen Young	18
1988 – Glen Young	29
1989 – Eric Metcalf	31
1990 – Eric Metcalf	52
1991 – Eric Metcalf	23
1992 – Randy Baldwin	30
1993 – Randy Baldwin	24
1994 – Randy Baldwin	28
1995 – Earnest Hunter	23
1999 – Ronnie Powell	44
2000 – Jamel White	43
2001 – Ben Gay	23
2002 – Andre Davis	50
2003 – Andre Davis	38
2004 – Richard Alston	46
2005 – Josh Cribbs	45
2006 – Josh Cribbs	61
2007 – Josh Cribbs	59
2008 – Josh Cribbs	44
2009 – Josh Cribbs	56
2010 – Josh Cribbs	40
2011 – Josh Cribbs	39
2012 – Josh Cribbs	43
2013 – Fozzy Whittaker	23
2014 – Marlon Moore	13

ONE-THOUSAND-YARD RECEIVERS

Mac Speedie	1,146 (1947)
Mac Speedie	1,028 (1949)
Paul Warfield	1,067 (1968)
Ozzie Newsome	1,002 (1981)
Ozzie Newsome	1,001 (1984)
Webster Slaughter	1,236 (1989)
Kevin Johnson	1,097 (2001)
Antonio Bryant	1,009 (2005)
Braylon Edwards	1,289 (2007)
Kellen Winslow	1,106 (2007)
Josh Gordon	1,646 (2013)

ONE-THOUSAND-YARD RUSHERS

Jim Brown	1,527 (1958)
Jim Brown	1,329 (1959)
Jim Brown	1,257 (1960)
Jim Brown	1,408 (1961)
Jim Brown	1,863 (1963)
Jim Brown	1,446 (1964)
Jim Brown	1,544 (1965)
Leroy Kelly	1,205 (1967)
Leroy Kelly	1,141 (1966)
Leroy Kelly	1,239 (1968)
Greg Pruitt	1,067 (1975)
Greg Pruitt	1,000 (1976)
Greg Pruitt	1,086 (1977)
Mike Pruitt	1,294 (1979)
Mike Pruitt	1,034 (1980)
Mike Pruitt	1,103 (1981)
Mike Pruitt	1,184 (1983)
Kevin Mack	1,104 (1985)
Earnest Byner	1,002 (1985)
Reuben Droughns	1,232 (2005)

CLEVELAND BROWNS A-Z   239

Jamal Lewis   1,304 (2007)
Jamal Lewis   1,002 (2008)
Peyton Hillis   1,177 (2010)

PASS COMPLETIONS LEADERS

1946 – Otto Graham	95
1947 – Otto Graham	163
1948 – Otto Graham	173
1949 – Otto Graham	161
1950 – Otto Graham	137
1951 – Otto Graham	147
1952 – Otto Graham	181
1953 – Otto Graham	167
1954 – Otto Graham	142
1955 – Otto Graham	98
1956 – Tommy O'Connell	42
1957 – Tommy O'Connell	63
1958 – Milt Plum	102
1959 – Milt Plum	156
1960 – Milt Plum	151
1961 – Milt Plum	177
1962 – Frank Ryan	112
1963 – Frank Ryan	135
1964 – Frank Ryan	174
1965 – Frank Ryan	119
1966 – Frank Ryan	200
1967 – Frank Ryan	136
1968 – Bill Nelsen	152
1969 – Bill Nelsen	190
1970 – Bill Nelsen	159
1971 – Bill Nelsen	174
1972 – Mike Phipps	144
1973 – Mike Phipps	148
1974 – Mike Phipps	117
1975 – Mike Phipps	162
1976 – Brian Sipe	178
1977 – Brian Sipe	112
1978 – Brian Sipe	222
1979 – Brian Sipe	286
1980 – Brian Sipe	337
1981 – Brian Sipe	313
1982 – Brian Sipe	101
1983 – Brian Sipe	291
1984 – Paul McDonald	271
1985 – Bernie Kosar	124
1986 – Bernie Kosar	310
1987 – Bernie Kosar	241
1988 – Bernie Kosar	156
1989 – Bernie Kosar	303
1990 – Bernie Kosar	230
1991 – Bernie Kosar	307
1992 – Mike Tomczak	120
1993 – Vinny Testaverde	130
1994 – Vinny Testaverde	207
1995 – Vinny Testaverde	241
1999 – Tim Couch	223
2000 – Tim Couch	137
2001 – Tim Couch	272
2002 – Tim Couch	273
2003 – Kelly Holcomb	193
2004 – Jeff Garcia	144
2005 – Trent Dilfer	199
2006 – Charlie Frye	252
2007 – Derek Anderson	298
2008 – Derek Anderson	142
2009 – Brady Quinn	136
2010 – Colt McCoy	135
2011 – Colt McCoy	265
2012 – Brandon Weeden	297
2013 – Jason Campbell	180
2014 – Brian Hoyer	242

PASSING YARDS LEADERS

1946 – Otto Graham	1,834
1947 – Otto Graham	2,753
1948 – Otto Graham	2,713
1949 – Otto Graham	2,785
1950 – Otto Graham	1,943
1951 – Otto Graham	2,205
1952 – Otto Graham	2,816
1953 – Otto Graham	2,722
1954 – Otto Graham	2,092
1955 – Otto Graham	1,721
1956 – Tommy O'Connell	551
1957 – Tommy O'Connell	1,229
1958 – Milt Plum	1,619
1959 – Milt Plum	1,992
1960 – Milt Plum	2,297
1961 – Milt Plum	2,416
1962 – Frank Ryan	1,541
1963 – Frank Ryan	2,026
1964 – Frank Ryan	2,404
1965 – Frank Ryan	1,751
1966 – Frank Ryan	2,974
1967 – Frank Ryan	2,026
1968 – Bill Nelsen	2,366
1969 – Bill Nelsen	2,743
1970 – Bill Nelsen	2,156
1971 – Bill Nelsen	2,319
1972 – Mike Phipps	1,994
1973 – Mike Phipps	1,719
1974 – Mike Phipps	1,384
1975 – Mike Phipps	1,749
1976 – Brian Sipe	2,113
1977 – Brian Sipe	1,233
1978 – Brian Sipe	2,906
1979 – Brian Sipe	3,793
1980 – Brian Sipe	4,132
1981 – Brian Sipe	3,876
1982 – Brian Sipe	1,064
1983 – Brian Sipe	3,566
1984 – Paul McDonald	3,472
1985 – Bernie Kosar	1,578
1986 – Bernie Kosar	3,854
1987 – Bernie Kosar	3,033
1988 – Bernie Kosar	1,890
1989 – Bernie Kosar	3,533
1990 – Bernie Kosar	2,562
1991 – Bernie Kosar	3,487
1992 – Mike Tomczak	1,693
1993 – Vinny Testaverde	1,797
1994 – Vinny Testaverde	2,575
1995 – Vinny Testaverde	2,883
1999 – Tim Couch	2,447
2000 – Tim Couch	1,483
2001 – Tim Couch	3,040
2002 – Tim Couch	2,842
2003 – Kelly Holcomb	1,797
2004 – Jeff Garcia	1,731
2005 – Trent Dilfer	2,321
2006 – Charlie Frye	2,454
2007 – Derek Anderson	3,787
2008 – Derek Anderson	1,615
2009 – Brady Quinn	1,339
2010 – Colt McCoy	1,576
2011 – Colt McCoy	2,733
2012 – Brandon Weeden	3,385
2013 – Jason Campbell	2,015
2014 – Brian Hoyer	3,326

PUNT RETURN YARDS LEADERS

1946 – Tom Colella	172
1947 – Otto Graham	121
1948 – Cliff Lewis	258
1949 – Cliff Lewis	174

1950 – Don Phelps	174	1989 – Gerald McNeil	496
1951 – Ken Carpenter	173	1990 – Stefon Adams	81
1952 – Ray Renfro	169	1991 – Webster Slaughter	112
1953 – Billy Reynolds	111	1992 – Eric Metcalf	429
1954 – Billy Reynolds	138	1993 – Eric Metcalf	464
1955 – Don Paul	148	1994 – Eric Metcalf	348
1956 – Ken Konz	187	1995 – Derrick Alexander	122
1957 – Billy Reynolds	114	1999 – Kevin Johnson	128
1958 – Bobby Mitchell	65	2000 – Dennis Northcutt	289
1959 – Bobby Mitchell	177	2001 – Kevin Johnson	117
1960 – Jim Shofner	105	2002 – Dennis Northcutt	367
1961 – Bobby Mitchell	164	2003 – Dennis Northcutt	295
1962 – Howard Cassady	47	2004 – Dennis Northcutt	432
1963 – Jim Shorter	134	2005 – Dennis Northcutt	368
1964 – Leroy Kelly	171	2006 – Dennis Northcutt	312
1965 – Leroy Kelly	265	2007 – Josh Cribbs	405
1966 – Leroy Kelly	104	2008 – Josh Cribbs	228
1967 – Ben Davis	229	2009 – Josh Cribbs	452
1968 – Charles Leigh	76	2010 – Josh Cribbs	168
1969 – Walt Sumner	72	2011 – Josh Cribbs	388
1970 – Reece Morrison	133	2012 – Josh Cribbs	457
1971 – Leroy Kelly	292	2013 – Travis Benjamin	257
1972 – Bobby Majors	96	2014 – Travis Benjamin	127
1973 – Greg Pruitt	180		
1974 – Greg Pruitt	349	**PUNT RETURNS LEADERS**	
1975 – Greg Pruitt	130		
1976 – Steve Holden	205	1946 – Bud Schwenk	12
1977 – Roily Woolsey	290	1947 – Otto Graham	10
1978 – Keith Wright	288	1948 – Cliff Lewis	26
1979 – Dino Hall	295	1949 – Cliff Lewis	20
1980 – Keith Wright	129	1950 – Don Phelps	13
1981 – Dino Hall	248	1951 – Ken Carpenter	14
1982 – Dwight Walker	101	Cliff Lewis	14
1983 – Dino Hall	284	1952 – Ray Renfro	22
1984 – Brian Brennan	199	1953 – Billy Reynolds	18
1985 – Clarence Weathers	218	1954 – Chet Hanulak	27
1986 – Gerald McNeil	348	1955 – Don Paul	19
1987 – Gerald McNeil	386	1956 – Don Paul	17
1988 – Gerald McNeil	315		

1957 – Billy Reynolds	24
1958 – Ken Konz	18
1959 – Bobby Mitchell	17
1960 – Jim Shofner	11
1961 – Bobby Mitchell	14
Jim Shofner	14
1962 – Jim Shofner	8
1963 – Jim Shofner	9
1964 – Walter Roberts	10
1965 – Walter Roberts	18
1966 – Leroy Kelly	13
1967 – Ben Davis	18
1968 – Charles Leigh	14
1969 – Reece Morrison	11
1970 – Reece Morrison	15
1971 – Leroy Kelly	30
1972 – Bobby Majors	16
1973 – Greg Pruitt	16
1974 – Greg Pruitt	27
1975 – Greg Pruitt	13
1976 – Steve Holden	31
1977 – Roily Woolsey	32
1978 – Keith Wright	37
1979 – Dino Hall	29
1980 – Keith Wright	29
1981 – Dino Hall	33
1982 – Dwight Walker	19
1983 – Dino Hall	39
1984 – Brian Brennan	25
1985 – Clarence Weathers	28
1986 – Gerald McNeil	40
1987 – Gerald McNeil	34
1988 – Gerald McNeil	38
1989 – Gerald McNeil	49
1990 – Stefon Adams	13
1991 – Webster Slaughter	17
1992 – Eric Metcalf	44
1993 – Eric Metcalf	36
1994 – Eric Metcalf	35

1995 – Keenan McCardell	13
1999 – Kevin Johnson	19
2000 – Dennis Northcutt	27
2001 – Dennis Northcutt	15
2002 – Dennis Northcutt	25
2003 – Dennis Northcutt	36
2004 – Dennis Northcutt	36
2005 – Dennis Northcutt	35
2006 – Dennis Northcutt	28
2007 – Josh Cribbs	30
2008 – Josh Cribbs	28
2009 – Josh Cribbs	38
2010 – Josh Cribbs	20
2011 – Josh Cribbs	34
2012 – Josh Cribbs	38
2013 – Travis Benjamin	22
2014 – Travis Benjamin	15

PUNTING YARDS LEADERS

1946 – Tom Colella	1,894
1947 – Chet Adams	2,096
1948 – Tom Colella	1,715
1949 – Horace Gillom	2,009
1950 – Horace Gillom	2,849
1951 – Horace Gillom	3,321
1952 – Horace Gillom	2,787
1953 – Horace Gillom	2,760
1954 – Horace Gillom	2,230
1955 – Horace Gillom	2,389
1956 – Fred Morrison	1,561
1957 – Ken Konz	2,396
1958 – Dick Deschaine	2,063
1959 – Junior Wren	996
1960 – Sam Baker	2,309
1961 – Sam Baker	2,296
1962 – Gary Collins	1,926
1963 – Gary Collins	2,160

1964 – Gary Collins	2,016	2006 – Dave Zastudil	3,563
1965 – Gary Collins	3,035	2007 – Dave Zastudil	2,046
1966 – Gary Collins	2,223	2008 – Dave Zastudil	3,410
1967 – Gary Collins	2,078	2009 – Dave Zastudil	2,188
1968 – Don Cockroft	2,297	2010 – Reggie Hodges	3,424
1969 – Don Cockroft	2,138	2011 – Brad Maynard	3,282
1970 – Don Cockroft	3,023	2012 – Reggie Hodges	3,766
1971 – Don Cockroft	2,508	2013 – Spencer Lanning	3,679
1972 – Don Cockroft	3,498	2014 – Spencer Lanning	4,119
1973 – Don Cockroft	3,321		
1974 – Don Cockroft	3,643		

RECEIVING YARDS LEADERS

1975 – Don Cockroft	3,317		
1976 – Don Cockroft	2,487	1946 – Dante Lavelli	843
1977 – Greg Coleman	2,389	1947 – Mac Speedie	1,146
1978 – Johnny Evans	3,089	1948 – Mac Speedie	816
1979 – Johnny Evans	2,844	1949 – Mac Speedie	1,028
1980 – Johnny Evans	2,530	1950 – Dante Lavelli	565
1981 – Steve Cox	2,884	1951 – Mac Speedie	589
1982 – Steve Cox	1,887	1952 – Mac Speedie	911
1983 – Jeff Gossett	2,854	1953 – Dante Lavelli	783
1984 – Steve Cox	3,213	1954 – Dante Lavelli	802
1985 – Jeff Gossett	3,261	1955 – Darrell Brewster	622
1986 – Jeff Gossett	3,423	1956 – Darrell Brewster	417
1987 – Jeff Gossett	779	1957 – Darrell Brewster	614
1988 – Max Runager	1,935	1958 – Ray Renfro	573
1989 – Bryan Wagner	3,817	1959 – Ray Renfro	528
1990 – Bryan Wagner	2,879	1960 – Gern Nagler	616
1991 – Brian Hansen	3,397	1961 – Ray Renfro	834
1992 – Brian Hansen	3,083	1962 – Rich Kreitling	659
1993 – Brian Hansen	3,632	1963 – Gary Collins	674
1994 – Tom Tupa	3,211	1964 – Paul Warfield	920
1995 – Tom Tupa	2,831	1965 – Gary Collins	884
1999 – Chris Gardocki	4,645	1966 – Gary Collins	946
2000 – Chris Gardocki	4,919	1967 – Paul Warfield	702
2001 – Chris Gardocki	4,249	1968 – Paul Warfield	1,067
2002 – Chris Gardocki	3,388	1969 – Paul Warfield	886
2003 – Chris Gardocki	3,019	1970 – Milt Morin	611
2004 – Derrick Frost	3,404	1971 – Fair Hooker	649
2005 – Kyle Richardson	3,181		

1972 – Frank Pitts	620	2014 – Andrew Hawkins	824
1973 – Milt Morin	417		
1974 – Steve Holden	452	**RECEPTIONS LEADERS**	
1975 – Reggie Rucker	770		
1976 – Reggie Rucker	676	1946 – Dante Lavelli	40
1977 – Reggie Rucker	565	1947 – Mac Speedie	67
1978 – Reggie Rucker	893	1948 – Mac Speedie	58
1979 – Dave Logan	982	1949 – Mac Speedie	62
1980 – Dave Logan	822	1950 – Mac Speedie	42
1981 – Ozzie Newsome	1,002	1951 – Dante Lavelli	43
1982 – Ozzie Newsome	633	1952 – Mac Speedie	62
1983 – Ozzie Newsome	970	1953 – Dante Lavelli	45
1984 – Ozzie Newsome	1,001	1954 – Dante Lavelli	47
1985 – Ozzie Newsome	711	1955 – Darrell Brewster	34
1986 – Brian Brennan	838	1956 – Darrell Brewster	28
1987 – Webster Slaughter	806	1957 – Darrell Brewster	30
1988 – Reggie Langhorne	780	1958 – Preston Carpenter	29
1989 – Webster Slaughter	1,236	1959 – Billy Howton	39
1990 – Webster Slaughter	847	1960 – Bobby Mitchell	45
1991 – Webster Slaughter	906	1961 – Ray Renfro	48
1992 – Michael Jackson	755	1962 – Jim Brown	47
1993 – Michael Jackson	756	1963 – Gary Collins	43
1994 – Derrick Alexander	828	1964 – Paul Warfield	52
1995 – Michael Jackson	714	1965 – Gary Collins	50
1999 – Kevin Johnson	986	1966 – Gary Collins	56
2000 – Kevin Johnson	669	1967 – Ernie Green	39
2001 – Kevin Johnson	1,097	1968 – Paul Warfield	50
2002 – Quincy Morgan	964	1969 – Gary Collins	54
2003 – Dennis Northcutt	729	1970 – Bo Scott	40
2004 – Dennis Northcutt	806	1971 – Fair Hooker	45
2005 – Antonio Bryant	1,009	1972 – Frank Pitts	36
2006 – Braylon Edwards	884	1973 – Frank Pitts	31
2007 – Braylon Edwards	1,289	1974 – Hugh McKinnis	32
2008 – Braylon Edwards	873	1975 – Reggie Rucker	60
2009 – Mohamed Massaquoi	624	1976 – Reggie Rucker	49
2010 – Ben Watson	763	1977 – Cleo Miller	41
2011 – Greg Little	709	1978 – Reggie Rucker	43
2012 – Josh Gordon	805	1979 – Dave Logan	59
2013 – Josh Gordon	1,646		

1980 – Mike Pruitt	63
1981 – Ozzie Newsome	69
1982 – Ozzie Newsome	49
1983 – Ozzie Newsome	89
1984 – Ozzie Newsome	89
1985 – Ozzie Newsome	62
1986 – Brian Brennan	55
1987 – Earnest Byner	52
1988 – Earnest Byner	59
1989 – Webster Slaughter	65
1990 – Webster Slaughter	59
1991 – Webster Slaughter	64
1992 – Michael Jackson	47
Eric Metcalf	47
1993 – Eric Metcalf	63
1994 – Derrick Alexander	48
1995 – Earnest Byner	61
1999 – Kevin Johnson	66
2000 – Kevin Johnson	57
2001 – Kevin Johnson	84
2002 – Kevin Johnson	67
2003 – Dennis Northcutt	62
2004 – Dennis Northcutt	55
2005 – Antonio Bryant	69
2006 – Kellen Winslow	89
2007 – Kellen Winslow	82
2008 – Braylon Edwards	55
2009 – Jerome Harrison	34
Mohamed Massaquoi	34
2010 – Ben Watson	68
2011 – Greg Little	61
2012 – Greg Little	53
2013 – Josh Gordon	87
2014 – Andrew Hawkins	63

RUSHING YARDS LEADERS

1946 – Marion Motley	601
1947 – Marion Motley	889
1948 – Marion Motley	964
1949 – Marion Motley	570
1950 – Marion Motley	810
1951 – Dub Jones	492
1952 – Marion Motley	444
1953 – Ray Renfro	352
1954 – Maurice Bassett	588
1955 – Fred Morrison	824
1956 – Preston Carpenter	756
1957 – Jim Brown	942
1958 – Jim Brown	1,527
1959 – Jim Brown	1,329
1960 – Jim Brown	1,257
1961 – Jim Brown	1,408
1962 – Jim Brown	996
1963 – Jim Brown	1,863
1964 – Jim Brown	1,446
1965 – Jim Brown	1,544
1966 – Leroy Kelly	1,141
1967 – Leroy Kelly	1,205
1968 – Leroy Kelly	1,239
1969 – Leroy Kelly	817
1970 – Leroy Kelly	656
1971 – Leroy Kelly	865
1972 – Leroy Kelly	811
1973 – Ken Brown	537
1974 – Greg Pruitt	540
1975 – Greg Pruitt	1,067
1976 – Greg Pruitt	1,000
1977 – Greg Pruitt	1,086
1978 – Greg Pruitt	960
1979 – Mike Pruitt	1,294
1980 – Mike Pruitt	1,034
1981 – Mike Pruitt	1,103

1982 – Mike Pruitt	516	1987 – Carl Hairston	8
1983 – Mike Pruitt	1,184	1988 – Clay Matthews	6
1984 – Boyce Green	673	Michael Dean Perry	6
1985 – Kevin Mack	1,104	1989 – Al Baker	7.5
1986 – Kevin Mack	665	1990 – Michael Dean Perry	11.5
1987 – Kevin Mack	735	1991 – Michael Dean Perry	8.5
1988 – Earnest Byner	576	1992 – Rob Burnett	9
1989 – Eric Metcalf	633	Clay Matthews	9
1990 – Kevin Mack	702	1993 – Anthony Pleasant	11
1991 – Kevin Mack	726	1994 – Rob Burnett	10
1992 – Kevin Mack	543	1995 – Anthony Pleasant	8
1993 – Tommy Vardell	644	1999 – John Thierry	7
1994 – Leroy Hoard	890	2000 – Keith McKenzie	8
1995 – Leroy Hoard	547	2001 – Jamir Miller	13
1999 – Terry Kirby	452	2002 – Mark Word	8
2000 – Travis Prentice	512	2003 – Kenard Lang	8
2001 – James Jackson	554	2004 – Ebenezer Ekuban	8
2002 – William Green	887	2005 – Alvin McKinley	5
2003 – William Green	559	Chaun Thompson	5
2004 – Lee Suggs	744	2006 – Kamerion Wimbley	11
2005 – Reuben Droughns	1,232	2007 – Kamerion Wimbley	5
2006 – Reuben Droughns	758	2008 – Shaun Rogers	4.5
2007 – Jamal Lewis	1,304	2009 – Kamerion Wimbley	6.5
2008 – Jamal Lewis	1,002	2010 – Marcus Benard	7.5
2009 – Jerome Harrison	862	2011 – Jabaal Sheard	8.5
2010 – Peyton Hillis	1,177	2012 – Jabaal Sheard	7
2011 – Peyton Hillis	587	2013 – Jabaal Sheard	5.5
2012 – Trent Richardson	950	2014 – Paul Kruger	11
2013 – Willis McGahee	377		
2014 – Terrance West	673	

SCORING LEADERS (POINTS)

SACKS LEADERS

		1946 – Dante Lavelli	48
		1947 – Marion Motley	60
1982 – Chip Banks	5.5	1948 – Edgar Jones	60
1983 – Clay Matthews	6	1949 – Marion Motley	48
1984 – Reggie Camp	14	1950 – Lou Groza	74
1985 – Chip Banks	11	1951 – Lou Groza	73
1986 – Carl Hairston	9	1952 – Lou Groza	89

1953 – Lou Groza	108	1992 – Matt Stover	92
1954 – Lou Groza	85	1993 – Matt Stover	84
1955 – Lou Groza	77	1994 – Matt Stover	110
1956 – Lou Groza	51	1995 – Matt Stover	125
1957 – Lou Groza	77	1999 – Terry Kirby	54
1958 – Jim Brown	108	2000 – Phil Dawson	59
1959 – Jim Brown	84	2001 – Phil Dawson	95
1960 – Sam Baker	80	2002 – Phil Dawson	100
1961 – Lou Groza	85	2003 – Phil Dawson	74
1962 – Jim Brown	108	2004 – Phil Dawson	100
1963 – Jim Brown	90	2005 – Phil Dawson	100
1964 – Lou Groza	115	2006 – Phil Dawson	88
1965 – Jim Brown	126	2007 – Phil Dawson	120
1966 – Leroy Kelly	96	2008 – Phil Dawson	108
1967 – Leroy Kelly	78	2009 – Phil Dawson	69
1968 – Leroy Kelly	120	2010 – Phil Dawson	97
1969 – Don Cockroft	81	2011 – Phil Dawson	92
1970 – Don Cockroft	70	2012 – Phil Dawson	116
1971 – Don Cockroft	79	2013 – Billy Cundiff	95
1972 – Don Cockroft	94	2014 – Billy Cundiff	94
1973 – Don Cockroft	90		
1974 – Don Cockroft	71		
1975 – Don Cockroft	72		
1976 – Don Cockroft	72		
1977 – Don Cockroft	81		
1978 – Don Cockroft	94		
1979 – Don Cockroft	89		
1980 – Don Cockroft	87		
1981 – Matt Bahr	61		
1982 – Matt Bahr	38		
1983 – Matt Bahr	101		
1984 – Matt Bahr	97		
1985 – Matt Bahr	77		
1986 – Matt Bahr	90		
1987 – Jeff Jaeger	75		
1988 – Matt Bahr	104		
1989 – Matt Bahr	88		
1990 – Jerry Kauric	66		
1991 – Matt Stover	81		

THREE-THOUSAND-YARD PASSERS

Brian Sipe	3,793 (1979)
Brian Sipe	4,132 (1980)
Brian Sipe	3,876 (1981)
Brian Sipe	3,566 (1983)
Paul McDonald	3,472 (1984)
Bernie Kosar	3,854 (1986)
Bernie Kosar	3,033 (1987)
Bernie Kosar	3,533 (1989)
Bernie Kosar	3,487 (1991)
Tim Couch	3,040 (2001)
Derek Anderson	3,787 (2007)
Brandon Weeden	3,385 (2012)
Brian Hoyer	3,326 (2014)

Team Statistics

COMPOSITE MONTHLY WON-LOST-TIED RECORDS, BEST TO WORST

Rank	Month	Won	Lost	Tied	PCT.
1.	October	160	108	2	.596
2.	November	150	117	7	.560
3.	September	99	93	2	.515
4.	December	93	119	2	.439
5.	January	3	5	0	.375

COMPOSITE WON-LOST RECORDS VS. OTHER TEAMS, BEST TO WORST (POSTSEASON)

Rank Team	Won	Lost	PCT.
1. Buffalo Bisons/Bills (original)	2	0	1.000
New York Yankees	2	0	1.000
Buffalo Bills (current)	1	0	1.000
New England Patriots	1	0	1.000
New York Jets	1	0	1.000
San Francisco 49ers	1	0	1.000
7. Dallas Cowboys	2	1	.667
St. Louis Rams	2	1	.667
9. Indianapolis Colts	2	2	.500
New York Giants	1	1	.500
11. Detroit Lions	1	3	.250
12. Green Bay Packers	0	1	.000
Minnesota Vikings	0	1	.000
Tennessee Titans	0	1	.000
15. Miami Dolphins	0	2	.000
Oakland Raiders	0	2	.000
Pittsburgh Steelers	0	2	.000
18. Denver Broncos	0	3	.000

FINALES
* Denotes official finale

YEAR	HOME	AWAY
1946	Cleveland 42, Buffalo 17	*Cleveland 66, Brooklyn 14
1947	Cleveland 37, San Francisco 14	*Cleveland 42, Baltimore 0
1948	Cleveland 14, San Francisco 7	*Cleveland 31, Brooklyn 21
1949	Cleveland 7, Buffalo 7	*Cleveland 14, Chicago 6
1950	Cleveland 13, Philadelphia 7	*Cleveland 45, Washington 21
1951	Cleveland 49, Chicago Cardinals 28	*Cleveland 24, Philadelphia 9
1952	Philadelphia 28, Cleveland 20	*New York 37, Cleveland 34
1953	Cleveland 62, New York 14	*Philadelphia 42, Cleveland 27
1954	*Detroit 14, Cleveland 10	Cleveland 34, Washington 14
1955	*Cleveland 35, Chicago Cardinals 24	Cleveland 30, Pittsburgh 7
1956	*Chicago Cardinals 24, Cleveland 7	Cleveland 24, New York 7
1957	Cleveland 31, Chicago Cardinals 0	*Cleveland 34, New York 28
1958	Cleveland 21, Washington 14	*New York 13, Cleveland 10
1959	San Francisco 21, Cleveland 20	*Cleveland 28, Philadelphia 21
1960	Cleveland 42, Chicago 0	*Cleveland 48, New York 34
1961	New York 37, Cleveland 21	*New York 7, Cleveland 7
1962	Cleveland 35, Pittsburgh 14	*Cleveland 13, San Francisco 10
1963	Cleveland 27, Dallas 17	*Cleveland 27, Washington 20
1964	Cleveland 38, Philadelphia 24	*Cleveland 52, New York 20
1965	Cleveland 24, Washington 16	*Cleveland 27, St. Louis 24
1966	Cleveland 49, New York 40	*Cleveland 38, St. Louis 10
1967	Cleveland 24, New York 14	*Philadelphia 28, Cleveland 24
1968	Cleveland 45, New York 10	*St. Louis 27, Cleveland 16
1969	Cleveland 20, Green Bay 7	*New York 27, Cleveland 14
1970	Dallas 6, Cleveland 2	*Cleveland 27, Denver 13
1971	Cleveland 31, Cincinnati 27	*Cleveland 20, Washington 13
1972	Cleveland 27, Buffalo 10	*Cleveland 26, New York Jets 10
1973	Cleveland 21, Pittsburgh 16	*Los Angeles 30, Cleveland 17
1974	Cleveland 7, San Francisco 0	*Houston 28, Cleveland 24
1975	Cleveland 40, Kansas City 14	*Houston 21, Cleveland 10
1976	Cleveland 13, Houston 10	*Kansas City 39, Cleveland 14

1977	Houston 19, Cleveland 15	*Seattle 20, Cleveland 19
1978	Cleveland 37, New York Jets 34 (OT)	*Cincinnati 48, Cleveland 16
1979	Cleveland 14, Houston 7	*Cincinnati 16, Cleveland 12
1980	Cleveland 17, New York Jets 14	*Cleveland 27, Cincinnati 24
1981	New York Jets 14, Cleveland 13	*Seattle 42, Cleveland 21
1982	Cleveland 10, Pittsburgh 9	*Pittsburgh 37, Cleveland 21
1983	*Cleveland 30, Pittsburgh 17	Houston 34, Cleveland 27
1984	Cincinnati 20, Cleveland 17 (OT)	*Cleveland 27, Houston 20
1985	Cleveland 28, Houston 21	*New York Jets 37, Cleveland 10
1986	*Cleveland 47, San Diego 17	Cleveland 34, Cincinnati 3
1987	Cleveland 38, Cincinnati 24	*Cleveland 19, Pittsburgh 13
1988	*Cleveland 28, Houston 23	Miami 38, Cleveland 31
1989	Cleveland 23, Minnesota 17 (OT)	*Cleveland 24, Houston 20
1990	Cleveland 13, Atlanta 10	*Cincinnati 21, Cleveland 14
1991	Houston 17, Cleveland 14	* Pittsburgh 17, Cleveland 10
1992	Houston 17, Cleveland 14	*Pittsburgh 23, Cleveland 13
1993	New England 20, Cleveland 17	* Pittsburgh 16, Cleveland 9
1994	*Cleveland 35, Seattle 9	Pittsburgh 17, Cleveland 7
1995	Cleveland 26, Cincinnati 10	Jacksonville 24, Cleveland 21
1999	*Indianapolis 29, Cleveland 28	Cincinnati 44, Cleveland 28
2000	Tennessee 24, Cleveland 0	Jacksonville 48, Cleveland 0
2001	Jacksonville 15, Cleveland 10	*Pittsburgh 28, Cleveland 7
2002	*Cleveland 24, Atlanta 16	Cleveland 14, Baltimore 13
2003	Baltimore 35, Cleveland 0	*Cleveland 22, Cincinnati 14
2004	San Diego 21, Cleveland 0	*Cleveland 22, Houston 14
2005	*Cleveland 20, Baltimore 16	Cleveland 9, Oakland 7
2006	Tampa Bay 22, Cleveland 7	*Houston 14, Cleveland 6
2007	*Cleveland 20, San Francisco	7 Cincinnati 19, Cleveland 14
2008	Cincinnati 14, Cleveland 0	*Pittsburgh 31, Cleveland 0
2009	*Cleveland 23, Jacksonville 17	Cleveland 41, Kansas City 34
2010	*Pittsburgh 41, Cleveland 9	Cincinnati 19, Cleveland 17
2011	*Pittsburgh 13, Cleveland 9	Baltimore 20, Cleveland 14
2012	Washington 38, Cleveland 21	*Pittsburgh 24, Cleveland 10
2013	Chicago 38, Cleveland 31	*Pittsburgh 20, Cleveland 7
2014	Cincinnati 30, Cleveland 0	*Baltimore 20, Cleveland 10

Official Finales – 32-33-1 (.492)

Official Home Finales – 9-6 (.600)

Official Away Finales – 23-27-1 (.461)

Home Finales – 41-24-1 (.629)

Away Finales – 30-35-1 (.462)

OPENERS

* Denotes official opener

YEAR	HOME	AWAY
1946	*Cleveland 44, Miami 0	Cleveland 20, Chicago 6
1947	*Cleveland 30, Buffalo 14	Cleveland 55, Brooldyn 7
1948	*Cleveland 19, Los Angeles 14	Cleveland 42, Buffalo 13
1949	Cleveland 21, Baltimore 0	*Buffalo 28, Cleveland 28
1950	New York Giants 6, Cleveland 0	*Cleveland 35, Philadelphia 10
1951	Cleveland 45, Washington 0	*San Francisco 24, Cleveland 10
1952	*Cleveland 37, Los Angeles 7	Cleveland 21, Pittsburgh 20
1953	Cleveland 37, Philadelphia 13	*Cleveland 27, Green Bay 0
1954	Cleveland 31, Chicago Cardinals 7	*Philadelphia 28, Cleveland 10
1955	*Washington 27, Cleveland 17	Cleveland 38, San Francisco 3
1956	New York 21, Cleveland 9	*Chicago Cardinals 9, Cleveland 7
1957	*New York 6, Cleveland 3	Cleveland 23, Pittsburgh 12
1958	Cleveland 35, Chicago Cardinals 28	*Cleveland 30, Los Angeles 27
1959	New York 10, Cleveland 6	*Pittsburgh 17, Cleveland 7
1960	Cleveland 28, Pittsburgh 20	*Cleveland 41, Philadelphia 24
1961	Cleveland 20, St. Louis 17	*Philadelphia 27, Cleveland 20
1962	*Cleveland 17, New York 7	Philadelphia 35, Cleveland 7
1963	*Cleveland 37, Washington 14	Cleveland 41, Dallas 24
1964	Cleveland 33, St. Louis 33	*Cleveland 27, Washington 13
1965	St. Louis 49, Cleveland 13	*Cleveland 17, Washington 7
1966	Green Bay 21, Cleveland 20	*Cleveland 36, Washington 14
1967	*Dallas 21, Cleveland 14	Detroit 31, Cleveland 14
1968	Los Angeles 24, Cleveland 6	*Cleveland 24, New Orleans 10
1969	Cleveland 27, Washington 23	*Cleveland 27, Philadelphia 20
1970	*Cleveland 31, New York Jets 21	San Francisco 34, Cleveland 31
1971	*Cleveland 31, Houston 0	Cleveland 14, Baltimore 13
1972	*Green Bay 26, Cleveland 10	Cleveland 27, Philadelphia 17
1973	*Cleveland 24, Baltimore 14	Pittsburgh 33, Cleveland 6

1974	Cleveland 20, Houston 7	*Cincinnati 33, Cleveland 7
1975	Minnesota 42, Cleveland 10	*Cincinnati 24, Cleveland 17
1976	*Cleveland 38, New York Jets 17	Pittsburgh 31, Cleveland 14
1977	Cleveland 30, New England 27 (OT)	*Cleveland 13, Cincinnati 3
1978	*Cleveland 24, San Francisco 7	Cleveland 24, Atlanta 16
1979	Cleveland 13, Baltimore 10	*Cleveland 25, New York Jets 22 (OT)
1980	Houston 16, Cleveland 7	*New England 34, Cleveland 17
1981	*San Diego 44, Cleveland 14	Cleveland 20, Cincinnati 17
1982	Philadelphia 24, Cleveland 21	*Cleveland 21, Seattle 7
1983	*Minnesota 27, Cleveland 21	Cleveland 31, Detroit 26
1984	Denver 24, Cleveland 14	*Seattle 33, Cleveland 0
1985	*St. Louis 27, Cleveland 24 (OT)	Dallas 20, Cleveland 7
1986	Cincinnati 30, Cleveland 13	*Chicago 41, Cleveland 31
1987	Cleveland 34, Pittsburgh 10	*New Orleans 28, Cleveland 21
1988	New York Jets 23, Cleveland 3	*Cleveland 6, Kansas City 3
1989	Cleveland 38, New York Jets 24	*Cleveland 51, Pittsburgh 0
1990	*Cleveland 13, Pittsburgh 3	New York Jets 24, Cleveland 21
1991	*Dallas 26, Cleveland 14	Cleveland 20, New England 0
1992	Miami 27, Cleveland 23	*Indianapolis 14, Cleveland 3
1993	*Cleveland 27, Cincinnati 14	Cleveland 19, L.A. Raiders 16
1994	Pittsburgh 17, Cleveland 10	*Cleveland 28, Cincinnati 20
1995	Cleveland 22, Tampa Bay 6	*New England 17, Cleveland 14
1999	*Pittsburgh 43, Cleveland 0	Tennessee 26, Cleveland 9
2000	*Jacksonville 27, Cleveland 7	Cleveland 24, Cincinnati 7
2001	*Seattle 9, Cleveland 6	Cleveland 23, Jacksonville 14
2002	*Kansas City 40, Cleveland 39	Cleveland 31, Tennessee 28 (OT)
2003	*Indianapolis 9, Cleveland 6	Baltimore 33, Cleveland 13
2004	*Cleveland 20, Baltimore 3	Dallas 19, Cleveland 12
2005	*Cincinnati 27, Cleveland 13	Cleveland 26, Green Bay 24
2006	*New Orleans 19, Cleveland 14	Cincinnati 34, Cleveland 17
2007	*Pittsburgh 34, Cleveland 7	Oakland 26, Cleveland 24
2008	*Dallas 28, Cleveland 10	Baltimore 28, Cleveland 10
2009	*Minnesota 34, Cleveland 20	Denver 27, Cleveland 6
2010	Kansas City 16, Cleveland 14	*Tampa Bay 17, Cleveland 14
2011	*Cincinnati 27, Cleveland 17	Cleveland 27, Indianapolis 19
2012	*Philadelphia 17, Cleveland 16	Cincinnati 34, Cleveland 27
2013	*Miami 23, Cleveland 10	Baltimore 14, Cleveland 6
2014	Cleveland 26, New Orleans 24	*Pittsburgh 30, Cleveland 27

Official Openers – 29-36-1 (.447)

Official Home Openers – 14-21 (.400)

Official Away Openers – 15-15-1 (.500)

Home Openers – 29-36-1 (.447)

Away Openers – 34-31-1 (.523)

GAMES IN WHICH BOTH TEAMS SCORED
FEWER THAN 10 POINTS
* Denotes postseason

Cleveland 7, New York 0	(Oct. 12, 1946, at N.Y.)
Cleveland 7, Buffalo 7	(Nov. 13, 1949, at Cle.)
New York Giants 6, Cleveland 0	(Oct. 1, 1950, at Cle.)
*Cleveland 8, New York Giants 3	(Dec. 17, 1950, at Cle.)
Cleveland 7, New York 0	(Oct. 25, 1953, at N.Y.)
Cleveland 6, Philadelphia 0	(Nov. 21, 1954, at Cle.)
Chicago Cardinals 9, Cleveland 7	(Sept. 30, 1956, at Chi.)
Cleveland 6, New York 3	(Sept. 29, 1957, at Cle.)
New York 7, Cleveland 7	(Dec. 17, 1961, at N.Y.)
Pittsburgh 9, Cleveland 7	(Nov. 10, 1963, at Pit.)
Dallas 6, Cleveland 2	(Dec. 12, 1970, at Cle.)
Cleveland 7, Oakland 3	(Nov. 18, 1973, at Oak.)
Cleveland 7, San Francisco 0	(Dec. 1, 1974, at Cle.)
Los Angeles 9, Cleveland 0	(Nov. 27, 1977, at Cle.)
Houston 9, Cleveland 3	(Sept. 13, 1981, at Cle.)
Indianapolis 9, Cleveland 7	(Dec. 6, 1987, at Cle.)
Cleveland 6, Kansas City 3	(Sept. 4, 1988, at K.C.)
Seattle 9, Cleveland 6	(Sept. 9, 2001, at Cle.)
Indianapolis 9, Cleveland 6	(Sept. 7, 2003, at Cle.)
New England 9, Cleveland 3	(Oct. 26, 2003, at N.E.)
Cleveland 9, Oakland 7	(Dec. 18, 2005, at Oak.)
Cleveland 8, Buffalo 0	(Dec. 16, 2007, at Cle.)
Cleveland 6, Buffalo 3	(Oct. 11, 2009, at Buf.)
Cleveland 6, Seattle 3	(Oct. 23, 2011, at Cle.)
Cleveland 7, San Diego 6	(Oct. 28, 2012, at Cle.)
Overall Regular Season – 12-10-2 (.542)	

Home Regular Season - 6-7-1 (.464)
Away Regular Season – 6-3-1 (.650)
Postseason – 1-0 (1.000)

HIGHEST-SCORING GAMES

TEN BY THE BROWNS

1. 66—Cleveland 66, Brooklyn 14	(Dec. 8, 1946, at Bro.)
2. 62—Cleveland 62, New York 14	(Dec. 6, 1953, at Cle.)
Cleveland 62, Washington 3	(Nov. 7, 1954, at Cle.)
4. 61—Cleveland 61, Los Angeles 14	(Oct. 14, 1949, at L.A.)
5. 55—Cleveland 55, Brooklyn 7	(Sept. 12, 1947, at Bro.)
6. 52—Cleveland 52, New York 20	(Dec. 12, 1964, at N.Y.)
7. 51—Cleveland 51, Chicago 14	(Nov. 17, 1946, at Cle.)
Cleveland 51, Pittsburgh 0	(Sept. 10, 1989, at Pit.)
Cleveland 51, Cincinnati 45	(Sept. 16, 2007, at Cle.)
10. 49—Cleveland 49, Chicago Cardinals 28	(Dec. 2, 1951, at Cle.)
Cleveland 49, Philadelphia 7	(Oct. 19, 1952, at Phi.)
Cleveland 49, Atlanta 17	(Oct. 30, 1966, at Atl.)
Cleveland 49, New York 40	(Dec. 4, 1966, at Cle.)

TEN BY BROWNS OPPONENTS

1. 58—Houston 58, Cleveland 14	(Dec. 9, 1990, at Hou.)
Cincinnati 58, Cleveland 48	(Nov. 28, 2004, at Cin.)
3. 56—San Francisco 56, Cleveland 28	(Oct. 9, 1949, at S.F.)
4. 55—Pittsburgh 55, Cleveland 27	(Oct. 17, 1954, at Pit.)
Green Bay 55, Cleveland 7	(Nov. 12, 1967, at G.B.)
6. 51—Minnesota 51, Cleveland 3	(Nov. 9, 1969, at Minn.)
Pittsburgh 51, Cleveland 35	(Oct. 7, 1979, at Cle.)
8. 49—Green Bay 49, Cleveland 17	(Oct. 15, 1961, at Cle.
St. Louis 49, Cleveland 13	(Sept. 26, 1965, at Cle.)
10. 48—New York 48, Cleveland 7	(Dec. 6, 1959, at N.Y.)
Cincinnati 48, Cleveland 16	(Dec. 17, 1978, at Cin.)
Jacksonville 48, Cleveland 0	(Dec. 3, 2000, at Jac.)

TEN BETWEEN BOTH TEAMS

1. 106—Cincinnati 58, Cleveland 48   (Nov. 28, 2004, at Cin.)
2. 96—Cleveland 51, Cincinnati 45   (Sept. 16, 2007, at Cle.)
3. 89—Cleveland 49, New York 40   (Dec. 4, 1966, at Cle.
4. 86—Pittsburgh 51, Cleveland 35   (Oct. 7, 1979, at Cle.)
5. 84—San Francisco 56, Cleveland 28   (Oct. 9, 1949, at S.F.)
   6. 82—Pittsburgh 55, Cleveland 27   (Oct. 17, 1954, at Pit.)
   Cleveland 48, New York 34   (Dec. 18, 1960, at N.Y.)
8. 80—Cleveland 66, Brooklyn 14   (Dec. 8, 1946, at Bro.)
9. 79—Cleveland 42, Washington 37   (Nov. 26, 1967, at Cle.)
   Cleveland 41, Tennessee 38   (Dec. 30, 2001, at Ten.)
   Kansas City 40, Cleveland 39   (Sept. 8, 2002, at Cle.)

HIGHEST-SCORING GAMES (POSTSEASON)

FIVE BY THE BROWNS

1. 56—Cleveland 56, Detroit 10   (NFL Championship, Dec. 26, 1954, at Cle.)

49—Cleveland 49, Buffalo 7   (AAFC Championship, Dec. 19, 1948, at Cle.)

3. 38—Cleveland 38, Los Angeles 14   (NFL Championship, Dec. 26, 1955, at L.A.)

Cleveland 38, Dallas 14   (Eastern Conference Championship, Dec. 28, 1969, at Dal.)

Cleveland 38, Indianapolis 21   (AFC Divisional Playoff Jan. 9, 1988, at Cle.)

FIVE BY BROWNS OPPONENTS

1. 59—Detroit 59, Cleveland 14   (NFL Championship, Dec. 29, 1957, at Det.)

2. 52—Dallas 52, Cleveland 14   (Eastern Conference Championship, Dec. 24, 1967, at Dal.)

3. 38—Denver 38, Cleveland 33   (AFC Championship, Jan. 17, 1988, at Den.)

4. 37—Denver 37, Cleveland 21   (AFC Championship, Jan. 14, 1990, at Den.)

5. 36—Pittsburgh 36, Cleveland 33   (AFC Wild Card, Jan. 5, 2003, at Pit.)

FIVE BETWEEN BOTH TEAMS

1. 73—Detroit 59, Cleveland 14	(NFL Championship, Dec. 29, 1957, at Det.)
2. 71—Denver 38, Cleveland 33	(AFC Championship, Jan. 17, 1988, at Den.)
3. 69—Pittsburgh 36, Cleveland 33	(AFC Wild Card, Jan. 5, 2003, at Pit.)
4. 66—Cleveland 56, Detroit 10	(NFL Championship, Dec. 26, 1954, at Cle.)
Dallas 52, Cleveland 14	(Eastern Conference Championship, Dec. 24, 1967, at Dal.)

HOME WON-LOST-TIED RECORDS

YEAR	Won	LOST	Tied	PCT.
1946	6	1	0	.857
1947	6	1	0	.857
1948	7	0	0	1.000
1949	5	0	1	1.000
1950	5	1	0	.833
1951	6	0	0	1.000
1952	4	2	0	.667
1953	6	0	0	1.000
1954	5	1	0	.833
1955	5	1	0	.833
1956	1	5	0	.167
1957	6	0	0	1.000
1958	4	2	0	.667
1959	3	3	0	.500
1960	4	2	0	.667
1961	4	3	0	.571
1962	4	2	1	.667
1963	5	2	0	.714
1964	5	1	1	.833
1965	5	2	0	.714
1966	5	2	0	.714
1967	6	1	0	.857
1968	5	2	0	.714
1969	5	1	1	.833
1970	4	3	0	.571
1971	4	3	0	.571
1972	4	3	0	.571
1973	5	1	1	.786
1974	3	4	0	.429
1975	3	4	0	.429
1976	6	1	0	.857
1977	2	5	0	.286
1978	5	3	0	.625

1979	5	3	0	.625
1980	6	2	0	.750
1981	3	5	0	.375
1982	2	2	0	.500
1983	6	2	0	.750
1984	2	6	0	.250
1985	5	3	0	.625
1986	6	2	0	.750
1987	5	2	0	.714
1988	6	2	0	.750
1989	5	2	1	.688
1990	2	6	0	.250
1991	3	5	0	.375
1992	4	4	0	.500
1993	4	4	0	.500
1994	6	2	0	.750
1995	3	5	0	.375
1999	0	8	0	.000
2000	2	6	0	.250
2001	4	4	0	.500
2002	3	5	0	.375
2003	2	6	0	.250
2004	3	5	0	.375
2005	4	4	0	.500
2006	2	6	0	.250
2007	7	1	0	.875
2008	1	7	0	.125
2009	3	5	0	.375
2010	3	5	0	.375
2011	3	5	0	.375
2012	4	4	0	.500
2013	3	5	0	.375
2014	4	4	0	.500
TOTAL	**274**	**199**	**6**	**.578**

ROAD WON-LOST-TIED RECORDS

YEAR	WON	LOST	Tied	PCT.
1946	6	1	0	.857
1947	6	0	1	1.000
1948	7	0	0	1.000
1949	4	1	1	.800
1950	5	1	0	.833
1951	5	1	0	.833
1952	4	2	0	.667
1953	5	1	0	.833
1954	4	2	0	.667
1955	4	1	1	.800
1956	4	2	0	.667
1957	3	2	1	.600
1958	5	1	0	.833
1959	4	2	0	.667
1960	4	1	1	.800
1961	4	2	1	.667
1962	3	4	0	.429
1963	5	2	0	.714
1964	5	2	0	.714
1965	6	1	0	.857
1966	4	3	0	.571
1967	3	4	0	.429
1968	5	2	0	.714
1969	5	2	0	.714
1970	3	4	0	.429
1971	5	2	0	.714
1972	6	1	0	.857
1973	2	4	1	.357
1974	1	6	0	.143
1975	0	7	0	.000
1976	3	4	0	.429
1977	4	3	0	.571

1978	3	5	0	.375
1979	4	4	0	.500
1980	5	3	0	.625
1981	2	6	0	.250
1982	2	3	0	.400
1983	3	5	0	.375
1984	3	5	0	.375
1985	3	5	0	.375
1986	6	2	0	750
1987	5	3	0	.625
1988	4	4	0	.500
1989	4	4	0	.500
1990	1	7	0	.125
1991	3	5	0	.375
1992	3	5	0	.375
1993	3	5	0	.375
1994	5	3	0	.625
1995	2	6	0	.250
1999	2	6	0	.250
2000	1	7	0	.125
2001	3	5	0	.375
2002	6	2	0	.750
2003	3	5	0	.375
2004	1	7	0	.125
2005	2	6	0	.250
2006	2	6	0	.250
2007	3	5	0	.375
2008	3	5	0	.375
2009	2	6	0	.250
2010	2	6	0	.250
2011	1	7	0	.125
2012	1	7	0	.125
2013	1	7	0	.125
2014	3	5	0	.375
TOTAL	**231**	**243**	**7**	**.489**

LOWEST-SCORING GAMES BETWEEN BOTH TEAMS

1. 6—New York Giants 6, Cleveland 0   (Oct. 1, 1950, at Cle.)
   Cleveland 6, Philadelphia 0   (Nov. 21, 1954, at Cle.)
3. 7—Cleveland 7, New York 0   (Oct. 12, 1946, at N.Y.)
   Cleveland 7, New York 0   (Oct. 25, 1953, at N.Y.)
   Cleveland 7, San Francisco 0   (Dec. 1, 1974, at Cle.)
6. 8—Dallas 6, Cleveland 2   (Dec. 12, 1970, at Cle.)
   Cleveland 8, Buffalo 0   (Dec. 16, 2007, at Cle.)
8. 9—Cleveland 6, New York 3   (Sept. 29, 1957, at Cle.)
   Los Angeles 9, Cleveland 0   (Nov. 27, 1977, at Cle.)
   Cleveland 6, Kansas City 3   (Sept. 4, 1988, at K.C.)
   Cleveland 6, Buffalo 3   (Oct. 11, 2009, at Buf.)
   Cleveland 6, Seattle 3   (Oct. 23, 2011, at Cle.)

LOWEST-SCORING GAMES (POSTSEASON)

FIVE BY THE BROWNS

1. 0 – New York 10, Cleveland 0   (Eastern Conference Playoff, Dec. 21, 1958, at N.Y.)
   Baltimore 34, Cleveland 0   (NFL Championship, Dec. 29, 1968, at Cle.)
3. 3 – Baltimore 20, Cleveland 3   (AFC Divisional Playoff, Dec. 26, 1971, at Cle.)
4. 7 – Detroit 17, Cleveland 7   (NFL Championship, Dec. 28, 1952, at Cle.)
   Minnesota 27, Cleveland 7   (NFL Championship, Jan. 4, 1970, at Minn.)

FIVE BY BROWNS OPPONENTS

1. 0 – Cleveland 27, Baltimore 0   (NFL Championship, Dec. 27, 1964, at Cle.)
2. 3 – Cleveland 14, New York 3   (AAFC Championship, Dec. 14, 1947, at N.Y.)
   Cleveland 8, New York 3   (American Conference Playoff, Dec. 17, 1950, at Cle.)
4. 7 – Cleveland 49, Buffalo 7   (AAFC Championship, Dec. 19, 1948, at Cle.)
   Cleveland 21, San Francisco 7   (AAFC Championship, Dec. 11, 1949, at Cle.)

F**IVE BETWEEN** B**OTH** T**EAMS**

1. 10 —New York 10, Cleveland 0   (Eastern Conference Playoff, Dec. 21, 1958, at N.Y.)
2. 11 —Cleveland 8, New York   (American Conference Playoff,
        Giants 3   Dec. 17, 1950, at Cle.)
3. 17 —Cleveland 14, New York 3   (AAFC Championship, Dec. 14, 1947, at N.Y.)
4. 23 – Cleveland 14, New York 9   (AAFC Championship, Dec. 22, 1946, at Cle.)
      Baltimore 20, Cleveland 3   (AFC Divisional Playoff, Dec. 26, 1971, at Cle.)

MOST ONE - SIDED GAMES

T**EN** V**ICTORIES**

1. 59 —Cleveland 62, Washington 3   (Nov. 7, 1954, at Cle.)
2. 52 —Cleveland 66, Brooklyn 14   (Dec. 8, 1946, at Bro.)
3. 51 —Cleveland 51, Pittsburgh 0   (Sept. 10, 1989, at Pit.)
4. 48 —Cleveland 55, Brooklyn 7   (Sept. 12, 1947, at Bro.)
      Cleveland 62, New York 14   (Dec. 6, 1953, at Cle.)
6. 47 —Cleveland 61, Los Angeles 14   (Oct. 14, 1949, at L.A.)
7. 45 —Cleveland 45, Washington 0   (Oct. 14, 1951, at Cle.)
8. 44 —Cleveland 44, Miami 0   (Sept. 6, 1946, at Cle.)
9. 42 —Cleveland 42, Baltimore 0   (Dec. 7, 1947, at Bal.)
      Cleveland 49, Philadelphia 7   (Oct. 19, 1952, at Phi.)
      Cleveland 42, Chicago 0   (Dec. 11, 1960, at Cle.)

T**EN** D**EFEATS**

1. 48—Green Bay 55, Cleveland 7   (Nov. 12, 1967, at G.B.)
      Minnesota 51, Cleveland 3   (Nov. 9, 1969, at Minn.)
      Jacksonville 48, Cleveland 0   (Dec. 3, 2000, at Jac.)
4. 44—Houston 58, Cleveland 14   (Dec. 9, 1990, at Hou.)
5. 43—Pittsburgh 43, Cleveland 0   (Sept. 12, 1999, at Cle.)
6. 42—Buffalo 42, Cleveland 0   (Nov. 4, 1990, at Cle.)
7. 41—New York 48, Cleveland 7   (Dec. 6, 1959, at N.Y.)
      Pittsburgh 41, Cleveland 0   (Dec. 24, 2005, at Cle.)
9. 37—Baltimore 44, Cleveland 7   (Nov. 26, 2000, at Bal.)
10. 36—St. Louis 49, Cleveland 13   (Sept. 26, 1965, at Cle.)
      Pittsburgh 42, Cleveland 6   (Oct. 5, 1975, at Cle.)

MOST ONE - SIDED GAMES (POSTSEASON)

FIVE VICTORIES

1. 46 – Cleveland 56, Detroit 10   (NFL Championship, Dec. 26, 1954, at Cle.)
2. 42 – Cleveland 49, Buffalo 7   (AAFC Championship, Dec. 19, 1948, at Cle.)
3. 27 – Cleveland 27, Baltimore 0   (NFL Championship, Dec. 27, 1964, at Cle.)
4. 24 – Cleveland 38, Los Angeles 14   (NFL Championship, Dec. 26, 1955, at L.A.)
    Cleveland 38, Dallas 14   (Eastern Conference Championship, Dec. 28, 1969, at Dal.)

FIVE DEFEATS

1. 45 – Detroit 59, Cleveland 14   (NFL Championship, Dec. 29, 1957, at Det.)
2. 38 – Dallas 52, Cleveland 14   (Eastern Conference Championship, Dec. 24, 1967, at Dal.)
3. 34 – Baltimore 34, Cleveland 0   (NFL Championship, Dec. 29, 1968, at Cle.)
4. 20 – Minnesota 27, Cleveland 7   (NFL Championship, Jan. 4, 1970, at Minn.)
    Pittsburgh 29, Cleveland 9   (AFC Divisional Playoff, Jan. 7, 1995, at Pit.)

POSTSEASON

Cleveland 14, New York 9	(AAFC Championship, Dec. 22, 1946, at Cle.)
Cleveland 14, New York 3	(AAFC Championship, Dec. 14, 1947, at N.Y.)
Cleveland 49, Buffalo 7	(AAFC Championship, Dec. 19, 1948, at Cle.)
Cleveland 31, Buffalo 21	(AAFC First-Round Playoff, Dec. 4, 1949, at Cle.)
Cleveland 21, San Francisco 7	(AAFC Championship, Dec. 11, 1949, at Cle.)
Cleveland 8, New York Giants 3	(American Conference Playoff, Dec. 17, 1950, at Cle.
Cleveland 30, Los Angeles 28	(NFL Championship, Dec. 24, 1950, at Cle.)
Los Angeles 24, Cleveland 17	(NFL Championship, Dec. 23, 1951, at L.A.)
Detroit 17, Cleveland 7	(NFL Championship, Dec. 28, 1952, at Cle.)
Detroit 17, Cleveland 16	(NFL Championship, Dec. 27, 1953, at Det.)
Cleveland 56, Detroit 10	(NFL Championship, Dec. 26, 1954, at Cle.)
Cleveland 38, Los Angeles 14	(NFL Championship, Dec. 26, 1955, at L.A.)
Detroit 59, Cleveland 14	(NFL Championship, Dec. 29, 1957, at Det.)
New York 10, Cleveland 0	(Eastern Conference Playoff, Dec. 21, 1958, at N.Y.)
Cleveland 27, Baltimore 0	(NFL Championship, Dec. 27, 1964, at Cle.)
Green Bay 23, Cleveland 12	(NFL Championship, Jan. 2, 1966, at G.B.)
Dallas 52, Cleveland 14	(Eastern Conference Championship, Dec. 24, 1967, at Dal.)
Cleveland 31, Dallas 20	(Eastern Conference Championship, Dec. 21, 1968, at Cle.)
Baltimore 34, Cleveland 0	(NFL Championship, Dec. 29, 1968, at Cle.)
Cleveland 38, Dallas 14	(Eastern Conference Championship, Dec. 28, 1969, at Dal.)
Minnesota 27, Cleveland 7	(NFL Championship, Jan. 4, 1970, at Minn.)
Baltimore 20, Cleveland 3	(AFC Divisional Playoff, Dec. 26, 1971, at Cle.)
Miami 20, Cleveland 14	(AFC Divisional Playoff, Dec. 24, 1972, at Mia.)
Oakland 14, Cleveland 12	(AFC Divisional Playoff, Jan. 4, 1981, at Cle.)
L.A. Raiders 27, Cleveland 10	(AFC First-Round, Jan. 8, 1983, at L.A.)
Miami 24, Cleveland 21	(AFC Divisional Playoff, Jan. 4, 1986, at Mia.)
Cleveland 23, New York Jets 20 (20T)	(AFC Divisional Playoff, Jan. 3, 1987, at Cle.)

Denver 23, Cleveland 20 (OT)	(AFC Championship, Jan. 11, 1987, at Cle.)
Cleveland 38, Indianapolis 21	(AFC Divisional Playoff, Jan. 9, 1988, at Cle.)
Denver 38, Cleveland 33	(AFC Championship, Jan. 17, 1988, at Den.)
Houston 24, Cleveland 23	(AFC Wild Card, Dec. 24, 1988, at Cle.)
Cleveland 34, Buffalo 30	(AFC Divisional Playoff, Jan. 6, 1990, at Cle.)
Denver 37, Cleveland 21	(AFC Championship, Jan. 14, 1990, at Den.)
Cleveland 20, New England 13	(AFC Wild Card, Jan. 1, 1995, at Cle.)
Pittsburgh 29, Cleveland 9	(AFC Divisional Playoff, Jan. 7, 1995, at Pit.)
Pittsburgh 36, Cleveland 33	(AFC Wild Card, Jan. 5, 2003, at Pit.)

Overall – 16-20 (.444)

Home – 13-6 (.684)

Away – 3-14 (.176)

POSTSEASON GAMES THE BROWNS LOST AND WHO THEY WOULD HAVE PLAYED HAD THEY WON

(Does not include NFL Championship games since there would not have been a next opponent)

New York 10, Cleveland 0 (Eastern Conference Playoff, Dec. 21, 1958, at N.Y.). Had the Browns won . . . vs. Baltimore in the NFL Championship at home

Dallas 52, Cleveland 14 (Eastern Conference Championship, Dec. 24, 1967, at Dal.). Had the Browns won . . . at Green Bay in the NFL Championship

Baltimore 34, Cleveland 0 (NFL Championship, Dec. 29, 1968, at Cle.). Had the Browns won . . . vs. New York Jets in Super Bowl III in Miami

Minnesota 27, Cleveland 7 (NFL Championship, Jan. 4, 1970, at Minn.). Had the Browns won . . . vs. Kansas City in Super Bowl IV in New Orleans

Baltimore 20, Cleveland 3 (AFC Divisional Playoff, Dec. 26, 1971, at Cle.). Had the Browns won . . . vs. Miami in the AFC Championship at home

Miami 20, Cleveland 14 (AFC Divisional Playoff, Dec. 24, 1972, at Mia.). Had the Browns won . . . at Pittsburgh in the AFC Championship

Oakland 14, Cleveland 12 (AFC Divisional Playoff, Jan. 4, 1981, at Cle.). Had the Browns won . . . at San Diego in the AFC Championship

Los Angeles Raiders 27, Cleveland 10 (AFC First Round, Jan. 8, 1983, at L.A.). Had the Browns won . . . at Miami in an AFC Second-Round Playoff

Miami 24, Cleveland 21 (AFC Divisional Playoff, Jan. 4,1986, at Mia.). Had the Browns won . . . vs. New England in the AFC Championship at home

Denver 23, Cleveland 20 (OT) (AFC Championship, Jan. 11, 1987, at Cle.). Had the Browns won . . . vs. New York Giants in Super Bowl XXI in Pasadena, California

Denver 38, Cleveland 33 (AFC Championship, Jan. 17,1988, at Den.). Had the Browns won . . . vs. Washington in Super Bowl XXII in San Diego

Houston 24, Cleveland 23 (AFC Wild Card, Dec. 24,1988, at Cle.). Had the Browns won . . . at Buffalo in an AFC Divisional Playoff

Denver 37, Cleveland 21 (AFC Championship, Jan. 14, 1990, at Den.). Had the Browns won . . . vs. San Francisco in Super Bowl XXIV in New Orleans

Pittsburgh 29, Cleveland 9 (AFC Divisional Playoff, Jan. 7, 1995, at Pit.). Had the Browns won . . . at San Diego in the AFC Championship

Pittsburgh 36, Cleveland 33 (AFC Wild Card, Jan. 5, 2003, at Pit.). Had the Browns won . . . at Oakland in an AFC Divisional Playoff

DOME GAMES

*Denotes retractable roof

Cleveland 21, Houston 10 (Dec. 7, 1970)

Cleveland 37, Houston 24 (Nov. 28, 1971)

Cleveland 23, Houston 17 (Oct. 22, 1972)

Cleveland 23, Houston 13 (Nov. 11, 1973)

Houston 28, Cleveland 24 (Dec. 15, 1974)

Detroit 21, Cleveland 10 (Nov. 9, 1975)

Houston 21, Cleveland 10 (Dec. 21, 1975)

Cleveland 21, Houston 7 (Nov. 7, 1976)

Cleveland 24, Houston 23 (Oct. 16, 1977)

Seattle 20, Cleveland 19 (Dec. 18, 1977)

Cleveland 24, New Orleans 16 (Oct. 8, 1978)

Houston 14, Cleveland 10 (Nov. 5, 1978)

Seattle 47, Cleveland 24 (Dec. 3, 1978)

Houston 31, Cleveland 10 (Sept. 30, 1979)

Cleveland 27, Seattle 3 (Oct. 12, 1980)

Cleveland 17, Houston 14 (Nov. 30, 1980)

Houston 17, Cleveland 13 (Dec. 3, 1981)

Seattle 42, Cleveland 21 (Dec. 20, 1981)

Cleveland 21, Seattle 7 (Sept. 12, 1982)

Cleveland 20, Houston 14 (Dec. 26, 1982)

Cleveland 31, Detroit 26 (Sept. 11,1983)

Houston 34, Cleveland 27 (Dec. 11, 1983)

Seattle 33, Cleveland 0 (Sept. 3, 1984)

Cleveland 27, Houston 20 (Dec. 16, 1984)

Cleveland 21, Houston 6 (Oct. 13,1985)

Seattle 31, Cleveland 13 (Dec. 8, 1985)

Cleveland 24, Houston 20 (Sept. 14, 1986)

Cleveland 23, Minnesota 20 (Oct. 26, 1986)

*Cleveland 22, Houston 14 (Jan. 2, 2005)

Cleveland 24, Indianapolis 9 (Nov. 2, 1986)

New Orleans 28, Cleveland 21 (Sept. 13, 1987)

Cleveland 40, Houston 7 (Nov. 22, 1987)

Houston 24, Cleveland 17 (Nov. 7, 1988)

Cleveland 17, Seattle 7 (Nov. 12, 1989)

Detroit 13, Cleveland 10 (Nov. 23, 1989)

Indianapolis 23, Cleveland 17 (OT)
(Dec. 10, 1989)

Cleveland 24, Houston 20 (Dec. 23, 1989)

New Orleans 25, Cleveland 20 (Oct. 14, 1990)

Houston 58, Cleveland 14 (Dec. 9, 1990)

Houston 28, Cleveland 24 (Nov. 17, 1991)

Cleveland 31, Indianapolis 0 (Dec. 1, 1991)

Indianapolis 14, Cleveland 3 (Sept. 6, 1992)

Cleveland 24, Houston 14 (Nov. 8, 1992)

Minnesota 17, Cleveland 13 (Nov. 22, 1992)

Detroit 24, Cleveland 14 (Dec. 13, 1992)

Indianapolis 23, Cleveland 10 (Sept. 26, 1993)

Seattle 22, Cleveland 5 (Nov. 14, 1993)

Atlanta 17, Cleveland 14 (Nov. 28, 1993)

Houston 19, Cleveland 17 (Dec. 12, 1993)

Cleveland 21, Indianapolis 14 (Sept. 25, 1994)

Cleveland 11, Houston 8 (Oct. 13, 1994)

Cleveland 14, Houston 7 (Sept. 17, 1995)

Detroit 38, Cleveland 20 (Oct. 8, 1995)

Minnesota 27, Cleveland 11 (Dec. 9, 1995)

St. Louis 34, Cleveland 3 (Oct. 24, 1999)

Cleveland 21, New Orleans 16 (Oct. 31, 1999)

Cleveland 24, New Orleans 15 (Nov. 24, 2002)

Indianapolis 13, Cleveland 6 (Sept. 25, 2005)

*Houston 19, Cleveland 16 (Oct. 30, 2005)   Minnesota 24, Cleveland 12 (Nov. 27, 2005)

Cleveland 17, Atlanta 13 (Nov. 12, 2006)   *Houston 14, Cleveland 6 (Dec. 31, 2006)

Cleveland 27, St. Louis 20 (Oct. 28, 2007)   *Arizona 27, Cleveland 21 (Dec. 2, 2007)

Detroit 38, Cleveland 37 (Nov. 22, 2009)   Cleveland 30, New Orleans 17 (Oct. 24, 2010)

*Cleveland 27, Indianapolis 19 (Sept. 18, 2011)   *Houston 30, Cleveland 12 (Nov. 6, 2011)

*Arizona 20, Cleveland 17 (OT) (Dec. 18, 2011)   *Indianapolis 17, Cleveland 13 (Oct. 21, 2012)

*Dallas 23, Cleveland 20 (OT) (Nov. 18, 2012)   Cleveland 31, Minnesota 27 (Sept. 22, 2013)

Cleveland 26, Atlanta 24 (Nov. 23, 2014)

Overall – 34-39 (.466)

SHUTOUTS
* Denotes postseason

Cleveland 44, Miami 0	(Sept. 6, 1946, at Cle.)
Cleveland 28, Buffalo 0	(Sept. 22, 1946, at Buf.)
Cleveland 7, New York 0	(Oct. 12, 1946, at N.Y.)
Cleveland 34, Miami 0	(Dec. 3, 1946, at Mia.)
Cleveland 28, Baltimore 0	(Sept. 21, 1947, at Cle.)
Cleveland 42, Baltimore 0	(Dec. 7, 1947, at Bal.)
Cleveland 21, Baltimore 0	(Sept. 11, 1949, at Cle.)
Cleveland 31, Brooklyn-New York 0	(Nov. 20, 1949, at Bro.-N.Y.)
Cleveland 31, Baltimore 0	(Sept. 24, 1950, at Bal.)
New York Giants 6, Cleveland 0	(Oct. 1, 1950, at Cle.)
Cleveland 45, Washington 0	(Oct. 14, 1951, at Cle.)
Cleveland 17, Pittsburgh 0	(Oct. 21, 1951, at Cle.)
Cleveland 10, New York Giants 0	(Nov. 18, 1951, at N.Y.)
Cleveland 28, Pittsburgh 0	(Dec. 9, 1951, at Pit.)
Cleveland 10, Chicago Cardinals 0	(Dec. 7, 1952, at Chi.)
Cleveland 27, Green Bay 0	(Sept. 27, 1953, at G.B.)
Cleveland 7, New York 0	(Oct. 25, 1953, at N.Y.)
Cleveland 6, Philadelphia 0	(Nov. 21, 1954, at Cle.)
Cleveland 16, Philadelphia 0	(Nov. 18, 1956, at Phi.)
Cleveland 24, Pittsburgh 0	(Nov. 10, 1957, at Cle.)
Cleveland 31, Chicago Cardinals 0	(Dec. 1, 1957, at Cle.)
*New York 10, Cleveland 0	(Dec. 21, 1958, at N.Y.)
Cleveland 42, Chicago 0	(Dec. 11, 1960, at Cle.)
*Cleveland 27, Baltimore 0	(Dec. 27, 1964, at Cle.)
Cleveland 24, Chicago 0	(Oct. 22, 1967, at Cle.)
*Baltimore 34, Cleveland 0	(Dec. 29, 1968, at Cle.)
Cleveland 28, Miami 0	(Oct. 25, 1970, at Mia.)
Cleveland 31, Houston 0	(Sept. 19, 1971, at Cle.)
Denver 27, Cleveland 0	(Oct. 24, 1971, at Cle.)
Chicago 17, Cleveland 0	(Oct. 15, 1972, at Cle.)
Pittsburgh 30, Cleveland 0	(Dec. 3, 1972, at Pit.)
Cleveland 20, Houston 0	(Nov. 5, 1972, at Cle.)
Cleveland 7, San Francisco 0	(Dec. 1, 1974, at Cle.)
Los Angeles 9, Cleveland 0	(Nov. 27, 1977, at Cle.)

Cleveland 20, Tampa Bay 0   (Nov. 13, 1983, at Cle.)
Cleveland 30, New England 0   (Nov. 20, 1983, at N.E.)
Seattle 33, Cleveland 0   (Sept. 3, 1984, at Sea.)
Cleveland 34, Cincinnati 0   (Oct. 18, 1987, at Cin.)
Cleveland 51, Pittsburgh 0   (Sept. 10, 1989, at Pit.)
Cincinnati 21, Cleveland 0   (Dec. 3, 1989, at Cle.)
Kansas City 34, Cleveland 0   (Sept. 30, 1990, at K.C.)
Buffalo 42, Cleveland 0   (Nov. 4, 1990, at Cle.)
Pittsburgh 35, Cleveland 0   (Dec. 23, 1990, at Pit.)
Cleveland 20, New England 0   (Sept. 8, 1991, at N.E.)
Cleveland 31, Indianapolis 0   (Dec. 1, 1991, at Ind.)
Denver 12, Cleveland 0   (Sept. 27, 1992, at Cle.)
Cleveland 32, Arizona 0   (Sept. 18, 1994, at Cle.)
Pittsburgh 43, Cleveland 0   (Sept. 12, 1999, at Cle.)
Baltimore 12, Cleveland 0   (Oct. 1, 2000, at Cle.)
Pittsburgh 22, Cleveland 0   (Oct. 22, 2000, at Pit.)
Jacksonville 48, Cleveland 0   (Dec. 3, 2000, at Jac.)
Cleveland 18, Cincinnati 0   (Nov. 25, 2001, at Cle.)
Baltimore 35, Cleveland 0   (Dec. 21, 2003, at Cle.)
San Diego 21, Cleveland 0   (Dec. 19, 2004, at Cle.)
Cleveland 22, Miami 0   (Nov. 20, 2005, at Cle.)
Pittsburgh 41, Cleveland 0   (Dec. 24, 2005, at Cle.)
Cincinnati 30, Cleveland 0   (Nov. 26, 2006, at Cle.)
Cleveland 8, Buffalo 0   (Dec. 16, 2007, at Cle.)
Cincinnati 14, Cleveland 0   (Dec. 21, 2008, at Cle.)
Pittsburgh 31, Cleveland 0   (Dec. 28, 2008, at Pit.)
Baltimore 16, Cleveland 0   (Nov. 16, 2009, at Cle.)
Cincinnati 30, Cleveland 0   (Dec. 14, 2014, at Cle.)

Overall Regular Season – 36-23 (.610)
Home Regular Season – 18-16 (.529)
Away Regular Season – 18-7 (.720)
Postseason – 1-2 (.333)

STREAKS

FIVE LONGEST WINNING IN A SEASON

1. 14 games—Sept. 3-Dec. 5, 1948 (0-0 to 14-0)
2. 11 games—Oct. 7-Dec. 16, 1951 (0-1 to 11-1)
         Sept. 27-Dec. 6, 1953 (0-0 to 11-0)
4.   8 games—Oct. 24-Dec. 12, 1954 (1-2 to 9-2)
         Oct. 20-Dec. 8, 1968 (2-3 to 10-3)

FIVE LONGEST LOSING IN A SEASON

1. 9 games—Sept. 21-Nov. 16, 1975 (0-0 to 0-9)
         Oct. 24-Dec. 26, 2004 (3-3 to 3-12)
3. 8 games—Oct. 14-Dec. 9, 1990 (2-3 to 2-11)
4. 7 games—Sept. 12-Oct. 24, 1999 (0-0 to 0-7)
         Sept. 24-Nov. 5, 2000 (2-1 to 2-8)
         Oct. 18-Dec. 6, 2009 (1-4 to 1-11)
         Nov. 17-Dec. 29, 2013 (4-5 to 4-12)

FIVE LONGEST WINNING TO START A SEASON

1. 14 games—Sept. 3-Dec. 5, 1948
2. 11 games—Sept. 27-Dec. 6, 1953
3.   7 games—Sept. 6-Oct. 20, 1946
4.   6 games—Sept. 15-Oct. 20, 1963
5.   5 games—Sept. 5-Oct. 5, 1947
         Sept. 28-Oct. 26, 1958

FIVE LONGEST LOSING TO START A SEASON

1. 9 games—Sept. 21-Nov. 16, 1975
2. 7 games—Sept. 12-Oct. 24, 1999
3. 5 games—Sept. 9-Oct. 7, 2012
4. 4 games—Sept. 13-Oct. 4, 2009
5. 3 games—Sept. 3-16, 1984
         Sept. 10-24, 2006
         Sept. 7-21, 2008
         Sept. 12-26, 2010

FIVE LONGEST WINNING TO END A SEASON

1. 14 games—Sept. 3-Dec. 5, 1948 (0-0 to 14-0)
2. 11 games—Oct. 7-Dec. 16, 1951 (0-1 to 11-1)
3. 6 games—Oct. 29-Dec. 10, 1950 (4-2 to 10-2)
4. 5 games—Nov. 10-Dec. 8, 1946 (7-2 to 12-2)
            Nov. 21-Dec. 19, 1971 (4-5 to 9-5)
            Nov. 23-Dec. 21, 1986 (7-4 to 12-4)

FIVE LONGEST LOSING TO END A SEASON

1. 7 games—Nov. 17-Dec. 29, 2013 (4-5 to 4-12)
2. 6 games—Nov. 21-Dec. 26, 1999 (2-8 to 2-14)
            Nov. 23-Dec. 28, 2008 (4-6 to 4-12)
            Nov. 27, 2011-Jan. 1, 2012 (4-6 to 4-12)
5. 5 games—Nov. 22-Dec. 20, 1981 (5-6 to 5-11)
            Nov. 19-Dec. 17, 2000 (3-8 to 3-13)
            Nov. 30-Dec. 28, 2014 (7-4 to 7-9)

TEAM TOP FIVES (GAME)
(POSTSEASON)

RUSHING YARDS

1. 251 (Jan. 4, 1986, at Miami)
2. 227 (Dec. 28, 1952, vs. Detroit)
3. 218 (Dec. 29, 1957, at Detroit)
4. 217 (Dec. 11, 1949, vs. San Francisco)
5. 215 (Dec. 19, 1948, vs. Buffalo)

PASSING YARDS

1. 494 (Jan. 3, 1987, vs. New York Jets)
2. 409 (Jan. 5, 2003, at Pittsburgh)
3. 356 (Jan. 17, 1988, at Denver)
4. 326 (Dec. 4, 1949, vs. Buffalo)
5. 298 (Dec. 24, 1950, vs. Los Angeles)

PASS COMPLETIONS

1. 34 (Jan. 3, 1987, vs. New York Jets)
2. 26 (Jan. 17, 1988, at Denver)
   26 (Jan. 5, 2003, at Pittsburgh)
4. 22 (Dec. 4, 1949, vs. Buffalo)
 22 (Dec. 24, 1950, vs. Los Angeles)

INTERCEPTIONS

1. 7 (Dec. 26, 1955, at Los Angeles)
2. 6 (Dec. 26, 1954, vs. Detroit)
3. 5 (Dec. 19, 1948, vs. Buffalo)
4. 5 (Dec. 24, 1950, vs. Los Angeles)
5. 4 (Dec. 21, 1968, vs. Dallas)

PUNTING YARDS

1. 363 (Dec. 17, 1950, vs. New York Giants)
2. 338 (Jan. 14, 1990, at Denver)
3. 310 (Jan. 3, 1987, vs. New York Jets)
4. 304 (Dec. 21, 1958, at New York)
5. 291 (Jan. 8, 1983, at Los Angeles Raiders)

PUNT RETURN YARDS
(Does not include the game against the Buffalo Bills on December 4, 1949)

1. 81 (Jan. 4, 1981, vs. Oakland)
2. 74 (Dec. 26, 1971, vs. Baltimore)
3. 70 (Jan. 5, 2003, at Pittsburgh)
4. 65 (Jan. 3, 1987, vs. New York Jets)
5. 61 (Dec. 11, 1949, vs. San Francisco)

KICKOFF RETURN YARDS

1. 180 (Jan. 6, 1990, vs. Buffalo)
2. 163 (Dec. 29, 1957, at Detroit)
3. 155 (Jan. 2, 1966, at Green Bay)
4. 132 (Dec. 23, 1951, at Los Angeles)
5. 130 (Jan. 14, 1990, at Denver)

TOTAL NET YARDS

1. 558 (Jan. 3, 1987, vs. New York Jets)
2. 464 (Jan. 17, 1988, at Denver)
3. 447 (Jan. 5, 2003, at Pittsburgh)
4. 404 (Jan. 9, 1988, vs. Indianapolis)
5. 398 (Dec. 4, 1949, vs. Buffalo)

TEAM TOP FIVES (SEASON)

SCORING (POINTS)

1. 415 (1964)
2. 403 (1966)
3. 402 (2007)
4. 394 (1968)
5. 391 (1986)

RUSHING YARDS

1. 2,639 (1963)
2. 2,557 (1947)
   2,557 (1948)
4. 2,526 (1958)
5. 2,488 (1978)

PASSING YARDS

1. 4,372 (2013)
2. 4,339 (1981)
3. 4,132 (1980)
4. 4,018 (1986)
5. 3,932 (1983)

PASS COMPLETIONS

1. 379 (2013)
2. 348 (1981)

3. 338 (2002)
4. 337 (1980)
5. 328 (2012)

INTERCEPTIONS

1. 41 (1946)
2. 33 (2001)
3. 32 (1947)
   32 (1968)
5. 31 (1950)
   31 (1960)

SACKS

1. 48 (1992)
   48 (1993)
3. 45 (1989)
4. 44 (1985)
5. 43 (1984)
   43 (2001)

PUNTING YARDS

1. 4,645 (1999)
2. 4,919 (2000)
3. 4,249 (2001)
4. 4,119 (2014)

4. 3,977 (2009)

PUNT RETURN YARDS

1. 606 (2012)
2. 563 (1993)
3. 537 (1946)
4. 523 (1974)
5. 503 (1947)

KICKOFF RETURN YARDS

1. 1,943 (2007)
2. 1,725 (1999)
3. 1,710 (2000)
4. 1,697 (1978)
5. 1,670 (2009)

TOTAL NET YARDS

1. 5,915 (1981)
2. 5,772 (1979)
3. 5,621 (2007)
4. 5,588 (1980)
5. 5,583 (1983)

VS. DOMED-STADIUM TEAMS AT HOME
* Denotes postseason
\# Denotes team with retractable roof

Cleveland 28, Houston 14 (Nov. 22, 1970)

Cleveland 31, Houston 0 (Sept. 19, 1971)

Cleveland 20, Houston 0 (Nov. 5, 1972)

Cleveland 42, Houston 13 (Oct. 21, 1973)

Cleveland 20, Houston 7 (Sept. 22, 1974)

Houston 40, Cleveland 10 (Oct. 12, 1975)

Cleveland 17, New Orleans 16 (Nov. 30, 1975)

Cleveland 13, Houston 10 (Dec. 5, 1976)

Houston 19, Cleveland 15 (Dec. 11, 1977)

Houston 16, Cleveland 13 (Oct. 1, 1978)

Seattle 29, Cleveland 24 (Nov. 11, 1979)

Cleveland 14, Houston 7 (Dec. 2, 1979)

Houston 16, Cleveland 7 (Sept. 15, 1980)

Houston 9, Cleveland 3 (Sept. 13, 1981)

Cleveland 20, New Orleans 17 (Oct. 18, 1981)

Minnesota 27, Cleveland 21 (Sept. 4, 1983)

Seattle 24, Cleveland 9 (Oct. 2, 1983)

Cleveland 25, Houston 19 (OT)
(Oct. 30, 1983)

New Orleans 16, Cleveland 14 (Oct. 28, 1984)

Cleveland 27, Houston 10 (Nov. 25, 1984)

Cleveland 28, Houston 21 (Dec. 15, 1985)

#Cleveland 34, Houston 17 (Oct. 20, 2002)

Cleveland 24, Atlanta 16 (Dec. 29, 2002)

St. Louis 26, Cleveland 20 (Dec. 8, 2003)

New Orleans 19, Cleveland 14 (Sept. 10, 2006)

#Houston 16, Cleveland 6 (Nov. 23, 2008)

Minnesota 34, Cleveland 20 (Sept. 13, 2009)

St. Louis 13, Cleveland 12 (Nov. 13, 2011)

Cleveland 26, New Orleans 24 (Sept. 14, 2014)

#Indianapolis 25, Cleveland 24 (Dec. 7, 2014)

Cleveland 24, Detroit 21 (Sept. 28, 1986)

Cleveland 13, Houston 10 (OT) (Nov. 30, 1986)

Houston 15, Cleveland 10 (Oct. 11, 1987)

Indianapolis 9, Cleveland 7 (Dec. 6, 1987)

*Cleveland 38, Indianapolis 21 (Jan. 9, 1988)

Cleveland 23, Indianapolis 17 (Sept. 19, 1988)

Seattle 16, Cleveland 10 (Oct. 9, 1988)

Cleveland 28, Houston 23 (Dec. 18, 1988)

*Houston 24, Cleveland 23 (Dec. 24, 1988)

Cleveland 28, Houston 17 (Oct. 29, 1989)

Cleveland 23, Minnesota 17 (OT)
(Dec. 17, 1989)

Houston 35, Cleveland 23 (Nov. 18, 1990)

Houston 17, Cleveland 14 (Dec. 15, 1991)

Houston 17, Cleveland 14 (Dec. 20, 1992)

Houston 27, Cleveland 20 (Nov. 21, 1993)

Cleveland 17, New Orleans 13 (Dec. 5, 1993)

Cleveland 34, Houston 10 (Nov. 27, 1994)

Cleveland 35, Seattle 9 (Dec. 24, 1994)

Houston 37, Cleveland 10 (Nov. 5, 1995)

Indianapolis 29, Cleveland 28 (Dec. 26, 1999)

Cleveland 24, Detroit 14 (Sept. 23, 2001)

Indianapolis 28, Cleveland 23 (Dec. 15, 2002)

Indianapolis 9, Cleveland 6 (Sept. 7, 2003)

Detroit 13, Cleveland 10 (Oct. 23, 2005)

#Cleveland 27, Houston 17 (Nov. 25, 2007)

#Indianapolis 10, Cleveland 6 (Nov. 30, 2008)

Atlanta 20, Cleveland 10 (Oct. 10, 2010)

Detroit 31, Cleveland 17 (Oct. 13, 2013)

#Houston 23, Cleveland 7 (Nov. 16, 2014)

Regular Season – 26-31 (.456)

Postseason – 1-1 (.500)

VS. NFL CHAMPIONS (1950-69) AND SUPER BOWL CHAMPIONS (1970-95, SINCE 1999) OF SEASON AT HAND

(Does not include the Browns' four seasons in the AAFC from 1946-49 and the 1950, '54, '55, and '64 seasons since they were the champions those years)

* Denotes postseason

Cleveland 38, Los Angeles 23 (Oct. 7, 1951, at L.A.)
*Los Angeles 24, Cleveland 17 (Dec. 23, 1951, at L.A)
Detroit 17, Cleveland 6 (Nov. 2, 1952, at Det.)
*Detroit 17, Cleveland 7 (Dec. 28, 1952, at Cle.)
*Detroit 17, Cleveland 16 (Dec. 27, 1953, at Det.)
New York 21, Cleveland 9 (Oct. 14, 1956, at Cle.)
Cleveland 24, New York 7 (Dec. 9, 1956, at N.Y.)
Detroit 20, Cleveland 7 (Dec. 8, 1957, at Det.)
*Detroit 59, Cleveland 14 (Dec. 29, 1957, at Det.)
Cleveland 38, Baltimore 31 (Nov. 1, 1959, at Bal.)
Cleveland 41, Philadelphia 24 (Sept. 25, 1960, at Phi.)
Philadelphia 31, Cleveland 29 (Oct. 23, 1960, at Cle.)
Green Bay 49, Cleveland 17 (Oct. 15, 1961, at Cle.)
*Green Bay 23, Cleveland 12 (Jan. 2, 1966, at G.B.)
Green Bay 21, Cleveland 20 (Sept. 18, 1966, at Cle.)
Green Bay 55, Cleveland 7 (Nov. 12, 1967, at G.B.)
Cleveland 30, Baltimore 20 (Oct. 20, 1968, at Bal.)
*Baltimore 34, Cleveland 0 (Dec. 29, 1968, at Cle.)
Minnesota 51, Cleveland 3 (Nov. 9, 1969, at Minn.)
*Minnesota 27, Cleveland 7 (Jan. 4, 1970, at Minn.)
*Miami 20, Cleveland 14 (Dec. 24, 1972, at Mia.)
Miami 17, Cleveland 9 (Oct. 15, 1973, at Cle.)
Pittsburgh 20, Cleveland 16 (Oct. 20, 1974, at Pit.)
Pittsburgh 26, Cleveland 16 (Nov. 17, 1974, at Cle.)
Pittsburgh 42, Cleveland 6 (Oct. 5, 1975, at Cle.)
Pittsburgh 31, Cleveland 17 (Dec. 7, 1975, at Pit.)
Pittsburgh 15, Cleveland 9 (OT) (Sept. 24, 1978, at Pit.)
Pittsburgh 34, Cleveland 14 (Oct. 15, 1978, at Cle.)
Pittsburgh 51, Cleveland 35 (Oct. 7, 1979, at Cle.)
Pittsburgh 33, Cleveland 30 (OT) (Nov. 25, 1979, at Pit.)
*Oakland 14, Cleveland 12 (Jan. 4, 1981, at Cle.)
Cleveland 15, San Francisco 12 (Nov. 15, 1981, at S.F.)
San Francisco 41, Cleveland 7 (Nov. 11, 1984, at Cle.)
Washington 42, Cleveland 17 (Oct. 13, 1991, at Was.)
St. Louis 34, Cleveland 3 (Oct. 24, 1999, at St.L.)
Baltimore 12, Cleveland 0 (Oct. 1, 2000, at Cle.)
Baltimore 44, Cleveland 7 (Nov. 26, 2000, at Bal.)

New England 27, Cleveland 16 (Dec. 9, 2001, at N.E.)
Tampa Bay 17, Cleveland 3 (Oct. 13, 2002, at T.B.)
New England 9, Cleveland 3 (Oct. 26, 2003, at N.E.)
New England 42, Cleveland 15 (Dec. 5, 2004, at Cle.)
Pittsburgh 34, Cleveland 21 (Nov. 13, 2005, at Pit.)
Pittsburgh 41, Cleveland 0 (Dec. 24, 2005, at Cle.)
Pittsburgh 10, Cleveland 6 (Sept. 14, 2008, at Cle.)
Pittsburgh 31, Cleveland 0 (Dec. 28, 2008, at Pit.)
Baltimore 23, Cleveland 16 (Sept. 27, 2012, at Bal.)
Baltimore 25, Cleveland 15 (Nov. 4, 2012, at Cle.)

Overall Regular Season—6-32 (.158)
Home Regular Season—0-15 (.000)
Away Regular Season—6-17 (.261)
Postseason—0-9 (.000) (Wins are not feasible)

VS. WEST-COAST TEAMS AT HOME
* Denotes postseason

Cleveland 31, Los Angeles 14 (Oct. 20, 1946)

San Francisco 34, Cleveland 20 (Oct. 27, 1946)

Los Angeles 13, Cleveland 10 (Oct. 12, 1947)

Cleveland 37, San Francisco 14 (Nov. 16, 1947)

Cleveland 19, Los Angeles 14 (Sept. 3, 1948)

Cleveland 14, San Francisco 7 (Nov. 14, 1948)

Cleveland 42, Los Angeles 7 (Oct. 2, 1949)

Cleveland 30, San Francisco 28 (Oct. 30, 1949)

*Cleveland 21, San Francisco 7 (Dec. 11, 1949)

Cleveland 34, San Francisco 14 (Nov. 12, 1950)

*Cleveland 30, Los Angeles 28 (Dec. 24, 1950)

Cleveland 37, Los Angeles 7 (Sept. 28, 1952)

Cleveland 23, San Francisco 21 (Nov. 15, 1953)

Cleveland 45, Los Angeles 31 (Nov. 24, 1957)

San Francisco 21, Cleveland 20 (Nov. 29, 1959)

Cleveland 20, Los Angeles 6 (Sept. 29, 1963)

Los Angeles 24, Cleveland 6 (Sept. 29, 1968)

San Diego 27, Cleveland 10 (Nov. 1, 1970)

Oakland 34, Cleveland 20 (Oct. 4, 1971)

Cleveland 16, San Diego 16 (Oct. 28, 1973)

Oakland 40, Cleveland 24 (Oct. 6, 1974)

Cleveland 7, San Francisco 0 (Dec. 1, 1974)

Cleveland 13, Oakland 7 (Oct. 12, 2003)

San Diego 21, Cleveland 0 (Dec. 19, 2004)

Cleveland 20, San Francisco 7 (Dec. 30, 2007)

Cleveland 23, Oakland 9 (Dec. 27, 2009)

Cleveland 7, San Diego 6 (Oct. 28, 2012)

Cleveland 21, San Diego 17 (Oct. 24, 1976)

Oakland 26, Cleveland 10 (Oct. 9, 1977)

Los Angeles 9, Cleveland 0 (Nov. 27, 1977)

Cleveland 24, San Francisco 7 (Sept. 3, 1978)

Cleveland 30, Los Angeles 19 (Nov. 26, 1978)

Seattle 29, Cleveland 24 (Nov. 11, 1979)

*Oakland 14, Cleveland 12 (Jan. 4, 1981)

San Diego 44, Cleveland 14 (Sept. 7, 1981)

San Diego 30, Cleveland 13 (Dec. 5, 1982)

Seattle 24, Cleveland 9 (Oct. 2, 1983)

San Francisco 41, Cleveland 7 (Nov. 11, 1984)

Los Angeles Raiders 21, Cleveland 20 (Oct. 20, 1985)

Cleveland 47, San Diego 17 (Dec. 21, 1986)

Cleveland 30, Los Angeles Rams 17 (Oct. 26, 1987)

Seattle 16, Cleveland 10 (Oct. 9, 1988)

San Diego 24, Cleveland 14 (Sept. 23, 1990)

Los Angeles Rams 38, Cleveland 23 (Dec. 2, 1990)

San Diego 14, Cleveland 13 (Nov. 15, 1992)

Cleveland 23, San Francisco 13 (Sept. 13, 1993)

Cleveland 35, Seattle 9 (Dec. 24, 1994)

Seattle 9, Cleveland 6 (Sept. 9, 2001)

Cleveland 20, San Diego 16 (Oct. 7, 2001)

San Diego 26, Cleveland 20 (Oct. 19, 2003)

Cleveland 33, Seattle 30 (OT) (Nov. 4, 2007)

San Diego 30, Cleveland 23 (Dec. 6, 2009)

Cleveland 6, Seattle 3 (Oct. 23, 2011)

Cleveland 23, Oakland 13 (Oct. 26, 2014)

Regular Season – 27-23-1 (.539)

Postseason – 2-1 (.667)

WON-LOST RECORDS (POSTSEASON)

YEAR	WON	LOST	PCT.
1946	1	0	1.000
1947	1	0	1.000
1948	1	0	1.000
1949	2	0	1.000
1950	2	0	1.000
1951	0	1	.000
1952	0	1	.000
1953	0	1	.000
1954	1	0	1.000
1955	1	0	1.000
1957	0	1	.000
1958	0	1	.000
1964	1	0	1.000
1965	0	1	.000
1967	0	1	.000
1968	1	1	.500
1969	1	1	.500
1971	0	1	.000
1972	0	1	.000
1980	0	1	.000
1982	0	1	.000
1985	0	1	.000
1986	1	1	.500
1987	1	1	.500
1988	0	1	.000
1989	1	1	.500
1994	1	1	.500
2002	0	1	.000
TOTAL	16	20	.444

WON-LOST-TIED RECORDS

YEAR	WON	LOST	TIED	PCT.
1946	12	2	0	.857
1947	12	1	1	.923
1948	14	0	0	1.000
1949	9	1	2	.900
1950	10	2	0	.833
1951	11	1	0	.917
1952	8	4	0	.667
1953	11	1	0	.917
1954	9	3	0	.750
1955	9	2	1	.818
1956	5	7	0	.417
1957	9	2	1	.818
1958	9	3	0	.750
1959	7	5	0	.583
1960	8	3	1	.727
1961	8	5	1	.615
1962	7	6	1	.538
1963	10	4	0	.714
1964	10	3	1	.769
1965	11	3	0	.786
1966	9	5	0	.643
1967	9	5	0	.643
1968	10	4	0	.714
1969	10	3	1	.769
1970	7	7	0	.500
1971	9	5	0	.643
1972	10	4	0	.714
1973	7	5	2	.571
1974	4	10	0	.286
1975	3	11	0	.214
1976	9	5	0	.643
1977	6	8	0	.429
1978	8	8	0	.500
1979	9	7	0	.563

1980	11	5	0	.688
1981	5	11	0	.313
1982	4	5	0	.444
1983	9	7	0	.563
1984	5	11	0	.313
1985	8	8	0	.500
1986	12	4	0	.750
1987	10	5	0	.667
1988	10	6	0	.625
1989	9	6	1	.594
1990	3	13	0	.188
1991	6	10	0	.375
1992	7	9	0	.438
1993	7	9	0	.438
1994	11	5	0	.688
1995	5	11	0	.313
1999	2	14	0	.125
2000	3	13	0	.188
2001	7	9	0	.438
2002	9	7	0	.563
2003	5	11	0	.313
2004	4	12	0	.250
2005	6	10	0	.375
2006	4	12	0	.250
2007	10	6	0	.625
2008	4	12	0	.250
2009	5	11	0	.313
2010	5	11	0	.313
2011	4	12	0	.250
2012	5	11	0	.313
2013	4	12	0	.250
2014	7	9	0	.438
TOTAL	**505**	**442**	**13**	**.533**

WEST COAST, ON THE

* Denotes postseason

Los Angeles 17, Cleveland 16 (Nov. 3, 1946)

Cleveland 14, San Francisco 7 (Nov. 10, 1946)

Cleveland 14, San Francisco 7 (Oct. 26, 1947)

Cleveland 27, Los Angeles 17 (Nov. 27, 1947)

Cleveland 31, Los Angeles 14 (Nov. 25, 1948)

Cleveland 31, San Francisco 28 (Nov. 28, 1948)

San Francisco 56, Cleveland 28 (Oct. 9, 1949)

*Los Angeles Raiders 27, Cleveland 10 (Jan. 8, 1983)

San Francisco 24, Cleveland 10 (Sept. 30, 1951)

Cleveland 38, Los Angeles 23 (Oct. 7, 1951)

*Los Angeles 24, Cleveland 17 (Dec. 23, 1951)

Cleveland 38, San Francisco 3 (Oct. 2, 1955)

*Cleveland 38, Los Angeles 14 (Dec. 26, 1955)

Cleveland 30, Los Angeles 27 (Sept. 28, 1958)

Cleveland 13, San Francisco 10 (Dec. 15, 1962)

Los Angeles 42, Cleveland 7 (Dec. 12, 1965)

Cleveland 33, San Francisco 21 (Nov. 3, 1968)

San Francisco 34, Cleveland 31 (Sept. 27, 1970)

Oakland 23, Cleveland 20 (Nov. 8, 1970)

Cleveland 21, San Diego 17 (Nov. 13, 1972)

Cleveland 7, Oakland 3 (Nov. 18, 1973)

Los Angeles 30, Cleveland 17 (Dec. 16, 1973)

San Diego 36, Cleveland 35 (Nov. 3, 1974)

Oakland 38, Cleveland 17 (Nov. 16, 1975)

San Diego 37, Cleveland 14 (Dec. 4, 1977)

Oakland 19, Cleveland 14 (Dec. 9, 1979)

Cleveland 27, Seattle 3 (Oct. 12, 1980)

Los Angeles 27, Cleveland 16 (Oct. 4, 1981)

Cleveland 15, San Francisco 12 (Nov. 15, 1981)

Seattle 42, Cleveland 21 (Dec. 20, 1981)

Cleveland 21, Seattle 7 (Sept. 12, 1982)

Cleveland 61, Los Angeles 14 (Oct. 14, 1949)

Cleveland 30, San Diego 24 (OT) (Sept. 25, 1983)

Seattle 33, Cleveland 0 (Sept. 3, 1984)

Los Angeles Rams 20, Cleveland 17 (Sept. 9, 1984)

Cleveland 21, San Diego 7 (Sept. 29, 1985)

Seattle 31, Cleveland 13 (Dec. 8, 1985)

Los Angeles Raiders 27, Cleveland 14 (Nov. 16, 1986)

San Diego 27, Cleveland 24 (OT) (Nov. 1, 1987)

San Francisco 38, Cleveland 24 (Nov. 29, 1987)

Cleveland 24, Los Angeles Raiders 17 (Dec. 20, 1987)

Cleveland 17, Seattle 7 (Nov. 12, 1989)

San Francisco 20, Cleveland 17 (Oct. 28, 1990)

Cleveland 30, San Diego 24 (OT) (Oct. 20, 1991)

Cleveland 28, Los Angeles Raiders 16 (Sept. 20, 1992)

Cleveland 19, Los Angeles Raiders 16 (Sept. 19, 1993)

Seattle 22, Cleveland 5 (Nov. 14, 1993)

Cleveland 42, Los Angeles Rams 14 (Dec. 26, 1993)

San Diego 31, Cleveland 13 (Dec. 3, 1995)

San Diego 23, Cleveland 10 (Dec. 5, 1999)

Seattle 20, Cleveland 19 (Dec. 18, 1977)

Seattle 47, Cleveland 24 (Dec. 3, 1978)

Seattle 34, Cleveland 7 (Nov. 30, 2003)

Cleveland 24, Oakland 21 (Oct. 1, 2006)

Oakland 26, Cleveland 24 (Sept. 23, 2007)

San Francisco 20, Cleveland 10 (Oct. 30, 2011)

Oakland 36, Cleveland 10 (Sept. 24, 2000)

Cleveland 13, San Francisco 12 (Sept. 21, 2003)

Cleveland 9, Oakland 7 (Dec. 18, 2005)

San Diego 32, Cleveland 25 (Nov. 5, 2006)

Oakland 24, Cleveland 17 (Oct. 16, 2011)

Cleveland 20, Oakland 17 (Dec. 2, 2012)

Regular Season – 28-31 (.475)

Postseason – 1-2 (.333)

COMPOSITE WON-LOST-TIED RECORDS VS.
OTHER TEAMS, BEST TO WORST

1.	Chicago Rockets	8-0-0	1.000
	Baltimore Colts (original)	7-0-0	1.000
	Brooklyn Dodgers	6-0-0	1.000
	Brooklyn-New York Yankees	2-0-0	1.000
	Miami Seahawks	2-0-0	1.000
6.	New York Yankees	5-0-1	.917
7.	Buffalo Bisons/Bills (original)	6-0-2	.875
8.	Atlanta Falcons	11-3-0	.786
9.	New Orleans Saints	12-4-0	.750
10.	Los Angeles Dons	6-2-0	.750
11.	Washington Redskins	33-11-1	.744
12.	Arizona Cardinals	33-13-3	.704
13.	Tampa Bay Buccaneers	6-3-0	.667
14.	Philadelphia Eagles	31-16-1	.656
15.	San Francisco 49ers	17-9-0	.654
16.	Chicago Bears	9-6-0	.600
17.	Buffalo Bills (current)	11-8-0	.579
18.	New York Jets	12-9-0	.571
19.	New York Giants	26-20-2	.563
20.	Dallas Cowboys	15-12-0	.556
21.	Tennessee Titans	34-28-0	.548
22.	New England Patriots	12-10-0	.545
23.	Indianapolis Colts	15-14-0	.517
24.	Kansas City Chiefs	11-11-2	.500
	Miami Dolphins	8-8-0	.500
26.	Oakland Raiders	10-11-0	.476
27.	St. Louis Rams	9-10-0	.474
28.	Cincinnati Bengals	39-44-0	.470
29.	Pittsburgh Steelers	58-66-0	.468
30.	San Diego Chargers	8-14-1	.370
31.	Green Bay Packers	7-12-0	.368

32. Seattle Seahawks	6-11-0	.353
33. Jacksonville Jaguars	5-11-0	.313
34. Minnesota Vikings	4-10-0	.286
35. Baltimore Ravens	8-24-0	.250
36. Detroit Lions	4-15-0	.211
37. Denver Broncos	5-19-0	.208
38. Carolina Panthers	1-4-0	.200